_____ *The* _____

CHARITY

as a

BUSINESS

*Managing in the voluntary sector,
learning from the private sector*

By David Clutterbuck & Dez Dearlove

A DIRECTORY OF SOCIAL CHANGE PUBLICATION

301.7068

The Charity as a Business
Managing in the voluntary sector,
learning from the private sector

by David Clutterbuck & Dez Dearlove

Published by the Directory of Social Change,
24 Stephenson Way, London NW1 2DP

The Directory of Social Change is registered
charity no. 800517

Designed and typeset by Linda Parker
Printed and bound by Page Bros, Norwich

British Library Cataloguing in Publication Data.
A catalogue record for this book is available from
the British Library

ISBN 1 873860 900

Contents

A note on terminology

One of the first problems we faced in researching and writing this book was one of definition.

Charities, the voluntary sector, not-for-profit organisations – attempts to describe in one simple phrase what we mean by this diverse sector often result in even more confusion. The fact is, all of the common terms are only partial descriptions.

"Charities" assumes a degree of philanthropy that may be conspicuously absent in, say, a golf or cricket club, or a railway preservation society. In theory, at least, a voluntary organisation should have a clear set of beneficiaries, rather than be for the general public good.

"Voluntary sector" ignores the fact that most charities are now heavily reliant on full-time managerial and administrative paid employees.

"Not-for-profit organisation" is a very negative term. It says nothing about what the organisation is for. Moreover, many charities quite clearly are in the businesses of generating profits, which they distribute for the benefits of the cause they represent. While the Church Commissioners, for example, have a duty to maximise the rental return on Church properties, they may temper that duty against social considerations.

"Cause-related organisations" comes closest to describing the whole sector. But it could be considered too broad a categorization, for it appears to include highly commercial companies, such as The Body Shop, which integrates business and environmental causes.

As part of our research, we explored with various charities and expert observers the term "cause-management organisation". This term has the breadth and relevance of "cause-related" but enables a distinction to be made between management of the cause and management of the business. This is, it must be admitted, a subtle distinction, but it provides a more forceful, accurate description.

Nonetheless, at the end of the day, we concluded that trying to introduce yet another term to the equation would probably merely add to the confusion. Such consensus as we could gather suggests that people within the sector – however it is defined – tend generally to feel most comfortable with the traditional term "voluntary sector". That therefore is the term we have generally adopted throughout this book. Exceptions are where we quote individuals or refer to the narrower legal definition of a charity.

David Clutterbuck and Dez Dearlove

What's happening to the voluntary sector?

The popular image of the voluntary sector is of enthusiastic volunteers rattling collection boxes on street corners. Exactly what these organisations do with the money they collect or how they do it is less well known. Indeed, few members of the public have an accurate picture of what goes on behind the scenes. It is taken for granted that charities and other voluntary organisations do a good job. The only time many people hear about the way these organisations are managed is when something goes wrong.

Yet good management is crucial to the voluntary sector. The problem is that while there is broad agreement on the need to manage resources efficiently, the special status of voluntary organisations presents many of them with a moral dilemma. Should they be spending money and resources on improving the quality of management? Or would the money be better spent on the organisation's main purpose of helping disadvantaged children, campaigning for the environment or feeding the hungry?

This dilemma is complicated by the fact that even though the people who run voluntary organisations know that better management will improve efficiency in the long-term, convincing those who support their cause that their donations should help pay for management training, or contribute towards the salaries of professional managers can be difficult. As a result, many voluntary organisations walk a thin line; working to improve management internally, whilst playing it down with the public. Smaller voluntary organisations often have little choice in the matter. They simply don't have the funds to employ professional managers or to send volunteers on management training courses.

As a result many managers in the business world still regard their voluntary counterparts as poor cousins, strong on good intentions but weak on management skills. They would be startled to learn that individual managers in the voluntary sector may be responsible for budgets that are larger than the entire turnover of their companies.

Today, the voluntary sector comprises 3.4 per cent of the UK's Gross Domestic Product. The charity sector alone has an estimated income of £16 billion per annum and employs around a quarter of a million people (1.5 million if you count volunteers).

A growing number of voluntary organisations now use sophisticated management techniques and employ professional managers. Moreover, changes in the way that many voluntary organisations are funded – in particular greater dependency on statutory funding and increased competition for other sources of funding – are placing ever greater pressure on them to improve their efficiency.

However, the voluntary sector has traditionally been wary of what it sees as the dog-eat-dog world of big business, preferring to develop its own style of management. On both sides of the fence, too, there is a lingering feeling that this traditional stand-off may not actually be such a bad thing since the philosophy of business management may be inappropriate to the aspirations of voluntary organisations. But this view of the voluntary and private sectors – that never the twain shall meet – supposes that management and the techniques that it encompasses are inseparable from the aim of the organisation using them. This is not true.

More accurately, professional management techniques may be regarded as tools to help organisations achieve a variety of objectives – be they profit-oriented or simply concerned with the efficient use of resources for another purpose. Best practice in management terms is in fact about the effective stewardship of scarce resources to achieve a stated aim. If it were not, then there would be little agreement about management techniques across different business sectors. But a cursory glance at management literature confirms that the language of management is becoming increasingly universal, not just across business sectors but across national borders. Ask a manager in London about modern management ideas such as Total Quality, or Empowerment, or Business Process Re-engineering, for example, and he or she is likely to be as familiar with the concepts as a manager in Frankfurt, New York or Tokyo.

Indeed, many of the management breakthroughs of the past 20 years have resulted from one sector of industry, or one country, adapting ideas from another. The influx of Japanese management techniques into Europe and the United States in recent years confirms that modern management is informed by best practice regardless of its place of origin.

Some voluntary organisations now recognise the benefits of adapting techniques from the private sector. For example, The Leonard Cheshire Foundation recently announced that three of its homes for people with disabilities had achieved BS5750 accreditation – the British Standards seal of approval on Total Quality Management. Less common are examples of business learning from the voluntary sector, although, as we shall see later in this book, the *potential* for such transfers of expertise is considerable.

In general, however, the voluntary sector has been slower to embrace the global language of management, or to adopt modern techniques used by the private sector. In part, this is because such techniques have tended to be viewed as a means to maximise the financial return on investment – something that was felt to sit uncomfortably with the objectives of voluntary organisations. Happily, this short-sighted view is now being rapidly overtaken by the realisation that it is precisely the need to maximise society's return on its investments that gives the best voluntary organisations their vitality.

Nevertheless, within the voluntary sector some resistance to "private sector" methods remains. Those who subscribe to this view assert that the nature of the work undertaken by voluntary organisations is so different from that carried out by the business community that comparisons are unhelpful. But is the voluntary sector so fundamentally different to the private sector?

Is the voluntary sector really a special case?

A growing number of organisations from both sides of the fence think not. They now recognise that both sides have much to gain from partnerships with one another; both in terms of working together to achieve common goals and through the transfer of resources, experience and skills between organisations and across sectors. There are a number of reasons for this shift in thinking.

For one thing, voluntary organisations are becoming more interested in 'management' as a concept. In recent years many have recruited managers from the private sector (too many, according to some critics!). This is a response to increases in the size, scope and complexity of their work.

At the same time, the environment in which voluntary organisations operate is changing rapidly. New legislation introduced in the 1992 and 1993 Charities Acts; their involvement in public sector contracts as providers of services; economic pressures; and increasing demands on their resources are leading to ever higher requirements of professionalism and accountability. Whereas those who run voluntary organisations might once have been accurately cast in the role of gifted amateurs (often from the ranks of the great and the good) the reality today is very different. Yet much still needs to be done in terms of management training and support for those who work in the voluntary sector.

The urgency with which training issues in particular need to be addressed is underlined by a recent report by the National Federation of Community Organisations ('Goalposts moving for voluntary organisations – urgency of voluntary management training'). The report states:

"Voluntary work is the infrastructure of the welfare state. Great Britain can boast the most active and successful voluntary sector. If this paper seems to indicate massive maladministration of the voluntary sector it must be plainly stated that the voluntary sector does not purposefully maladministrate – quite the contrary – volunteers are very moral and responsible people wishing to do things right.

"What in fact we see is the total lack of attention to supervision, to standards of advice and information, a massive absence of direction and resources to help in the management training of voluntary organisations.

Legislation and agencies have 'shifted the goalposts'. It is not scare mongering to say that if we don't take this subject seriously, the consequences will be for many that the 'game is over'.

"It is no longer a question of 'where can we find resources for management training'. The imperative is we know what will happen if the resources are not made available."

Strong words indeed. But there are other factors, too, which require that the differences between the voluntary, private and public sectors be re-examined. The truth is that the ground occupied by these three sectors is shifting.

In some areas – such as moves to establish minimum standards of protection for employees through equal opportunities legislation – the aims and aspirations of the voluntary and private sectors are moving closer together. In others, where public sector services are being withdrawn or contracted out, voluntary organisations are now in direct competition with private sector companies, forcing both to review their management processes. The trend toward 'contracting out' public services brings its own management pressures, with voluntary service providers required to make accurate costing forecasts and demonstrate efficiency in all their activities. To do so, they must employ professional management techniques.

At the same time there has been an important sea change in the way some in the business community view their involvement with the voluntary sector. A growing number of companies are moving away from old-fashioned views of community involvement as a philanthropic activity. These companies recognise instead that the health of their businesses and their 'licence to operate' increasingly depends upon their willingness to shoulder a degree of social responsibility. The more enlightened companies no longer look upon the communities in which they operate as 'outside of themselves'; rather, they understand that the people (and their families) who are stakeholders in their businesses – their customers, employees, shareholders and suppliers – are also members of those communities. These companies increasingly identify the welfare of the community with the best interests of their businesses.

Commentators also observe that there is simple symbiosis involved. Many in business and government agree that much of the know-how the voluntary sector lacks can be obtained through partnerships with the private sector. But what many of the same people have been much slower to recognise is that in many areas – such as empowering employees, and running de-centralised operations – where the business world and the public sector are currently struggling to come to grips with the issues, the voluntary sector has a great deal of experience and much to teach. In the United States, there is a growing recognition of this fact. To quote American management writer Peter Drucker from his article 'What Business can learn from non-profits', Harvard Business Review, July-August 1989):

"The Girl Scouts, the Red Cross, the pastoral Churches – our voluntary organisations – are becoming America's management leaders. In two areas, strategy and the effectiveness of the board, they are practising what most American businesses only preach."

British perceptions – and in many cases practices – in this area may lag behind those in America, but the UK appears to be moving in a similar direction.

In this book we take as our starting point the simple idea that in order to manage voluntary organisations more effectively in the future it is necessary to re-evaluate the characteristics that distinguish them from companies. In particular, we believe it is time to question the claims of the voluntary sector that it is a special case, and to re-assess the barriers which in the past have obstructed the application of conventional management disciplines. Many of those barriers, on closer inspection, turn out to be illusory. However, there are important caveats for how far voluntary organisations should go in adopting private sector models of management. Underpinning all of this, there is a pressing need to assess the relevance of management techniques in the context of the new requirements of our society.

It is only through a better understanding of these issues that we can begin to test whether management techniques and ideas from other sectors have anything to offer the voluntary sector.

What do we mean by the voluntary sector?

The voluntary sector includes everything outside of the private and public sectors of the UK economy. In other words, the term is used as a catch-all for the myriad organisations that don't fit into either of the other two sectors. Indeed, with its enormous diversity it is not unfair to describe the voluntary sector as something of a grab-bag.

Voluntary organisations vary enormously in size, scope and aims. Their activities include provision of higher education, private education, medical research, welfare and health services, housing for rent, animal welfare, environmental campaigns and many others. Organisations vary in size from the small self-help group or campaign to the large welfare bureaucracies and fundraising organisations. They may be local, regional, national or international.

The diversity of the voluntary sector is summed up by Sandy Adirondack in her book 'Just About Managing' (London Voluntary Service Council 1992):

"It is not in any way homogenous. It encompasses the small group of local women coming together to support each other through a miscarriage, and international agencies such as Save the Children or Greenpeace; groups with annual incomes ranging from a few pounds to many millions; groups with no paid workers and others with hundreds of employees; groups committed to collective and co-operative working arrangements and those with rigid hierarchies; groups ranging politically from far right to far left – and everything in between.

"It includes groups which primarily provide a service, those which primarily campaign, and those which do both; groups engaged in research or action or both. And it covers an incredible range of sectors: Arts, children, disability, education, elderly, employment, environment, health, housing, human rights, peace, prison, reform, sport welfare and dozens of others."

Types of voluntary organisations

Further difficulties arise when it comes to dividing voluntary organisations into categories. Within the broad boundaries of the voluntary sector, a number of different criteria have been suggested to classify what amounts to a very disparate group of organisations. These include categorisation:

♦ By **source of income**.

♦ In terms of **who benefits**.

♦ According to **mission**.

♦ In terms of **accessibility of participation**.

♦ By **area of activity**.

However, one of the most useful (and simplest) models for categorising voluntary organisations is that developed by management writer and academic Charles Handy.

Handy's categorisation criteria combine many of the elements listed above (who benefits, accessibility of participation etc), but focus on the notion that there are three *purposes* for which voluntary organisations exist:

♦ To **link people** in similar circumstances.

♦ To **provide services**.

♦ To **campaign**.

According to Handy, each of these purposes carries implicit assumptions, which will determine the sort of management structure and processes that are appropriate.

From this analysis Handy distinguishes three *types* of voluntary organisation:

♦ **Mutual support organisations**: exist primarily in order to put people with a particular problem or enthusiasm in touch with similar people who can give them understanding, advice, support and encouragement. This, he says, is how many voluntary organisations start out. Typical organisations of this kind would be the Samaritans, Downs Syndrome Association or Alcoholics Anonymous.

♦ **Service delivery organisations**: are those "in the business of providing services to those in need". They usually employ large numbers of paid staff. Typical organisations of this kind would be holiday associations, special schools, residential care providers or law centres.

♦ **Campaigning organisations**: are organisations created to campaign for a cause, or to act as a pressure group for a particular interest. For example, Greenpeace, Friends of the Earth or Amnesty International.

The types of activity they engage in, Handy argues, carry with them an assumption about the nature of the organisation and how it ought to be managed. So, for example:

Mutual aid groups need only the minimum amount of organisation: to service their members; to find reasons for meetings; and to publicise themselves. Anyone who is interested can join and "no-one is going to vet them, analyse their job record or give them an aptitude test". In the main, mutual aid groups do not want to be managed and tend to regard administration as a distraction.

Service delivery organisations, on the other hand, are very different. They are instrumental in getting things done and are all about creating an organisational methodology to achieve their service aims. In Handy's words: "They take pride in being professional, effective and low-cost. It follows that they need to be selective about their recruits, demanding in their review of standards, prepared to reprimand where necessary, even to dismiss someone whose work is inadequate."

Unlike a mutual aid group, you cannot by choice join the core of a service delivery organisation. These organisations tend to resemble more closely the structures of organisations in the public and private sectors. For example, they have formal job definitions with formal responsibilities and accountability. It is important, too, that the organisation is able to continue operating in the same way if individuals leave. This has implications for personnel management practices such as succession planning, and contingency planning.

Campaigning organisations are different again because they tend to be led rather than managed. They require administration but this is secondary to their mission. As Handy puts it: "The essence of the [campaigning] organisation is that of adherence to a cause, focused on a leader, often a charismatic one whose personality infects the organisation. The only qualification for belonging is that you believe, and the more believers the better."

Handy's typology suggests that each of the three sets of assumptions that underpin the three sorts of organisations are different, and that there are different ways to structure and manage an organisation depending on what sort of organisation you are.

Over time, however, he suggests that there is a tendency for mutual aid organisations to move into service delivery, or for service delivery organisations to begin to campaign. "The logic is clear", he says, "but the clash of assumptions can be heard from miles away."

Mencap provides a good example of this process at work. Explains chief executive Fred Heddell:

"Mencap will be 50 years old in 1996. It started as self-help groups for parents of mentally handicapped children. In its early years, it was about

campaigning and lobbying for education. The organisation still consists of autonomous local groups affiliated to the Royal Society (Mencap).

"Mencap pioneered the idea of care in the community and in recent years service provision has become the bulk of its activities. Budgets for 1994 are £70 million (trebled over three years) and now instead of a handful, we have 5,000 staff. Only £5 million of our income is voluntary contributions; the rest comes from statutory sources, which have expectations of quality and price. So Mencap has had to evolve from being a campaigning organisation to being run like a business."

Mencap has also had to move from a parent group to one that also stands for the rights of those with mental handicaps. The values and concerns of these two groups are often at odds.

The stresses and strains of this transition have been considerable, not least because it takes time to convince the charity's constituents that the changes are for the better.

Our own analysis suggests that, in addition to Handy's three categories there are also:

♦ **Fundraising organisations**: operations, such as Red Nose Day, which are solely concerned with fundraising without a specific cause in mind, distributing cash to a variety of causes. The Round Table effectively operates in this manner. Included in this category are also the various commercial and semi-commercial agencies that assist voluntary organisations in fundraising.

♦ **Grant-making organisations**: trusts and foundations that exist solely to provide funding for specified causes. The origins of these may be very wide – from a personal legacy to a foundation established by a company to separate community and business activities. Their remit may equally vary from very wide to very narrow.

♦ **Trading organisations**: essentially a specialised form of fundraising, these need to be managed as separate businesses and to develop a business-like culture.

In practice, a voluntary sector organisation may involve a complex mix of different operations, each requiring a different structure, culture and objectives to be effective. The problem for many voluntary sector organisations lies in deciding which activity is the prime reason for existing and which are simply support mechanisms. In the Mencap case above, is the prime reason for existing to promote the welfare of mentally handicapped people or to provide welfare services? And in whose interests should it operate – those of the mentally handicapped, their parents and siblings, or society as a whole? Even where it is clear to all where the organisation's priorities lie, there is still the danger that the support operations may exert too great an influence over the culture and resource allocation of the organisation as a whole.

A critical role for leaders of voluntary organisations is to recognise the conflicts that occur from a multiplicity of purposes. They must develop management styles and systems that permit a constructive balance between the need for the organisation to control its support operations and the need to give those operations the freedom to achieve their objectives in the most effective manner. In the private sector, this would be viewed as a classic dilemma of centralisation versus decentralisation.

Charities

Since charities are by far the largest grouping in the voluntary sector, it is worth going into some detail about them.

It is generally understood that a voluntary organisation is an institution or organisation for helping those in need. More specifically charities must be established for the benefit of the public, or a sufficiently important section of the public, rather than for the benefit of private individuals. And: "to qualify as a charity an organisation must be for the relief of poverty, or for the advancement of education, or for the advancement of religion, or for other purposes beneficial to the community not falling under any of the preceding heads" ('Charities Digest' 1991)

To become a charity, both the Charity Commission and the Inland Revenue must be satisfied that the purpose of the organisation falls entirely under one or more of the headings above. Over the years, however, some flexibility and new purposes have been accepted as charitable where they are similar to existing charitable purposes or where they are seen to be within the spirit of the charitable sector.

As vague as these definitions are, however, it is not surprising that many people find it easier to think of all voluntary organisations as charities. The confusion over what is and is not a charity is demonstrated by Dr Diana Leat in her publication 'Managing Across Sectors'.

She observes: "If the mythical man in the street were asked to say which of the following – Oxfam, Age Concern, the Medical Research Council, Eton, Amnesty International, the Arts Council and Save the Children Fund – is not a charity, he would probably plump for Eton, the Medical Research Council or the Arts Council. In fact, the only organisation in the list above which is not a charity is Amnesty International." Although to confuse the issue further, Amnesty itself operates a charity called the Prisoners of Conscience Research Trust.

Again, however, the most important point to make is that charities come in all shapes and sizes. Most of us are familiar with the very large charities. Organisations such as Barnardos and the RSPCA are household names and have enormous financial and human resources at their disposal. But the vast majority of charities have very low incomes, no paid staff and only a handful of volunteers or members.

As the Chief Charity Commissioner put it recently: "Charities range in scope and size from the international Save the Children Fund to organisations like St Tiggywinkles, where they look after poorly hedgehogs and concussed deer." (ref 2)

Sources of charitable income

Of the £16 billion estimated total income of charities in the UK, 20 per cent – £3.2 billion – is from donations (including legacies); 54 per cent – £8.7 billion – is from fees and charges (including local and central government money paid as fees for services); 15 per cent – £2.5 billion – from investments and rent; 6 per cent – £1.0 billion – from government grants; and 5 per cent – £0.8 billion – from other income. (Source 'Charity Trends' 1992).

But these aggregated figures conceal very wide differences within the charities sector. A survey of the distribution of charitable income in 1975 revealed that the top 5 per cent of charities commanded 83 per cent of the total. The big household names which constitute a tiny minority of all charities actually consume the lion's share of charity income, employ the majority of staff and involve the majority of volunteers. For example, in the year ending February 1994 the National Trust had an income of £151 million, involved thousands of volunteers, had over 2 million members and employed about 3,000 paid staff. Some other charities, such as universities, are bigger still.

The composition of charities' incomes also varies widely. Some – such as the Medical Research Council and the Arts Council, for example – are almost entirely dependent on government grants, while others – such as public schools (also charities) derive virtually all their income from fees. Other charities – large and small – are almost solely dependent upon fundraising from corporate and individual donors.

The difference between the sources of income is illustrated by the following example: Age Concern England, with an income of over £10.8 million in 1993 derived about a third of its income from government sources and almost half from voluntary sources, the remainder coming from trading; by contrast, the Wellcome Trust, with a total income of £199 million in the same year did no fundraising and received no government grants, deriving its entire income from its very substantial assets (£5,241 million in 1993).

The picture that emerges from all this is one of vast diversity within the voluntary sector. In this respect it can be said to mirror the private sector. In fact, as we will try to demonstrate later, there are often greater similarities between comparable sized organisations across these sectors than within them. So, for example, many smaller voluntary organisations have more in common with fast growing entrepreneurial companies than with the established voluntary sector giants such as Save the Children. Similarly, many small businesses have more in common with small voluntary organisations than with the ICIs and IBMs of the business world.

Dr Diana Leat has been involved in research in the voluntary sector for over 20 years. She confirms that differences across sectors, and similarities within sectors, are often exaggerated.

"Reading case studies of the computer company Apple in its early years I was struck by its commonality with voluntary organisations. It had an

ethos of passion, informality, emphasising creativity and a 'we're at the forefront' culture that said 'we're going to change the world'. To a certain extent it did!"

The collapse of sector boundaries

The voluntary sector in Britain was created piece-meal. In the main, its history is one of new organisations and movements created from the grassroots level. This is both its greatest strength and its greatest weakness.

On the positive side, the absence of complex command structures or central planning control has allowed the voluntary sector to react rapidly to social needs as they arise. Indeed, many would argue that the voluntary sector is at its most effective when reacting to new challenges. In many areas of public life it continues to lead the way today; for example, in addressing the problems of homelessness, where Shelter and other voluntary organisations have done much to raise public awareness and challenge government policy.

On the negative side, however, it can be argued that the way in which the voluntary sector has developed has deprived voluntary organisations of effective management structures and created a cultural bias towards 'action' and against long-term planning and management. In some areas it has also led to duplication of welfare provision, and prevented constructive rationalisation through mergers and other forms of restructuring. Indeed, the structure of voluntary organisations could be said to make mergers almost impossible.

Yet the overriding principle of the voluntary sector – that private individuals should be able to organise themselves to provide social benefits not provided by the State – has served Britain extremely well. That is not to say there isn't room for improvement.

Many of the older established voluntary organisations such as Save the Children and the Salvation Army have grown into very large organisations with an annual income of £ millions. In many ways the management challenges they face are not very different to those faced by any other large international organisation.

But with about 4,000 new charities registered every year, there are also clearly some very young voluntary organisations around. Many of these have been created to meet new social needs. Aids charities such as the Terrence Higgins Trust, for example, are a relatively new phenomenon.

At the same time, commentators have noted a growth in government-inspired and often wholly state-funded voluntary organisations in Britain as in the United States. Organisations such as the NHS trusts form part of what has been called 'third party government' in which central and local government uses third parties to pursue its policy aims. The effects of the policies of successive UK governments since 1979 are likely to accelerate this trend. For example, the Government increasingly pays existing charities to carry out social responsibilities, as in the case of Care in the Community. However, many inside and outside the voluntary sector voice concerns that moves towards a contractor/provider relationship with government will undermine the independence of the voluntary sector.

Yet the tradition of independence from the State does not in itself explain why voluntary organisations are a special case. Indeed, much of the private sector also evolved in this way.

There are a number of other reasons put forward to explain why voluntary organisations require a different management approach to other organisations. These are discussed in more detail in Appendix 2. In practice, most of these reasons can be countered with practical examples. Two clear conclusions emerge from a review of this issue.

Firstly, the voluntary sector is not so fundamentally different to the for-profit sector as is commonly thought. Secondly, the profit motive, far from being a simple guiding principle for private sector management, is in itself problematic, not least because of difficulties over defining time scales.

At the same time, it is apparent that in many areas the two sectors are now moving closer together. For example, companies now have to manage much more carefully the social dimension of their activities, be it in the area of providing equal opportunities for employees, protecting the environment, or contributing to the social infrastructure – while voluntary organisations are increasingly accountable for investment decisions and fulfilling contractual obligations.

The voluntary ethos

There is a view that the tangible differences between the way voluntary sector organisations and businesses are managed are less important that the philosophy that underpins them. This intangible difference is sometimes referred to as the 'voluntary' or 'voluntary sector ethos'. Yet it is extremely difficult to define.

Diana Leat's description of the voluntary ethos as one of "participation and equality" is a valiant attempt. But as Sandra Greaves, former editor of 'Third Sector' magazine, points out: "In reality it's a whole mish-mash of issues such as equal opportunities and others. Not all voluntary sector organisations actually subscribe to it."

There is a strand in the voluntary ethos, too, that is rooted in the notion of a more ethical approach to running an organisation. While this may have some validity in practice, it is misleading to suggest that voluntary organisations are any freer from the constraints and pressures that incline companies to act unethically. Companies and voluntary organisations are only as ethical as the people who work for them. It is dangerous to assume that because people work in the voluntary sector they automatically have more integrity.

At the same time, many companies are moving away from hierarchical, non-democratic management styles towards a more participative and democratic approach. A growing number also have ethical codes to influence the actions of all their employees. Many of these companies now regularly update their ethical codes to stay abreast of changes in the business and social environment. In 1993, for example, National Westminster Bank revised and extended its ethical code to take account of new developments in the banking world, particularly those brought about by new technology.

Many voluntary organisations – perhaps the majority – do not have formal ethical codes. Rather, they rely on the unwritten and often unspoken notion of the voluntary ethos to ensure probity in their activities. There is a danger in this approach that it blinds voluntary organisations to the need to adopt best practice in ethical management.

The importance of purpose

To understand the genuine differences between the voluntary sector and other sectors, we need to dig deep, to the level of organisation purpose. Says Judy Welemensky, formerly Chief Executive of NCVO and The National Schizophrenia Fellowship and currently a specialist consultant: "A voluntary organisation isn't necessarily about volunteers, although most have at least a Board made up of volunteers. It is an organisation run for a social purpose. It may make a profit, but that is secondary to the social purpose. In effect, a voluntary organisation is defined by what it is trying to achieve." A useful concept, she suggests, is "social profit" – the non-financial benefits to the community that occur as a result of voluntary organisations' activities.

In trying to define the purpose of a voluntary organisation, we arrived at the following:

♦ To promote **awareness of social issue**(s).

♦ To preserve **heritage/culture** (e.g. Welsh Language Society; trusts to maintain old railways/ships).

♦ To provide **welfare** for a specific audience (e.g. for distressed gentlefolk).

♦ To provide **collective support** (e.g. Mencap, victims' relatives etc).

♦ To **add value to society**, in part or whole.

By comparison, the purpose of a business would generally involve some or all of the following:

♦ To **create wealth**/add to GDP (general).

♦ To **make profits** for shareholders/owners (specific).

♦ To serve **defined customer groups**.

♦ To **add value for its stakeholders**.

A business may also – depending on its culture and leadership – have as a purpose:

♦ To contribute to **societal betterment**.

The purpose of government, on the other hand, can be seen as:

♦ To establish **rule of law**.
♦ To create the **fiscal environment** for creation of wealth/ increase in GDP.
♦ To ensure and **promote community services**.
♦ To **protect the state**.
♦ To **add value to the nation**.

All three sectors:

♦ Provide **employment**.
♦ **Educate and campaign** to further their aims.
♦ Provide **services directly**.
♦ Provide **services through third parties**.

A voluntary organisation's purpose can be:

♦ **Ethical**: aimed at promoting a specific moral framework.
♦ **Substantive**: aimed at delivering specific benefits to target group(s).
♦ **Political**: aimed at promoting the interests of specific groups in society.

They may have all three purposes – or just one.

Organisations in all three sectors have to be *business-like*, in the sense that they are expected to:

♦ Exercise financial probity.
♦ Have effective leadership.
♦ Be good employers.
♦ Develop clear, viable strategies.
♦ Report to stakeholders.
♦ Promote their purpose effectively.
♦ Make people accountable.
♦ Deliver continuous quality improvement.
♦ Be open, honest and ethical.

Who are the stakeholders?

	Government	Private sector	Voluntary sector
Taxpayers		x	
The public	x	x	?
Shareholders		x	
Customers/clients	x	x	x
Suppliers	x	x	x
Employees	x	x	x
Volunteers			x
Public interest groups	x	x	x
Members	x		x

How business-like should voluntary organisations be?

One of the dangers voiced by many of the people we interviewed was that, in adopting best business practice, voluntary organisations may lose the spontaneity and commitment to the cause that sets them apart from business. Our perception is that the dangers are much less significant if voluntary organisations seek not to become more *business-like*, but to become *effectively managed*. Problems arise when voluntary organisations attempt to a*dopt the characteristics* of businesses rather than simply *absorb and adapt management best practice.*

There is more than a semantic difference here. Being business-like implies solely managing for profit, the relentless pursuit of efficiency and, in the modern context, the requirement to hang on to customers. Management structure, systems and culture all support these basic assumptions. All three assumptions are to a greater or lesser extent alien to the effective voluntary organisation. It manages finance for probity, security and the ability to pursue the cause and in trust for those who have funded it; it tempers the need for efficiency by accepting broader social consequences of its role as employer; and it will often have as a primary aim the rehabilitation and therefore a loss of customers or market. For example, the tuberculosis charities have largely achieved their aims in the UK. To continue to serve a useful purpose, they must turn their attention to those parts of the world where the disease still lingers, or to other similar diseases – if their constitution allows them to do so.

Because the organisational purpose is different, effective voluntary organisations will tend to develop their own kinds of structures, systems and cultures. These may, on the surface at least, be very similar to those of some private sector or public sector organisations – there is no less variety or versatility of approach to resolving business problems in the voluntary sector. Voluntary organisations with a substantial trading arm, for example, will be under greater pressure to copy best commercial practice than those who rely on public donations to support their activities. That pressure will often be stronger if trading is a primary activity (for example, the admissions to National Trust properties) than peripheral (for example, National Trust gifts and catering).

A critical dilemma for some voluntary organisations is how to compete in the no-man's land of public funded welfare. Where the government seeks to fulfil laudable social objectives through external agents, private sector organisations and voluntary organisations can find themselves in competition for the same funding. It is tempting for the voluntary organisation to seek to become more like its private sector competitors, if only to achieve the levels of efficiency and productivity they need to compete. The cost, however, can be high. The voluntary organisation's strengths (the powerful resource of volunteers and fundraising) can be a disadvantage in the sense that government agencies may expect them to carry out tasks on the cheap.

The experience of private sector organisations is that attempting to follow two cultural paths simultaneously leads almost always to ineffectiveness and failure. Where the need arises for a voluntary organisation to run a business (be that as a primary purpose or peripheral activity), it should be run as a business, as a separate subsidiary or joint venture, with its own management team, business processes and culture. The role of the voluntary organisation then becomes one of owner/principal stakeholder. We will explore this in more detail in the discussion of voluntary sector governance, on pages 39-43.

References

1. Charles Handy, *'Understanding Voluntary Organisations'*, Penguin 1988, p13,

2. *Charity Choice 4th Edition 1991: The Encyclopaedia of Charities*, Abercorn Hill Associates, London 1990.

3. *Resourcing the Voluntary Sector: The Funders' Perspective'*, 1993,

4. Dr Diana Leat, *'Managing Across Sectors: Similarities and Differences Between For-Profit and Voluntary Non-profit Organisations'*, VOLPROF, City University Business School, March 1993.

Chapter 1

A crisis of leadership?

Key issues

♦ *What kind of leaders do voluntary sector organisations need?*

♦ *Should they be like business leaders?*

♦ *How do the structures of voluntary organisations constrain or empower their leaders?*

♦ *Does change management require a different sort of leadership?*

Two themes concerning the leadership of voluntary sector organisations occurred frequently in our interviews. The first was that there is, in reality or potentially, a leadership crisis in the sector. The crisis originates at two levels; across the sector as a whole and at the head of individual organisations.

The sector, so the argument goes, lacks the kind of unified voice that industry is able to exert through trade associations, chambers of commerce, the Confederation of British Industry or the Institute of Directors. Neither the Charity Commission nor the National Council for Voluntary Organisations (NCVO) fulfils this role and there is still relatively little experience among voluntary organisations in collaborating to exert influence, except perhaps for short-term campaigns and a few specific issues such as Medical Research.

In individual voluntary organisations, leadership calibre varies considerably (as in other sectors). The criteria for selecting leaders often include factors absent from the private sector. For example, while the Royal National Institute for the Deaf did not *have* to appoint a deaf chief executive, the recent appointment made a powerful statement about the capabilities of deaf people in employment. It may be difficult for the Institute to appoint someone of normal hearing to the chief executive slot in the future. However, the argument goes, voluntary organisations are increasingly having to grapple with complex decisions about their purpose and how they achieve it; about internal and external relationships; and about planning for the long-term. The implication is that a greater degree of professionalism is needed throughout the management structure, starting at the top. Yet a significant minority of the people we interviewed questioned the wisdom of importing waves of managers from the private sector. The primary cause for their concerns are that knowledge of management needs to be balanced with deep understanding of the voluntary sector; and that prescriptions for the private sector may prove poisonous when taken as medicine in the voluntary sector.

The second recurring theme was that the voluntary sector has a great many effective leaders, whose style is very different from that of the archetypal corporate executive in the private sector. Personally and passionately involved, these leaders earn respect more by capturing hearts and minds than by controlling complex structures. The fear that "professionalising" leadership will dilute these qualities is a very real one, which has yet to be confronted and debated in most voluntary organisations.

Why should these issues be so critical now? One reason is that changes in charities legislation are both forcing a reevaluation of voluntary organisations' reasons for being and what they do. At the same time, the legislation is making it easier for voluntary organisations to become more business-like.

Good management starts at the top

It has become a cliché to say that good management starts at the top of an organisation, but it is true nonetheless. And it is as true of voluntary organisations as it is of private and public sector organisations.

Who are the leaders? The senior authority in a charity is the Board of Trustees. The extent, to which they offer leadership will depend upon how they view their role. Are they there as a managing Board, determining policy and instructing the chief executive? As an advising and monitoring group? Or as the "shareholders" of the organisation? Clearly, some of these roles will demand leadership by the trustees, others not.

In general, where trustees are significantly involved in the strategic planning and representation of the organisation, they can be regarded as executive and therefore part of the *management* structure. Because this is not usually the case, we will concentrate our discussion of leadership issues on the role of the senior executives. More detailed discussion of the role of the trustees can be found in Chapter 2.

The larger voluntary organisations have sophisticated management structures with a clearly identifiable layer of senior managers. However, for many of the smaller voluntary organisations the notion of a tier of 'top management' is hard to imagine. In these small organisations, the top management may consist of the founder and/or a couple of friends. Yet no matter how involved these people are with the day-to-day activities of the organisation, they still fulfil the essential role of top management by providing leadership and direction.

These people are the 'movers and shakers', translating what needs to be done into action. But regardless of how many movers and shakers an organisation has, there is always one person or a small group of people more influential than the others. They may be executives, an influential trustee – perhaps someone with a strong personality – or the founder.

That person or group – whether they are called the chief executive, the senior management team or simply Frank or Caroline – are the leaders.

The issues that confront these people are by and large those that face the business world. Among them:

♦ **How the organisation copes when it outgrows its founders**. The problems faced by the Richmond Fellowship when trustees and the founder disagree are echoed in hundreds of smaller companies, where the entrepreneurial style of the founder clashes with the need for professional management.

♦ **The critical importance of the relationship between the chairman and the chief executive**. Some hospital trusts have experienced great difficulty through lack of role clarity between these two powerful individuals. Relatively little is known about how chairmen and chief executives develop effective working relationships. The authors are currently carrying out research in this area.

♦ **The remuneration of top management**. In the private sector, it has long been the practice to reward non-executive directors (who in effect act as trustees on behalf of the shareholders). This practice has carried over into National Health Trusts. However, the practice is not without its critics. The excessively high pay awards given to some executive directors of large companies is due in part to the incestuous relationship between remuneration committees. ("I'll approve your pay package because I know it will have a knock-on effect on mine".) Now that voluntary organisations can also (under 1994 changes in the rules) pay trustees, the door has opened to establishing boards similar to those in the private sector. Voluntary organisations that follow that path would do well to learn from the mistakes of the private sector and build in mechanisms to avoid controversy and public perceptions of misuse of funds.

To understand the issues that confront voluntary leaders in larger organisations it is necessary to examine the management structures and responsibilities in more detail. This we will do later in this chapter. But here we focus on some general points about leadership which have relevance for voluntary organisations of all sizes.

What makes an effective leader?

The question of what makes a good leader has exercised the minds of men and women throughout history. Much of what has been written on the subject this century has concentrated on the personality traits that distinguish effective leaders from the also-rans. But whereas we once looked to the political and military arenas for illustrations of exemplary leadership, today we increasingly turn our attention towards the people who manage companies and other large organisations.

These leadership figures clearly serve a purpose. They create a focus for action. Without leadership, the collective power of a group of people in an organisation cannot be effectively harnessed to further its aims. But just what it is that makes leadership work in practice remains unclear. Indeed, there are probably as many theories and models of leadership as there are organisations to lead.

In the past few years, however, management theorists in particular have begun to look at the other side of the leadership equation, focusing more on what motivates the people who follow. Their findings suggest that what people look for in a leader varies with the values that the followers aspire to. What this means in practice is that leaders are only as good as their fit with the needs of the people they lead. It is the dynamics of the relationship between leaders and their followers that is now the centre of much discussion.

Credibility

In a recent book on the subject, two American management writers – James Kouzes and Barry Posner – claim that credibility is the factor that determines the strength of the leader-follower relationship:

"The heroic leadership myth has been shattered. What people want is leadership that is consistent with the principles and values articulated by the leader, and is genuinely respectful of the intelligence and contributions of the followers."

If Kouzes and Posner are right, then the axis on which effective leadership turns is the ability to create and sustain credibility. The problem is that inside organisations all too often the roles of leader and follower are viewed in isolation from each other. Yet at different times we are all leaders and all followers. Voluntary leaders in particular need to understand the essential give and take of the two roles if they are to be good at their jobs because typically they are required to fulfil both.

Paradoxical as it may sound, the most effective voluntary leaders lead by following; they are effective as leaders in so much as they follow the needs of beneficiaries, donors, employees and volunteers. It is this that gives them their credibility.

And according to Kouzes and Posner, effective leaders aren't born that way, they must learn to be credible. This, they claim, depends on the leader's ability to master six key disciplines:

- ♦ **Discovering yourself**.
- ♦ **Appreciating followers** (or constituents).
- ♦ **Affirming shared values**.
- ♦ **Developing capacity**.
- ♦ **Serving a purpose**.
- ♦ **Sustaining hope**.

Leaders then must first be clear in their own minds about their values and standards, and be confident that they have the competence to deliver what they believe in.

Next, they must recognise they are engaging in a relationship with followers which requires a deep understanding of what they, the followers, need. To do so they must learn to listen – something managers everywhere are traditionally poor at.

Third, leaders – whilst at the same time acknowledging the diversity of their followers – must find the common ground that unites the organisation and build a consensus on that firm ground.

Then, leaders must ensure that those who follow have the skills, knowledge and information to carry out their strategy by providing them with the appropriate training and development to do so.

Fifth, they must recognise that as leaders they are the servants of the organisation and must embody their own standards and values in everything they do if they are to fulfil their role.

Finally, and perhaps most importantly of all, leaders must inspire enthusiasm and optimism. In difficult times they must make themselves available to support their followers and realise that they are the ultimate keepers of the flame of hope.

The role of any leader, then, is to articulate a credible vision of the future which inspires the loyalty of his or her followers. To do so, that vision must serve their individual and collective aspirations and values. To put it simply, a leader can only lead people where they want to go. The corollary to this is that only a true leader can inspire people to push out the boundaries of their imagination to achieve their aspirations for the organisation.

The contribution of the true leader is therefore to define what the place their followers want to get to will look like, and to map out a route that will take them there. They also have to lead their funders who are a separate (but crucial) constituency from their customers. Oxfam, for example, is currently involved in consultation over whether it should be involved in helping the poor in the UK. Many within the organisation see poverty as an issue that transcends national borders, but some funders believe Oxfam should remain a Third World charity only. The task facing voluntary leaders then is often one of managing a coalition. They achieve this dual role by way of a mission. Whether that mission is one of defeating an oppressive enemy in warfare, feeding the world's hungry, or championing the rights of Black South Africans – all of which could be said to fit with a vision of a better world – the rest depends upon the willingness of the people to follow.

In business this truism about leadership is sometimes confused with other considerations such as financial rewards or fear of redundancy. But the fact remains that people will only follow where they want to go. The carrot of a higher salary, or the stick of a threat to their job, may influence their choice in the short-run. In the long-run, however, there is a limit to how many carrots and how many sticks people will allow to dilute their real aims. That is why the most effective manipulations of this kind alternate between threats and bribes in order to keep people off balance and out of touch with their real aspirations. In this way false leaders seek to control people through the two primary emotions of fear and greed.

Those who try to coerce people in this way may succeed for a while. But sooner or later they experience a difficult patch. To survive this difficult period in their leadership they require loyalty from their followers. But it is loyalty that their crude methods fail to inspire.

Voluntary leaders typically have fewer carrots and sticks at their disposal anyway, but a sense of loyalty among their followers is no less important for them. People will remain loyal if they believe in the vision of the leader. And no leader can afford to lose faith with the people they serve, or to forget that their success as a leader depends on their followers. In this way leader and followers are bound together by the organisation's mission. Indeed, no matter how successful a leader is, he or she would be wise to remember Winston Churchill's famous comment on his contribution to Britain's war effort: "The nation had the lion's heart. I had the luck to give the roar."

So it is with all effective leaders. Alone they cannot hope to change the world; that requires the heart of the people who follow them. What the leader can do is provide the roar.

What makes a good voluntary leader?

The many interviews and conversations we've had with people in the voluntary sector suggest there are three key characteristics exhibited by successful voluntary leaders. Typically, these people are:

♦ Entrepreneurial.

♦ Inspirational.

♦ Ethical.

Entrepreneurial

Exceptional voluntary leaders are often what the business world would describes as entrepreneurs. They are innovative, open to new opportunities and have the ability to make ideas work in practice. Evidence suggests that this has always been true.

Writing in The Times, April 8 1993 on the occasion of the 75th anniversary of Save the Children Fund , Libby Purves describes its co-founder Eglantyne Jebb as

"One of those doughty late-Victorian bluestocking spinsters in the tradition of Florence Nightingale, born to shake the world out of complacency.

"She was ahead of her time in harnessing the power of the media; a year out of the Great War, she hired the Royal Albert Hall for an appeal; she ran poster campaigns, enlisted the Pope, took full pages in The Times, and toured the country summoning newspapermen to harrowing screenings of a short film about the famine in Russia in 1920. She got herself arrested

for illegally distributing leaflets attacking the Allied blockade and harangued the court until the prosecutor gave a contribution."

According to Save the Children's archivist Rodney Breen, Jebb: "surrounded herself with professionals"; and "thought a charity should be run like a business". The first year's campaigning raised £400,000, the equivalent today of £8 million.

Today's voluntary leaders continue to push out the boundaries of the imagination. Listen for example to Business in the Community's chief executive Julia Cleverdon's description of a good voluntary leader:

"It's a misapprehension that entrepreneurs are found only in the private sector, the best voluntary leaders display many of the same characteristics. A real entrepreneur is David Robinson at Community Links. He bought the town hall at Canning in East London for £1 and refurbished it to turn it into a new centre for the Community Links project. If you want to capture the imagination of the private sector, you just have to send them to see David. He's done more as a flypaper to bring in the private sector than just about anyone I can think of in the voluntary sector. What David Robinson does is:

- *He sees issues through the customers eyes.*
- *He makes it easy for you to help – by knowing the actionable next steps. For example, he doesn't say to McAlpines 'we're trying to build such and such', he says 'well actually we need some bricks, can you help?' Then he says, 'we can probably arrange to collect them', and the next thing you know you're saying 'no that's alright we'll deliver them.'*

- *He never forgets what he's really trying to achieve i.e. what the purpose is. For example, a while ago he wrote me a letter asking if I knew what was happening on the voluntary sector side about the National Lottery, to which the answer was that I didn't. I called NCVO and they weren't sure, so I called CAF and they weren't either. So I went back to David and said it's a good point you've raised I'm looking into it. He came back immediately saying he didn't think I was moving fast enough and that BitC should take over and run it as a charitable trust! That is typical of him. He has a real terrier-like quality that once he gets his teeth into something he won't let go.*"

Inspirational

We have all at some time or other been inspired by someone. The intriguing thing about inspiration is that it motivates people to go that extra mile when they would otherwise be at the limits of their endurance. In voluntary organisations, which are often under-staffed and under-resourced, that extra spurt of inspired effort is often what makes the difference between success and failure.

In most cases, too, people who inspire us do so not because of the task but how they set about it. It is their attitude to the job in hand, and their ability to enthuse us with a greater purpose that inspires us to try harder.

Talking to a cross-section of people who work for voluntary organisations, it was surprisingly easy to tell which of them were inspired by their jobs. Curiously, however, it often seemed to have little to do with the tasks they performed or even the sort of work the organisation was engaged in. Rather it was much more to do with the emotion they felt towards what their organisation was trying to achieve. In the course of our research it became increasingly clear to us that the way some organisations are run inspires the people who work for them, while in others, for whatever reason and despite the worthiness of their cause, it does not.

CASE STUDY ➤ The Reanoke Symphony Orchestra

The story of what happened when a new conductor joined a financially strapped orchestra on the East Coast of America as told in the American management publication 'On Achieving Excellence' provides an interesting example of what inspiration can do.

In the space of one year, conductor Victoria Bond transformed the Reanoke Symphony Orchestra in Virginia from a poorly attended 2,400 seat symphony hall into a season sell-out, with very few changes to the previously demoralised 100 musicians.

Explaining how she did it, she says that before the first rehearsal she asked each musician for their CV and a personal written statement about how they felt towards the orchestra and who they were as musicians. In this way she was able to get an idea of what they were capable of on paper before she heard them play live.

"I wanted to know with whom I was dealing", she says, "before making any changes. I was impressed that there were a lot of PhDs from major conservatories. In fact, I realised these people seemed a lot better on paper than they sounded on the tape I'd heard of their last performance. So there was a lot of latent talent that was not being tapped."

The next step was to immediately establish what she expected of the orchestra. Her approach was what one might expect of someone working in a creative environment. She compared the performance at rehearsal with the way she felt the piece should sound in her mind given the quality of the musicians.

As she explains: "It was like bringing together two pictures that are slightly different. It was important to assess each person's ability quickly, to judge whether their performance didn't coincide with my standard because he or she didn't have the ability or because the player wasn't trying hard enough. In most cases it was the latter." Her leadership task then became that of inspiring the musicians to give of their best.

Her methods included asking individual musicians to sustain a note at exactly the level of quietness she had in her head until she was satisfied. The players quickly realised that they couldn't get away with any sloppiness in their playing because every one of them would be heard. More difficult, Bond says, was gaining their trust and confidence.

Dealing with artists or any other very committed group of people can be difficult, she observes, because it is not always easy to separate their performance from who they are. As a result, unless carefully handled, feedback can be seen as a battle of wills rather than something that will help them produce their best performance. Also, because of the constraints on time, she was forced to hand out criticism in front of their peers.

The key to inspiring musicians in particular, she says, lies in recognition. However, as with many voluntary organisations there are no financial bonuses she could use as incentives. Instead, she used other ways to reward players who performed well. For example, choosing them to perform solos or concertos and always treating them with courtesy and respect as artists.

"I like to perform from memory without sheet music", she explains, "that way I can maintain eye contact and feel the energy level of each musician. I always give a player who has had an important solo a bow, and if he or she has played particularly beautifully, I look that player in the eye and smile – that's tremendously effective."

At the same time, Bond was aware that her personality was what would attract and inspire people within the orchestra and in the local community to trust her. To foster community interest she became active in the community, demonstrating that she was not "one of those austere ivory tower people". For example, she rode on a float in the Christmas parade. She became an ambassador for the local branch of the Lung Association. She gave speeches to professional organisations and charities, preferring to let their interests guide the content of her talks rather than baffling them with the finer points of classical music.

To get younger people interested in classical music she introduced a note of irreverence. During a high school concert the principal cellist rode into the hall dressed as a motorcycle cop with siren blaring and gave her a ticket for speeding – playing *presto* in an *allegro* zone!

Ethical

It may seem self-evident that voluntary leaders require a high level of personal integrity. Yet many of the problems and particularly scandals that voluntary organisations face are created out of an unwillingness by leaders to take a realistic view of ethical issues including how much they are paid and the temptations they face in their jobs.

Consider, for example, the outcry surrounding America's best known charity United Way when it was revealed that its national president William Arimony was paid a salary of $436,000 a year and spent $1 million on limousine rides, Concorde flights and starting questionable United Way-related service companies.

Whatever the rights and wrongs of Arimony's conduct, the seeds of the scandal were sown by an attitude at the highest levels of the charity that meant that his salary and expenses were not publicly discussed.

Contrast that with the straight-talking approach when we interviewed Jane Tewson, chief executive of Charity Projects:

"How much am I paid? My salary is £35,000 a year. It's not that much compared to directors or a chief executive of an organisation with a similar turnover, but I still feel a bit guilty sometimes.

"You wouldn't believe the number of backhanders offered in the voluntary sector, especially around red nose day. You have to be cleaner than clean.

"We want charities to be more open. We publish how much money goes to each project – that should be best practice for all charities. Charities should be more open otherwise scandal stories will always be there."

Significantly, too, the leadership characteristic that has come top of virtually every survey Kouzes and Posner have carried out on the subject in over 10 years of research in North America, Europe, Australia and the Far East, is honesty.

It is the combination of these three elements – being entrepreneurial, inspirational and ethical – that gives the best voluntary leaders their credibility. It is their credibility that entitles them to lead.

A leader is of little use, however, unless he or she knows in which direction the organisation should be moving. It's all very well to think in terms of leading people to the promised land, but you must have some idea of where that promised land lies. The most important task for a leader is to define a vision – not necessarily of the promised land itself, but of a staging post along the way. In defining that vision, the leader sets the organisation a mission which it must accomplish to make the vision a reality.

The role of true leaders, then, is to create a mission that will sustain their followers through good and bad times. To do so, that mission must reflect a vision of a better future that the followers can understand. In Churchill's case that mission was clear: "Victory at all costs, victory in spite of all terror, victory however long and hard the road may be; for without victory there is no survival."

Yet many voluntary organisations would appear to have a ready-made mission which is the reason for their existence. This is an extremely valuable asset for a leader. As Julia Cleverdon, chief executive of Business in the Community, explains:

"I wouldn't say it's a cinch, but being a leader when you've got a really good cause is a lot easier than motivating someone on an assembly line making widgets. Voluntary organisations usually have a vision that people will buy into. In leadership terms that makes things a lot easier."

Indeed, to qualify as a charity an organisation must have a vision or cause. It must be for the relief of poverty, the advancement of education, or for some other purpose beneficial to the community. All charities have a mission which fits one or other of these categories. Many, of course, are much more specific. So, for example, the mission of Save the Children seems very clear, as does that of The Royal Society for the Prevention of Cruelty to Animals (RSPCA).

But while these missions have a wide appeal and are very effective for recruiting followers to the cause, they are too broad in scope to inspire changes in focus that may be necessary to ensure their long-term aims. In fact, these vague missions are only one step closer to reality than working towards the woolly notion of a better world. Without refinement, they are not practical goals. They beg clarification. For example, how is Save the Children to actually set about saving the children? And which children? How is the RSPCA to prevent cruelty to animals? And again which animals? Where? These are the sorts of questions that voluntary leaders must address. In doing so, it is useful to distil key goals into a meaningful mission statement.

Mission statements

A mission statement is a statement of general intent which creates a focus for all the organisation's activities. But although a great many organisations have mission statements, some are much better than others.

Bad mission statements generally fall into two categories: either they are so anodyne as to be all but worthless for any practical purposes; or they are handed down from on high and fail to inspire the imagination of the people further down the organisation whose day-to-day activities determine whether the mission is accomplished.

Good mission statements, on the other hand, are ones which have enough substance to be meaningful to everyone within the organisation and capture the mood of its people. Indeed, the best mission statements articulate the vision the organisation has of itself in the future, and express genuinely held values and beliefs that everyone in the organisation can align with.

For example, a good mission statement is that of Charity Projects, best known for its wholly owned subsidiary Comic Relief – and Red Nose Day. It was set up to:

Help disadvantaged people in the United Kingdom and Africa realise their aspirations and potential.

Its chief merit lies in its simplicity. It states what the organisation is trying to achieve, which parts of the world its efforts are focused on, and the guiding principles behind its work. Had the organisation stated its mission as 'raising money to provide aid', the purpose would still have been worthy but the message much less inspirational.

Or take the example of an hospital emergency room in America which states:

It's our mission to give assurance to the afflicted.

Again the message is simple and gets to the root of what the organisation really exists for. People coming to an emergency room may require many different sorts of treatment ranging from being rushed to an operating theatre, a series of tests, or being sent home with a couple of pain killers. But what all require is assurance.

Alternative mission statements for the same organisation could be: 'Our mission is to provide health care', or 'our mission is to treat critically ill people'. But these are not nearly so emotive, or precise.

The mission statement of the Salvation Army is another example of an inspirational message:

To make citizens out of the rejected.

Again, it has a ring to it that engages the hearts and minds of those who work each day to achieve it.

Sometimes mission statements are not self-evident to outsiders. For example most hospices see their mission as the management of pain and of the meaning of life, and not providing hospital services for the terminally ill. This distinction of what an organisation is for will underpin what it does.

As the American management writer Peter Drucker points out, the acid test of a mission statement is that it has meaning for everyone in the organisation so that every single person involved can say 'this is my contribution to what **we're** trying to achieve'.

At first sight, some voluntary organisations may feel they are too small to warrant a mission statement, particularly if they are run by only a handful of volunteers. Yet a mission statement can be a valuable tool for an organisation of any size because in creating it the leaders are compelled to think very hard about what it is the organisation exists to do, something they may otherwise be too busy to do. In distilling that objective into one or two phrases the leaders have to be clear about their core aims and the followers are able to see more clearly what it is they are working towards even if at times all hands are required on deck just to keep the organisation afloat.

Another excellent mission statement is that of the YMCA, which exists to:

Support young people in mind, spirit and body by acting before a problem becomes a crisis.

The strength of this mission lies in the fact that it really gets to the essence of the organisation's purpose and has allowed it to adapt to changing needs as its activities have moved beyond the popular image of sports clubs and old-fashioned accommodation for men.

Finally, a mission statement which we particularly liked is that of VOLPROF, the Centre for Voluntary Sector and Not-for-Profit Management at City University Business School. Its highly commendable mission is:

To explore the boundaries between for-profit and not-for-profit organisations and to promote the interchange of relevant management theories and practices through education, research and development.

Designing a mission statement

A dilemma for voluntary organisations in designing and implementing a mission statement is the extent, to which it takes into account the aspirations of the sector as a whole, rather than just those of its own stakeholders. As Tim Dartington of NCVO explains:

"Ian Bruce, director at VOLPROF and director general of the RNIB, has pointed out that 50% of top charities have general managers whose developmental careers were in the private sector. This poses a problem of leadership, because leaders need to understand where the sector as a whole is going. There's a temptation to set visions like those of IBM or Unilever, rather than seek unique statements that reflect the voluntary tradition and purpose."

Where the best voluntary sector mission statements might differ from the private sector, perhaps, is in the way they perceive their own role in the future. It is almost inconceivable that a company would aspire to reach a point where customers no longer have need of its services. But it would be a laudable goal for many voluntary organisations to work towards a point when they were needed less or not at all – for example, because a disease had been eliminated, or poverty in a certain area had been dramatically reduced. Part of its mission would therefore be to eventually make itself obsolete.

The fact remains, however, that establishing a mission statement is significantly easier for a voluntary organisation, because it does have a shared purpose. People join because they have shared values, or common cause, or both. Where they can learn from the private sector, once again, is in how *not* to design and use missions. Many companies have distributed to all employees high-minded statements of vision and value, but the evidence suggests very strongly that these rarely succeed in becoming a tool for motivating people, nor a touchstone for assessing decisions. Experience of business missions that do achieve these objectives is that they are:

♦ **Simple** – easy to understand and apply to everyday situations.

♦ **Challenging** but **realistic**.

♦ **Reinforcing** people's instinctive beliefs about what is right.

Mission statements

In designing a mission statement, a voluntary organisation should keep the following guidelines in mind:

♦ *Consult widely, both inside the organisation and outside.*

What is it you stand for (the cause)? What do you promise to do for your beneficiaries (the service)? What's special about the way that you do it? Is each of these long-term, immutable or make-shift and temporary?

♦ *Don't confuse vision and values.*

A mission is a combination of the vision (what we aim to do) and the values (the operating principles we will use to take us there).

♦ *Strive for simplicity of wording and concept.*

The longer and more complex the statement is, the less meaningful it will be. If it needs explaining in more detail, then find other ways to do so.

♦ *Make the vision visionable*

If it doesn't bring to people's minds a picture of what success looks like, then it isn't working. Does it stir emotions, provide challenge, make people want to give commitment?

♦ *Credibility is critical*

Will people inside and outside the organisation see it as "challenging but achievable" or as "pie in the sky"? The more it reflects the path you are already taking, rather than one you aspire to, the more credibility it will have. Can the organisation realistically live up to these aspirations? What changes will you have to make to ensure it does?

Voluntary sector versus private sector leaders

The idea that the private sector may have something to learn from the voluntary sector about the development of effective leaders still has very little currency, but is increasingly being recognised.

Management workshops

Consultant Judy Welemensky recalls attending a company's management workshop, at NCVO.

"I was paid £26,000 a year at the time and the middle managers of the oil company running the course were paid an average of £45,000. One of our set tasks was to call the director of a local education authority and make some policy suggestions. The oil company managers couldn't make the call, because they didn't know how to get started in a challenging new environment. Managers in the voluntary sector have to deal with a wider range of complexities and situations, with more opportunity and requirement to experiment and be flexible. Early in my career, I worked for a community relations council. I used to call on the director of housing or the chair of council committees without thinking anything of it. Then I joined a private sector company, where most of the time I couldn't even get access to my own boss.

"The lack of hierarchy consciousness within the voluntary sector means that managers have to exert influence and authority largely through persuasion, competence and personality, rather than through position. On the question of leadership style, I think it's becoming clear that voluntary organisations require a very diffuse sort of leadership. There's a big difference between a leader who says I've listened hard to what you've told me, and one who is actually part of what's going on. It's quite a difficult role to fill and the best voluntary sector leaders have to tolerate great complexity and ambiguity which requires different skills. That said, I don't think all voluntary sector leaders are good at managing these sorts of issues, but I believe there are some excellent voluntary sector leaders.

"This transition from hierarchical structures to empowered groups of individuals is one that leading private sector companies are struggling to achieve."

Leadership practice

Amanda Jordan, Senior Executive – Group Community Relations at National Westminster Bank, explains how the bank has benefited from observing leadership practice in the voluntary sector:

"Our chairman, Lord Alexander of Weedon has stated that involvement in the voluntary sector is important in helping us change our culture. We used to have a control culture. We had manuals for doing everything – a very strong management development ethos, but for management within the system. All that is going as we move towards decentralisation and empowerment. That requires different skills, which are rife in the voluntary sector. For example, our managers need to become multidisciplinary, so they can look after a variety of different functions. In the voluntary sector, by comparison, if you want to put on an exhibition, you manage the whole process yourself. A survey for Age Concern for example compared their managers with managers at similar levels in the National Health Service. It found that, on average, the Age Concern managers dealt with much wider range of tasks.

"Of 740 bank staff who responded to a questionnaire about their activities as school governors or trustees of voluntary organisations, 80% said they had developed their leadership capability as a result of their involvement."

Structure of voluntary organisations

We have talked so far about the leadership role in voluntary organisations in general terms. To see how leadership is exercised it is necessary to consider the structure of voluntary organisations.

There is no simple blueprint for the management structure of voluntary organisations. They may be structured in a wide variety of different ways, reflecting differences in size, resources and aims. Yet there are some common features.

Every voluntary organisation has a governing body which is legally and financially responsible for its actions. This body, which may be called variously the management committee, board of trustees, or board of directors (in the case of a charitable company), will generally be responsible for the major strategic decisions and ensuring the organisation meets its legal obligations. In some cases, however, the governing body may delegate responsibility to a separate management committee. The governing body has a number of key roles. It is responsible for:

♦ Ensuring that the organisation keeps **within its constitutional objectives** and does not act "ultra vires".

♦ Ensuring **funds are properly managed** and used for the purposes, for which they were raised.

Any breach is a breach of trust and trustees can be held personally liable for any such breach except where they can show that they acted with diligence and in good faith. What can go wrong and the implications for the trustees is clearly illustrated by the Charity Commission's investigation of War on Want. Their report is required reading for anyone wanting to understand the trustee role and how things can go wrong.

The governing body is responsible for ensuring that the organisation knows what it is supposed to be doing, and complies with the legal requirements incumbent upon it. In the main, those who serve on management committees will be trustees although they may be referred to by other names such as 'members of the committee', 'management committee members', 'directors', 'council members', 'executive committee members' or 'governors'. These people are either appointed or elected to serve in this capacity and are unpaid (except in very exceptional circumstances). The management committee as a whole constitutes the leadership of the voluntary organisation. In many ways the management committee fulfils a similar role to that of the board of directors in a for-profit company. The management committee is concerned with directing the efforts of the organisation, securing its long-term future and ensuring probity.

Where required, the management committee may be subdivided into sub-committees or standing committees responsible for specific aspects of the organisation's activities such as fundraising or project development. Alternatively, working parties may be set up to handle specific short-term tasks such as developing an equal opportunities policy, drawing up new guidelines, or reviewing the organisation's procedures in a certain area. Sometimes the constitution provides for this, but normally it is done under a general power of delegation. It should be noted that trustees can delegate their tasks but not their responsibility. They are certainly where the buck stops.

Decisions made by the management committee – the directing part of the organisation – are then transmitted into action by the executive management team which is responsible for the day-to-day running of the organisation and is led by the senior member of staff. Typical job titles for this role include chief executive, "director" (but not necessarily in the same legal sense as in a limited company), general secretary, manager or co-ordinator. The role is similar to that of a managing director or chief executive officer in a company. The voluntary sector chief executive is responsible for implementing the decisions of the management committee, just as a private sector chief executive implements the decisions of the board of directors.

Beyond the management committee, voluntary organisations are made up of a combination of paid employees and volunteers. The balance between paid workers and volunteers will vary with size, funding and the scope of the organisation's activities. Many small voluntary organisations are run entirely by volunteers. Conversely, some very large voluntary organisations have a sophisticated management pyramid made up almost entirely of paid full-time staff. In these large organisations paid employees are often professional managers performing tasks in much the same way as their counterparts in the private and public sectors.

For example, in large organisations there will be departmental heads or line managers, whose role is to cascade the implementation process down to the members of their teams. These line managers will be responsible for particular aspects of the day-to-day running of the organisation such as personnel, finance or administration. They will report directly to the chief executive and may work closely with standing committees or working parties from the management committee.

Depending on the size and complexity of the organisation, there may be further layers of management such as supervisors, co-ordinators or team leaders responsible for managing the people carrying out the day-to-day tasks. Typically, however, the structures of voluntary organisations are much flatter than traditional private sector management hierarchies, with fewer tiers of management between the workers and senior managers.

However, one of the most interesting developments in the private sector over the last few years has been the move away from highly hierarchical structures towards flatter management structures more closely resembling those in voluntary organisations. It is already becoming clear, however, that many companies are experiencing difficulties in adjusting to these flatter structures. This is another area where the private sector could learn much from the experience of the voluntary sector. We will say more about this in Chapter 9.

Management structure of a voluntary organisation

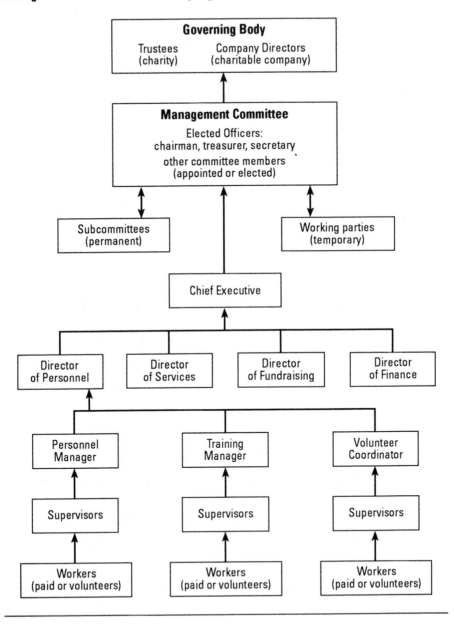

Finally, beneath the supervisory tiers of management there are the workers, who may be paid employees or volunteers, and who are individually responsible for managing their own work. Paid workers may be viewed in much the same way as employees in the private and public sectors. Volunteers, on the other hand, are unique to the voluntary sector.

The layers of management in the diagram correspond with the following management responsibilities:

♦ **Governing body** (where separate from the management committee): responsibility for the ethical climate and meeting legal requirements.

♦ **Management committee**: responsibility for the organisation as a whole, (setting and monitoring long and medium term strategy and developing policies).

♦ **Chief executive** (and senior management team): responsibility for the day-to-day management of the organisation's work: what the organisation does, how it does it, and how well the work is done, managing the people who do the work, and allocating the resources available.

♦ **Line managers/supervisors**: responsibility for managing a department, team or project to achieve set objectives.

♦ **Workers**: individual responsibility for managing themselves and their work.

It is in terms of their ability to meet these responsibilities that the effectiveness of the management structure and leadership of any voluntary organisation must be assessed. Yet, in the eyes of the law at least, the leadership buck stops with the trustees. This can create problems, as we will see in Chapter 2.

Corporate governance and the voluntary organisation

Although corporate governance has mainly hit the headlines as an issue for private sector quoted companies in recent years, it is an equally live issue for both public and voluntary organisations. A 1994 report from the Chartered Institute of Public Finance and Accountancy (Corporate Governance in the Public Services) found that the structures to ensure that executives of public sector bodies behaved responsibly, honestly and wisely in their decision-making were far from adequate. In particular, public organisations' resources could often be diverted to inappropriate purposes. Maintains Noel Hepworth, director of CIPFA, "We have to look for alternative structures which harmonise with but are not part of, the political process."

A major issue in making voluntary organisations more accountable to stakeholders is the governance structure. Typically, the governing body is made up of a self-perpetuating oligarchy of trustees (membership by invitation only) or members elected by constituents around the country. The governing body often has a number of weaknesses:

- Its members may be **insufficiently informed** to understand the issues; or so closely involved with grass roots issues they cannot see the big picture.

- To accommodate all constituencies, it is often **too large** to permit constructive debate or to exert effective control over the executive team.

- It is largely an **amateur** body, so members are often unable to understand the complexities of strategic planning, financial control, marketing or employment law.

- In most cases, it represents **only some of the stakeholder groups** – often the recipients of the service are not included in the decision-making structure at all.

- There are often **no provisions for removing** someone from the governing body, and for many organisations the power of appointing new members to the governing body rests entirely with existing members.

The governing body also has a number of strengths, not least that:

- It often comprises or encourages **grassroots representation** (particularly in membership organisations with formal election procedures).

- It often attracts **high calibre people** from business and other useful disciplines.

- It provides a route for **dissenting stakeholders** to register their concerns about executive decisions and actions (something frequently much more difficult in private sector and government organisations).

"Who creates strategy and vision?" may become an important issue here. The governing body is frequently if not usually inadequate to the task; yet the executives may not have the power and resources to do so either. It is not surprising, therefore, that voluntary organisations often require a strong, visionary leader (perhaps more so than a private sector organisation) to give genuine purpose and direction to their activities.

The executive team of voluntary organisations is as often as not an informal grouping of senior people who meet to consider operational matters. There are strong parallels with National Health Trusts, where the formal Board of trustees consists of five executives, five non-executives and an independent chairperson. Considerable discussion goes into which of the key functional areas of hospital management gets left off the Board. The executive team usually includes all the main hospital disciplines, but has no legal status or responsibilities – it is simply a convenient operational structure.

The debate over what an effective leadership structure for a voluntary organisation should be will continue for a long time. However, our view is that the most effective structures will provide direction and focus at the appropriate levels and will be generated to take account of, but not necessarily copy, good practice in the private sector.

An attractive option for the larger voluntary organisation would be a four-tier structure of governance, as follows:

1. The Constituents or Stakeholders

These are the volunteers, local committees, fund providers and "clients" in an equitable mix that ensures no-one is disempowered.

The constituents will elect the Supervisory Board with one third retiring each year.

2. The Supervisory Board or Council

Equivalent to the governing body in some voluntary organisations and the management committee in others, this body should:

♦ Be accountable to the constituents for performance of the organisation.

♦ Be small enough to make effective decisions but large enough to allow for proper discussion/diversity of views (i.e. between 6 and 12 people).

♦ Consist of people who are manifestly competent to fulfil the role.

♦ Meet with the executive team on a regular basis.

The chief executive will normally represent the executive team at the Supervisory Board meetings. One of the lessons from private sector experience is that the larger this body is, the less effective it tends to be.

In the private sector, a continuing source of debate surrounds the issue of who the Supervisory Board members should be. The German model of corporate governance assumes, as does the US model by and large, that this body should be entirely non-executive, with the exception in some cases of the chief executive. In the UK, private sector companies mix executives and non-executives in a wide variety of proportions.

There seems no reason why voluntary organisations in the UK should not avail themselves of equally diverse forms of governing bodies, as long as they fulfil the criteria above.

3. The executive team/management board

Formally constituted as the responsible management of the organisation, as in the European model of corporate governance. Appointed by the chief executive and chairman with the approval or delegated authority of the Supervisory Board, they will have responsibility for:

♦ Developing strategy and plans for the organisation.

♦ Delivering performance on the key strategic objectives.

4. The operational organisation

Voluntary organisations, which have a mix of radically different activities may find it most practical to adopt a "holding company" approach — especially when the organisation's activities include both cause-management and the running of a "business". For example, Oxfam's shops are essentially a retail business; as are those for the Royal Society for the

Protection of Birds (RSPB). They compete for trade with other High Street outlets. Mencap's homes for mentally handicapped people are in competition with those of other, commercial organisations. Separating out cause-management operations from trading activities and service provision allows each to have the style and intensity of management it needs.

This four-tier structure is not so different from what happens in some of the best run voluntary organisations at the moment. However, clearly articulating roles and responsibilities should make it much easier to achieve the organisation's objectives.

Smaller voluntary organisations may find this kind of structure far too top heavy. They can, nonetheless, adopt the basic principles of:

♦ Clarity of role between stakeholders, trustees, executives and operational management.

♦ Representation of stakeholders wherever practical.

♦ Management accountability.

However voluntary organisations' capacity to make radical changes to their structures is often limited by their constitution. It may often require permission from the Charity Commission to amend the constitution.

Keeping leaders under control

One of the uncomfortable lessons private sector companies have learned in recent years is the danger of allowing too much power to concentrate in the hands of one individual or a small cabal. Well-publicised cases, such as the collapse of the Maxwell empire, illustrate how easy it is for the autocratic, strong-willed leader to conceal fundamental problems within the organisation, especially when the roles of chairman and chief executive are combined.

Maxwell was finally unmasked when new non-executives he was obliged to take onto his board insisted on having information that was previously unavailable to the directors. As we shall explore in the next chapter, part of the role of the trustees is to exercise those same controlling powers over the leader's excesses and there are lessons for the voluntary sector in how they do so (when they use their powers effectively, which is not always!).

Contrary to much popular commentary, Sir Adrian Cadbury, whose committee on the financial aspects of corporate governance has stirred a radical re-examination of the composition and role of boards in UK quoted companies, is not totally against combining the roles of chief executive and chairman. There are circumstances (for example, when the business is in trouble and needs a rapid turnaround) when it may well be the best solution. Says Cadbury:

"It is the way in which the board as a whole works, which sets the framework for those at its head. It is the counterbalance provided by the other board members, which will determine whether the combination of

the two powers confer an unacceptable degree of power on one person or not."

The lesson for both private and voluntary sector organisations is that the trustees or directors must ensure that a genuine balance of power exists. On the one hand, this requires them to ensure that they as a group are of the calibre and influence and have the time to challenge (in all senses of the word) the executive leadership; on the other, it behoves them to appoint leaders with the strength of character to insist on the right to carry out delegated powers without undue interference.

The latter point is particularly relevant for professional bodies run by councils of trustees. We have seen several of the professional institutes for managers become paralysed because their councils would not set clear policy nor allow the chief executive room to set his or her own. The result in every case has been a drawn out tussle, which usually ends with the removal of the chief executive and the appointment of a more malleable individual to the post. This new appointee rarely lasts more than two years. Seen as lackey to the council, he or she is unable to demonstrate leadership and is in turn replaced – usually with another strong character, who may start the whole cycle again. Managing the balancing of power is perhaps the most difficult, yet one of the most critical responsibilities the trustees have. Significantly, it hardly ever comes onto the Council agenda. It should.

Managing change in the voluntary sector

Nowhere is the leader's calibre tested more than when the organisation has to go through radical change. In all the cases of successful major change we have examined, there has been a strong, committed and capable top team providing the drive and energy for organisational renewal.

Effective change management in a voluntary organisation is, in general, not unlike that in a private sector organisation. Indeed, this is one of many areas, where the private sector can potentially learn from voluntary sector experience. Key factors in successful major change include:

♦ Being very **clear about the objectives** of the changes and explaining them clearly to everyone involved.

♦ Taking time to **bring people on board**.

♦ **Planning changes** in detail and **involving people**, who will be affected, in designing the solutions.

♦ Making sure people have the **skills, confidence and support** to behave in the new ways.

♦ Being very clear about **what is expected** of everyone affected.

♦ Having **fair and reliable systems** to measure **progress and performance** against the new objectives.

The following cases illustrate most of these points.

CASE STUDY ▶ SCIP

At SCIP, the leading provider of resource materials for industry/school projects the appointment of a new chief executive coincided with a financial crisis. Most of SCIP's costs had been met by the DTI over the previous three years, but a sudden change of government policy in 1992 meant that the funding was in jeopardy – and therefore that the future of the organisation itself was in severe doubt.

Carol Kay, the new CEO, found that her staff:

"were used to the comfortable world of core funding. They were resistant and reluctant to accept the reality. People didn't think entrepreneurialy about the situation because they had never had to before. There was no concept that the organisation even needed managing, because people were used to working away on their own projects.

"Outside SCIP, education was in flux, with controversy over the National Curriculum. Schools had their own budgets, but they had never previously had to pay SCIP for its services and didn't know they had the money to support the infrastructure the Local Education Authorities had previously provided. At the same time, our business partners were caught in the recession.

"People started saying SCIP would go down. I realised that the financial imperative would have to be our discipline from then on. A very vigorous cost-cutting exercise reduced the number of staff from 21 to 16 and cut salaries. We installed new financial systems and offered the University of Warwick, where SCIP is based, a business plan with five options for survival."

Through persuasion, example and sheer determination, Kay gradually overcame her colleagues distaste for selling their services and generated new forms of income – from affiliation fees, sponsorship, consultancy contracts and sales of product.

One of the biggest challenges was to motivate staff who ranged from feeling defeated – they perceived they had been working hard to no avail – to being outright hostile. Kay spent much of her time working with them, explaining the new requirements and attempting to develop new skills and boost their confidence. The result was a rapid turnaround from no funding to near break-even. The University continues to support SCIP in expectation that it will return to self-sufficiency.

CASE STUDY ▶ Mencap

At Mencap, the crisis evolved from the rapid growth of the Society's care in the community activities. Basically, the organisation didn't have the management skills or systems to control a £70 million a year service providing operation. A critical report from the Department of Health in 1991 forced Mencap to look critically at itself and to bring in more professional managers.

Explains chief executive Fred Heddell:

Three years ago we were victims of our own success. We had a crisis of too rapid growth. Sir Brian Rix retired in 1987, recognising we needed new blood to manage the new problems. The trustees appointed a retired admiral, who was soon out of his depth. Our cash flow difficulties got worse; there were long delays in invoicing because the centre took all the decisions.

We recognised that we would have to decentralise accountability, starting with finance. The way it used to work was that the area manager negotiated contracts and had responsibility for a number of projects. He spent most of the money. Below him the project manager could also spend money. But getting money in was another matter entirely. Instructions to invoice had to go through the divisional manager to the central finance department. The people in the field weren't trusted to pay in their own cheques. Even when money came in, it went to a separate part of the finance department, so no-one knew what was happening.

Now the responsibility for invoicing rests with the budget holder. We reduced size of central finance dept from 52 people to just 3. There are another 14 finance people across the country. And these people also handle payroll and audit, which used to be contracted out.

We supported the project managers and area managers with information and training. They learnt that to keep projects viable, they had to make sure they didn't overspend. If money doesn't come into a home, the manager has a problem paying the wages.

Not everyone liked being made accountable. Says Heddell:

There was quite a lot of conflict to decentralisation, but it is now universally accepted that this was the right move. The main resistance came from managers with social services backgrounds, who were reluctant to be made accountable for their own budgets.

We have had to be tough with some people who filibustered. One way we got through to them was to say: "If you care about the people in your houses, financial security is crucial. If you leave that to someone else it isn't assured. So you have to take it on board." Finance is now marketed as a resource, not a policeman.

Then we were able to move onto the quality issues. We now have thick volumes of standards for the homes. We are able to build those standards into the contracts we make with local authorities. We are developing a much more professional approach to planning. We have adopted a more rigorous approach to training and to hiring. Even volunteers go through a strict interview and selection process. We have moved from a self-help group to a charity to a business.

These radical changes in the organisation inevitably required changes at the top. The top two layers of managers changed. The entire executive board has gone and so have six of the seven regional directors. It was, says finance director Roger Smythe "a painful business. After all, Fred is here because he cares about people."

Perhaps the most important lesson from this experience is the need for patience. Explains Smythe:

Change takes a lot longer in a charity. The Board of Trustees are elected people from the UK affiliates. Senior paid employees are not directors in the legal sense. Trustees take a very detailed interest in major changes. If you add in the statutory responsibilities you have for provision of services, you have even more delay factors. It's like Lynford Christie training with weights; when you finally run without them, you go a lot faster!

We had multiple stakeholders to consult: social services, people living in the homes, people managing them, parents and so on. It all took time. Everyone feels they own Mencap, so changes are resisted that much more.

Patience with people inside the organisation was important, too. Says Heddell:

"Some people were blocking development, but most of them left remarkably amicably. One or two accepted demotion: they had great commitment to the organisation. People were prepared to examine their own shortcomings and lack of experience."

The vast majority of people have risen to the challenge, with the few incompetent people being removed locally.

One thing I've learned working in a voluntary organisation is not to get too het up about resistance. You achieve a lot through patience and persistence.

Summary

Is there a crisis of leadership? It is clear to us that there are a number of issues in the voluntary sector which need to be urgently addressed if a leadership crisis is to be avoided. In the future it will be increasingly important for the sector to speak with one voice on major government policy issues. The creation of an effective lead body that could represent the sector to government, as the Confederation of British Industry does for business, would greatly improve its influence.

There are also important issues in the area of corporate governance which need to be faced by voluntary organisations. The most pressing of these relates to the accountability of current management structures. Opportunities exist in this area to learn from the recent debate on corporate governance in the private and public sectors.

At the same time, changes in legislation embodied in the Charities Acts are likely to throw into sharper relief the issue of good leadership at the level of individual voluntary organisations. However, there is a real danger here that voluntary leaders might move too far towards the private sector model. Indeed, there are signs that leadership is an area where companies can learn a great deal from best practice in the voluntary sector.

The best voluntary leaders have high credibility with their followers and articulate a clear and achievable mission. Typically, they are highly:

♦ Entrepreneurial.

♦ Inspirational.

♦ Ethical.

Checklist

1. Does your organisation have a **clear mission** that is relevant today?

2. Who are its **true leaders**? Are those people credible to others?

3. Who is **accountable for the ethical conduct** of the organisation? Does the current management structure enable them to carry out their duties?

4. What **changes does your organisation face** in the next few years? What steps are being taken to prepare for those changes?

References

1. James M. Kouzes and Barry Z. Posner, *'Credibility: how leaders gain and lose it' why people demand it'*, published by Jossey Bass 1993, (available outside the US from Maxwell Macmillan International Publishing Group, New York).

2. Widget Finn, *'Experience that blooms in fresh pastures'*, April 8 1993, p.18.

3. Peter Drucker, *'Managing the Non-profit Organisation'*, Butterworth Heinemann Ltd, 1990.

4. *'On Achieving Excellence'*, February 1989.

Chapter 2

What are trustees there for?

Key issues

♦ *Who are trustees responsible to?*

♦ *What competencies do they need?*

♦ *How can they be made more effective?*

The concept of 'trusteeship' dates back to the Middle Ages when knights leaving for the Crusades would appoint agents to manage their land and property affairs while they were away. Today's charity trustees are people who are entrusted to look after money, land, or property donated to a charity for a specific purpose. It is their responsibility to ensure that it is used effectively to achieve the end for which it was intended.

The Charities Act 1960 defines charity trustees as those individuals who are responsible for the general control and management of the charity, whatever their title. They have ultimate responsibility for the organisation – a point confirmed by the Nathan Report on Effectiveness and the Voluntary Sector. In theory, then, if not always in practice, the trustees direct the efforts of the organisation by interpreting and articulating its mission, values and overall objectives.

The problem with this text book view of trusteeship is that it doesn't always work like that. Ask any group of trustees from different organisations what their roles are and you will receive a wide range of answers. The answers are not necessarily wrong – a trustee of a National Health Trust with 2,000 employees is dealing with a very different organisation to the trustee of a local community association with a handful of part-time employees, for example. Nonetheless, in spite of the increased volume of guidance about the roles of trustees in recent years, there is still a great deal of confusion and uncertainty. The confusion arises from a whole variety of causes. Some of the most critical are the following.

Inadequate focus on what trustees can contribute

Most of the advice available refers to legal responsibilities and the proper conduct of a charity's affairs. Less readily available is advice on what trustees can do, as a group or individually, to add value to the organisation they serve. It's a lot easier for managers and volunteers, who can usually see tangible results from their efforts. But for trustees (in their trustee role at least) their contribution is much more difficult to describe. It is often impossible to say "I was responsible for making that happen".

To add value, you have to be clear about what value is. That means:

♦ Developing a clear and deep **understanding** of what various stakeholders expect and need.

♦ **Measuring** the degree, to which those needs are being met through the organisation's activities.

♦ Assessing the **efficiency**, with which the organisation is adding value.

♦ Stimulating changes to **increase value**.

Inadequate information and training

Trustees are almost always unpaid and part-time. They therefore have a limited amount of time available to perform their role. Furthermore, many receive little or no formal training in the skills required of them – another shortcoming pointed out by the Nathan Report – and no proper induction into the organisation. As a result, many voluntary trustees are unclear about their responsibilities and unsure about how the organisation really works or what it is trying to achieve.

As Widget Finn pointed out in an article in The Times: ('Training taken on trust', 31 March 1994):

"*There are one million trustees responsible for the management of charities in the UK. Charity boards, once the province of the great and the good, are now recruiting people from all walks of life. Trustees, like company directors, have considerable financial and legal responsibilities and yet many have no previous management experience.***"**

Managerial responsibilities of trustees

There is an important distinction to be made between the governance role of trustees and the role of management in voluntary organisations. Trustees are responsible for certain aspects of the management of the organisation, but must execute their responsibilities through the appropriate channels as designated by the management structure.

If the organisation has only a few members of staff, then trustees are likely to be involved in the day-to-day management of work. But in larger organisations where there are many members of staff, the day-to-day management tasks should be delegated to these people and the role of trustees becomes that of ensuring the organisation is well managed, rather than performing management tasks themselves.

In either case, it is important that trustees remember that their primary focus should be that of governance rather than management. Governance is about setting policy and longer term strategy, and monitoring and evaluating performance. Keeping this in mind can help both trustees and members of staff decide which issues they should be concentrating on.

That said, trustees have a number of managerial responsibilities including:

♦ **Strategic planning**.

♦ **Accountability** to funders and other stakeholders such as beneficiaries, volunteers and staff.

♦ **Senior staff** selection.

♦ **Monitoring and evaluating** the work of the organisation.

♦ Managing the organisation's **assets** including investments, property and land.

♦ Managing the organisation's **finances** including approving the budget, ensuring that sufficient funds are available to meet outgoings and establishing reserves or contingency funds where appropriate.

♦ **Representing** the views of the organisation.

These responsibilities may be discharged either through direct involvement or by delegating to staff. In the latter case, however, the trustees remain responsible for overseeing the work of those to whom it has been delegated.

The link between the trustees and the management

The leadership provided by the management committee is transmitted to the rest of the organisation via the chief executive. The strength of the relationship which exists between the chief executive and his or her management committee is therefore a crucial factor in determining the effectiveness of the trustees and the organisation as a whole.

If this relationship becomes strained, it is all too easy for the views of the trustees or directors serving on the management committee and the views of the people further down the organisation to become out of step.

At the same time, the individual trustees or directors must have confidence in the chief executive's ability to execute their joint decisions. Without that confidence the organisation cannot function effectively. Trustees have neither the time or the authority to implement decisions. In the best voluntary organisations leadership is provided by the management committee acting through the chief executive, with the chief executive acting as the focus for action. Yet, the legal framework within which trustees operate places strict limits on their ability to delegate their legal responsibilities.

As Stephen Lloyd, a partner with Bates, Wells & Braithwaite, solicitors specialising in charity law, notes in an illuminating article in 'NGO Finance' (Issue 9, Sept 1992):

"There is a paradox at the heart of trusteeship. Unpaid charity trustees have to labour under the strictest legal duties, stricter than highly paid executive directors! Trustees are in effect unpaid non-executive [part-

time] directors. But whereas the board of a commercial company may comprise a mixture of executive [full-time] and non-executive directors, a charity board is made up entirely of non-executives."

In larger voluntary organisations, this can cause problems if the trustees and those responsible for the day-to-day management of the organisation do not know what each other are doing or disagree about what the organisation should be doing.

In smaller voluntary organisations where there are no paid managers and the management and direction role are often combined, other problems may arise. Small voluntary organisations often experience severe problems as they grow. Rather like small companies run by entrepreneurial founders, small voluntary organisations are prone to growing pains as the quantity of work and the need for a strategic overview creates a pressure to split the strategic directing role and the day-to-day hands-on management role, which have previously been combined. As Sandra Greaves, former editor of 'Third Sector' magazine, explains:

"The old problem for a small business of loosening the entrepreneur's grip when the company becomes too big for one person to manage exists in the voluntary sector, too. How you edge out the founder becomes a difficult issue. And if the founder becomes a trustee with an executive manager put in charge of running the charity then you can get the classic boardroom power clash as the founder tries to hang on to power."

Other issues revolve around the trustee's backgrounds. Shirley Otto points to "the problems that arise where trustees try to control, following private sector models of hierarchy and command structures which are inappropriate to the voluntary sector." This problem can equally occur from the appointment of a private sector chief executive, whose views on appropriate structures and systems clash with those of an experienced voluntary sector board of trustees.

Who should be on the Board?

Says Greaves:

"Beyond that there are the control problems of executive versus non-executive roles. There are still a lot of charities saddled with out-dated models of the trustee board, with the great and the good, or trustees recruited via the Old Boy Network. It's getting better but a lot of voluntary organisations still don't even write a job description before they elect trustees. They should clarify the role and say this is an operational decision, this is a strategy decision – this is the stage at which trustees should become involved."

As Greaves indicates, questions such as who should become trustees and what their precise function should be are at the heart of improving the effectiveness of the trustee role. There is a growing feeling, too, that the pool from which trustees are drawn should be expanded to represent a broader cross-section of the UK population.

One aspect of this is that many in the voluntary sector believe that the notion of self-advocacy – having representatives of the end-user group, or beneficiaries, serving as trustees – is critical to the legitimacy of a voluntary organisation. Only in this way, the argument goes, can the management committee truly represent the interests of those it seeks to serve.

Jane Tewson, chief executive of Charity Projects, believes there is much to be said for this view:

"I always think that if you want to know how committed to the beneficiaries a charity is you should ask how many of the people they're trying to help actually sit on the board."

Mike Tuffrey, editor of 'Community Affairs Briefing', sees another dimension to the issue:

"Should trustees be independent or not? If you take the view that they should not be paid, and should not be benefiting directly, then you're left with the great and the good. But how then do you ensure that the organisation genuinely serves the need it exists for?

"You can have client group trustees to represent the beneficiaries' views. But if you take the example of a charity I'm involved with, L'Arche, the beneficiaries are people with learning difficulties; it's impractical to have these people as trustees. Yet regular consultation should be built into the trustees' terms of reference. That way decisions aren't made without reference to end-users. These problems exist above the level of management, therefore they are constitutional issues."

Another issue relating to who should be on the Board is how to use famous names. Very often these are people who have neither the time nor the inclination to fulfil directorial duties. Their time may be far better spent as ambassadors, putting the charity's case and creating public awareness of its activities and objectives. Observes John Williams of consultants Fishburn, Hedges, Bays & Williams:

"Big charities often don't use well enough the stature and influence of people they bring onto their boards. One good idea is to create a separate Board of Patrons. For example, National Children's Homes: Action for Children has a body of VIPs ranging from Angus Ogilvy to Angela Rippon."

Bringing the Trustees and the Patrons together from time to time keeps the Patrons informed about the charity's goals and current issues.

Representative trustees

The question of who should **not** be on the board also has another important dimension. By law, a trustee must always act in the best interests of the organisation of which they are a trustee. This means that the notion that they can sit on the board expressly as the representative of another organisation – be it a company, a government agency or another voluntary organisation – is untenable in law.

Yet many voluntary organisations currently have representative trustees either to include sectional interests from amongst their members (as is the case with the National Trust) or for funders to keep a watchful eye on the proceedings. These representative trustees need to be informed of their responsibilities and that their primary loyalty as trustees is to the organisation on whose board they sit.

The situation can best be likened to that of an individual who holds non-executive directorships on the boards of competing companies. The problem is not that they will on a regular basis face a conflict of interest so much as that one **could** arise.

In practice there are more effective ways of overseeing a grant than appointing a representative trustee, who is unlikely to contribute much anyway. If other organisations have a valid reason for being involved with board discussions, their representatives should not have trustee status, rather they should be consulted or invited to attend meetings if appropriate.

Legal gobbledygook

Trustees are exposed to onerous legal responsibilities which are in many ways similar to those incumbent on company directors. However, recent research has revealed a disturbing lack of awareness on the part of many trustees about the nature of those responsibilities.

For example, a survey by a working party on trustee training set up by NCVO (National Council of Voluntary Organisations) and the Charity Commission in 1992 revealed yawning gaps in their knowledge about their role. Only one in three of the trustees surveyed even realised they were trustees!

The working party concluded that in part this reflects a language problem, with the roles of many people who are trustees not named as such in their job titles. In some organisations, for instance, members of the management committee were unclear whether they were trustees or not. In charitable companies, respondents often saw themselves as directors without knowing whether they were also trustees. Says Sandra Greaves: "In the voluntary sector, because of the way it has developed over the years, it's actually quite an easy mistake to make."

When you consider, too, that the Charities Act 1992 introduced important changes to the legislative framework governing the responsibilities of trustees, it is clear that the current situation is a recipe for disaster.

How can trustees be more effective?

In many respects the role of voluntary trustees is similar to that of non-executive directors on the boards of companies. Both have onerous legal responsibilities for what the organisation does but face severe difficulties because of the limitations placed upon them. For example, both non-executive directors and trustees:

♦ Are **part-time**.

♦ Meet **infrequently**.

♦ Must **rely on the executive management** team to implement decisions.

♦ Are often appointed because of their **standing in the community**.

♦ Frequently have **little practical experience** of what the organisation does.

The opportunities for learning across sectors are therefore considerable. As Diana Leat observes:

"Whatever name you give them, the role of voluntary trustees has great similarities with that of non-executive directors in the private sector. They face very similar problems.

"But because they are in different sectors it is possible to miss the similarities and therefore to miss out on the interchange between sectors where there is great potential to learn."

Some companies have begun to see the light. For example, BP Exploration, the Metropolitan Police, and City solicitors Freshfields actively encourage promising managers to become voluntary trustees as part of their career development. David Hemsworth, commercial director of the Action Resource Centre (ARC), told The Times in April 1993:

"Companies are discovering that charities are very good for getting at the parts conventional management courses do not reach, and professional advisers who act as unpaid trustees can gain inside knowledge of how the voluntary sector works."

CASE STUDY ➤ Oasis Children's Venture

Simon Pring, a solicitor in his 20s, is on the management committee of the South London-based Oasis Children's Venture. Pring was put in touch with the venture through Lawyers in the Community, a scheme run by ARC which encourages City lawyers to become involved with small local community projects.

Oasis runs projects for local children including an environmental garden and go-kart track. Like many small charities it was started by a group of local people who wanted to do something positive in the community – but were in danger of getting tangled up in paperwork and falling foul of their legal obligations.

Says Oasis committee member Andrew Sawdon: "Our projects are affected by everything from changes in local authorities' grants schemes and food and safety regulations to the Children's Act. It's very helpful to have a lawyer on the committee who can offer professional advice as part of the overall team."

Some firms realise, too, that along with the management development benefits there can be other advantages to their business. For example, according to Pesh Framjee who heads the firm's charity unit, accountants Binder Hamlyn encourage staff to work on charity management committees because with 350 charity clients it makes sense to learn how they function.

In the main, however, the voluntary sector has been slower to see the connection between non-executives and trustees. But we believe there is potential for voluntary organisations to learn from the recent debate about how companies can make non-executive directors more effective. The NCVO and Charity Commission working Party on trustee training drew the same conclusion, including in its final report a section on non-executives under the heading 'relevant experience from other sectors in the UK'.

In the last few years a number of developments – including the Cadbury Report on corporate governance and scandals such as the Maxwell and BCCI affairs – have turned the spotlight on to non-executives. The resulting debate on the role of these independent part-time directors, we believe, has produced some useful pointers for improving the effectiveness of trustees.

Our own research, carried out in conjunction with Peter Waine of headhunters Hanson Green, into the role of non-executive directors in the private sector led us to conclude that the effectiveness of the role could be greatly enhanced by applying a number of simple management techniques.

One difference between trustees and non-executives is perhaps the expectation that a non-executive is expected to demonstrate independence – especially from management. The problem for many charity boards, says John Williams of Fishburn, Hedges, Bays & Williams is that they are made up in large part of people with a personal interest – for example, they may be relatives of mentally or physically handicapped people. Such boards, he explains "lack the neutral, external voice that questions what is being done and how".

Consultant Shirley Otto, a specialist in voluntary sector management, argues that trustees are there to represent the beneficiaries. Accepting this as a general statement, to what extent can people who have a personal interest represent the beneficiaries? Is there an argument for a strong outsider, able to weigh the views of those most intimately involved against perspectives from society at large? Can any organisation become insular and still be effective?

In a series of articles for 'The Sunday Times' (September and October 1993), the authors looked at key areas in which the non-executive director role could be improved. In particular we highlighted the need for:

♦ Greater awareness of their legal responsibilities.

♦ Proper induction into the organisation.

♦ On-going training.

Another issue to emerge in subsequent research is how well non-executives are trained to ask the right questions. We believe that attention to these four areas could yield corresponding improvements in the contribution of voluntary trustees. Taking these in turn:

How non-executives add value to the organisation

As we saw briefly in Chapter 1, the degree to which non-executive directors maintain the balance of power in the organisation is a critical factor in their effectiveness. Asa Demb and Friedrich Neubauer, two professors at the IMD business schools in Switzerland, describe the three key areas in which non-executives add value as:

♦ Auditing and monitoring executive management. (Companies often have other people to monitor their management, from Stock Exchange regulators to market analysts – voluntary sector organisations are generally much more reliant on the trustees, although there may be external monitoring by the Charity Commission or public agencies, to whom hey are contracted.)

♦ Strategy review: scrutinising management proposals from a broader perspective. (In the case of many voluntary organisations, proposals are considered from a narrower perspective, because trustees see themselves as representatives. The need for trustee education on managing the strategic process is high.)

♦ Corporate governance: choosing the external standards to which the organisation must respond... answering the question 'who is the organisation creating value for?'.

Trustee Boards: a health check

♦ Do the trustees meet sufficiently often to develop into a team?
♦ Do the trustees receive regular and sufficient information to:
  - understand the key organisational and competitive issues?
  - understand the internal and external influences and constraints on the organisation?
  - make informed judgements on financial and strategic issues?
♦ Do executives and other senior managers feel they can approach the trustees with their concerns?
♦ Is discussion at the trustee meetings:
  - to the point?
  - open and lively?
  - challenging but not conflict-generating?
♦ Does the board evaluate the quality of its decision-making?
♦ Is there a clear distinction between executive and non-executive roles?
♦ Are the chairman and chief executive roles separated? If so, is the dialogue between these two people constructive and built around common goals?
♦ Do trustee meetings result in a genuine and searching assessment of executive proposals?
♦ Do trustees have their own secretarial and administrative support, separate from the management resource?
♦ Does the structure of the organisation prevent the emergence of an inner circle of power and influence?

Trustees' legal responsibilities

In the debate on the Second Reading of the Charities Bill in the House of Lords, Lord Morris recalled an incident from his youth. Many years previously when he had been asked to serve as a trustee of a charity, he told the House, he had been unsure what was involved. On seeking the advice of a solicitor, he was told:

"The law knows no higher duty than that of trustee."

Yet many people currently serving as trustees are unaware of just what that high duty entails.

The Charities Acts of 1992 and 1993 were intended to clarify the situation and make trustees more accountable. Yet many of the legal aspects of the role remain vague.

Indeed, anecdotal evidence suggests that many trustees still regard the role as one of patron of the charity or charities they serve. As such, they mistakenly see their primary contribution as lending their name to the cause.

Most telling of all, perhaps, was a recent survey of lawyers involved in management committees through the Action Resource Centre's 'Lawyers in the Community' scheme. This showed that even the legal professionals admit to important gaps in their knowledge which reduce their effectiveness as trustees.

So what are the legal obligations and potential liabilities of trustees? The Charity Commissioners' pamphlet on the subject (ref CC3) summarises the trustee's duties succinctly by stating that he, or she, should exercise the same degree of care in discharging his trusteeship 'as the prudent man of business' would in supervising his own affairs. Yet many businessmen work six and seven days a week to supervise their affairs, while trustees are part-time.

The same pamphlet also emphasises the strict limitations the law places upon trustees against excessive delegation of their duties. Indeed, the capacity to delegate at all depends on the terms of the trust deed. Many charities have extremely limited powers of delegation in areas such as managing investments which make it technically impossible to sell shares unless the trustees sanction it.

Trustees are obliged to meet regularly in order to discharge their duties of supervision. But just how frequently is open to interpretation. Most charities only hold trustees meetings three or four times a year. Yet it is not clear whether that is sufficient in the eyes of the law.

Trustees have to act in the best interests of the organisation they serve, putting aside personal interests. It follows therefore that it is a trustee's duty to deal with a crisis should it occur at any time of the day or night.

However, the reality of trustees' management of charities is very different from the legal theory. Trustees do not exercise the same degree of supervision as the prudent man of business (who ever he might be). They simply don't have time to.

Rather, as Stephen Lloyd, a specialist charity lawyer, asserts in an article in 'NGO Finance':

"Trustees do delegate, often far more than the trust deed sanctions or the law allows. They have to. If they did not they would not continue in office, given the degree of supervision they would have to exercise. Trustees have to trust their staff."

Lloyd points out that although the Charity Commissioners fight this and have tried in a number of recent inquiries to impose a virtual doctrine of strict liability, whereby trustees would be liable for the mistakes, errors or negligent acts of the staff, (1. see references) their role would be impossible without a high degree of trust between the trustees and voluntary staff:

"Chief executives have to be allowed to manage. Charity staff have to be allowed to get on with their job, subject to some supervision from the trustees. A trustee sticking his or her nose into everything would be counter-productive."

However, changes in the legal responsibilities of trustees contained in the Charities Act 1992 are in part an effort to make trustees more accountable for the management of voluntary organisations.

In a speech on 5 November 1991 announcing the Charities Act 1992, John Major said:

"The Act will provide a statutory framework for the proper management and public accountability of charities ... Our aim is not to tie people up in red tape but to open wider the floodgates of giving, by ensuring even greater public confidence in charities themselves."

If this aim is to be achieved, however, it is essential that trustees have a better grasp of their legal duties, including the implications of three new pieces of legislation.

The NHS and Community Care Act 1990

Since April 1993 when the NHS and Community Care Act came into effect, local authorities have had overall responsibility for care in the community of the elderly, disabled people and other vulnerable groups such as people with drug and alcohol problems.

This has meant that funds which were previously administered by central government departments such as social security have been transferred to local councils. These directorates of social services are now in charge of everything from care assessments to the purchasing and contracting of services. The service providers are meant to be a mixture of voluntary private and public sector agencies. The implications for the voluntary sector are enormous.

As Kate Kirkland, head of the NCVO's trustees services unit told 'Investors Chronicle' in March 1993, the contract culture integral to the changes places new burdens on charity trustees. The potential for cases of contracts being entered into which national trustees have not signed – or contracts which make trustees liable for failure to deliver adequate services – highlight the financial and legal implications.

The Charities Acts 1992 and 1993

The Charities Act 1992 replaced the provisions of an earlier Act introduced in 1985. The Charities Act 1993 – most of the provisions of which came into force on 1st August 1993 – contains no new legislation but consolidates, or brings together, the provisions of the 1960 Act, Part 1 of the 1992 Act and the provisions of the Charitable Trusts Incorporation Act 1872, into a single piece of legislation. In summary, the Charities Act 1993:

♦ **Strengthens the Charity Commission's powers** to inquire into charities and gives it additional powers to deal with abuse and mismanagement and to protect charity property.

♦ Introduces a **new regime for accounting** by charities – all registered charities will have to submit an annual report and accounts to the Charity Commission.

♦ Gives the public **the right to ask** to see the annual accounts of a charity.

♦ Makes it an offence for charity trustees not to **submit their annual reports** and accounts to the Commission or to submit false information.

♦ Requires charities to state the fact that the charity is **a registered charity** on some of its official documents.

♦ Requires charitable companies wishing to **alter their objects** (purpose), or any provision in their memorandum or articles of association relating to the way in which the company's assets and property may be applied, to obtain written permission from the Commission.

♦ Sets out improved procedures for returning **unspent appeal money**.

♦ **Disqualifies** people convicted of offences involving dishonesty or deception (unless the conviction is legally regarded as spent), undischarged bankrupts and people disqualified from company directorship, from acting as charity trustees.

♦ Sets out a new statutory regime for **disposals of charity land**.

The 1992 Act regulates public collections for charities and other voluntary organisations, and the activities of professional fundraisers and commercial companies when they raise funds to benefit voluntary organisations.

To enable the Charity Commission to devote greater resources to monitoring charities and advising trustees, the new legislation relieves the Commission of certain duties, in particular it:

♦ Makes trustees **more directly responsible** for the management of a charity's investments by allowing the Official Custodian for Charities to return to charities the investments held on their behalf.

♦ Places the responsibility for **land transactions** on trustees by relieving the Charity Commission of the need to give consent to most charity land transactions.

All of this points to a clear conclusion. Not only do trustees need to be aware of the extent of their legal responsibilities, including those under the Charities Acts 1992 and 1993, they also require adequate training about the practical implications of the job.

Most particularly, legal advice and professional support should be made available to them in the execution of their duties. One way, for example, would be to recruit people from the appropriate professions and management disciplines onto management committees. These people could then pass on their knowledge to other trustees.

But unless voluntary organisations find ways to support trustees in these areas it seems likely that they will find it increasingly difficult to persuade high calibre people to become trustees.

Yet, the simple fact is that more than 70% of voluntary organisations in the UK have fewer than 20 staff and precious few resources to spare on recruiting and supporting trustees.

It was in response to this need that the NCVO commissioned Aston University to find out what trustees wanted to help them do their job. Over half of those surveyed requested a handbook and training days on special topics. A third wanted resource materials and a quarter wanted access to professional advice. To take account of these needs the NCVO launched the Trustee Helpline and the Good Trustee Guide in 1993.

The Charity Commission also launched the 'Crucial' Guide to Trusteeship, a free 24 minute video introduction to the role and responsibilities of trustees presented by comedian Lenny Henry. The video is also available with subtitles for people with hearing difficulties.

Trustee liability insurance

While it is clearly no substitute for trustees carrying out their duties effectively, insurance is available to protect trustees against personal liability for their wrongful actions as trustees. In general, such insurance provides protection against honest mistakes but not against acts which trustees knew, or should have known, were wrong. Nor does it indemnify them against any personal liability for claims and debts (which exist where the charity is established as an unincorporated body – a trust, association or society).

As well as indemnifying the trustees, most policies also indemnify the charity against liability arising from the wrongful actions of trustees and sometimes of staff and other agents. Some policies explicitly differentiate between these, enabling a choice about whether or not to cover the trustees, the charity or both.

Providing this sort of protection for trustees could go some way towards overcoming their concerns about taking on the responsibilities of the role. However, liability insurance tends to be expensive and voluntary organisations have to take a view as to whether it is a cost-effective option. They also (if they are charities) have to obtain the permission of the Charity Commission if the premiums are to be paid out of the charity's funds – as this is deemed to be a personal benefit to the trustees. There are no restrictions on trustees themselves paying for their own liability insurance to protect against possible personal loss, but again the decision is one that can only be made at the individual level.

Induction for trustees

Few companies would dream of taking on new employees without providing them with relevant background information about the organisation they are joining. Nor for that matter would most voluntary organisations. Yet it is not uncommon for company non-executive directors and voluntary trustees to find themselves dropped in at the deep-end with very little preparation for their role. As a result, they may find themselves expected to rubber-stamp decisions on matters they have little or no information about.

While it may not be practical to expect all new trustees to attend formal induction days (because of their commitments elsewhere), there are a number of tools available to voluntary organisations to ensure that trustees have a thorough grounding in the history and aims of the organisation. These include:

♦ Induction **packs**.

♦ Induction **meetings** (usually followed by social events).

♦ Trustee **mentors**.

♦ **Visits** to projects.

Induction packs

An induction pack contains relevant documents and information to help orientate a newcomer to an organisation. The NCVO recommends that the following be included in a trustee induction pack:

♦ A **brief history** of the organisation.

♦ The **memorandum and articles of association**.

♦ **Standing orders**.

♦ **Roles and responsibilities** of trustees, including trustee job descriptions.

♦ The **annual report and accounts** for the previous three years.

♦ A recent **set of board papers** and minutes.

♦ Details of **board and committee structure**.

♦ The organisation's **staff structure**.

♦ **Terms of reference** for the board of **trustees** and all **sub-committees**.

♦ Dates of **forthcoming meetings**.

♦ The **chief executive's job description**.

♦ Names, addresses, telephone and fax numbers of **other trustees**.

♦ Major **policy documents**.

Alternatively, voluntary organisations can develop their own induction packs. For example, the British Institute of Radiology provides all new trustees with an induction pack which Tim Gill at the NCVO Trustee Helpline describes as "a model of good practice".

Other organisations recognise the benefits of providing new trustees with information packs that include introductory materials on management. For example, the national organisation Mind has developed its own 'management information pack' for trustees.

Induction meetings

Some voluntary organisations hold induction meetings where new trustees are briefed about the origins and aims of the organisation and current projects. Often, these will be held in the evening to make it easier for trustees to attend, and may be followed by a social event to allow newcomers to get to know the other trustees and key members of staff.

SCOPE (formerly The Spastics Society), for example, has taken this approach for a number of years and has recently gone one step further by holding pre-induction meetings for people interested in becoming trustees. These are informal evening sessions at which would-be trustees are briefed about the organisation and their duties as trustees before committing themselves.

Trustee mentors

Formal and informal mentoring programmes to help induct newcomers into organisations have been common for some time. Until quite recently, mentoring was used primarily to assist graduates in making the transition from an academic to a working environment. However, a number of companies now use mentors – either internal or external – to support the development of senior managers and board directors who can otherwise become isolated at the top of an organisation.

In the case of new trustees, mentoring could provide an effective means to learn about the way the organisation works. A new trustee could be matched with an experienced trustee able to fill in the gaps in their knowledge and who could also explain from first hand experience some of the nuances of the way the management committee operates in practice. A mentor could also provide an invaluable sounding board for a new trustee by providing a fast-track not only to what is going on but to the politics and personalities that inevitably play a part in the workings of any committee.

In addition, by matching a new trustee who lacks certain skills with someone who is strong in that area, voluntary organisations could greatly improve the quality of trusteeship. For example, a trustee who lacks financial expertise might be matched with someone with professional accounting qualifications.

Another recent innovation is the creation of networks of trustees and non-executive directors. These networks allow non-executives and trustees to share best practice and common experiences in areas such as equal opportunities policy. Such networks offer a model that may be usefully borrowed by voluntary organisations, either to support the induction of trustees or to achieve specific goals such as increasing the number of women in top management positions.

Networks

The Oxford Regional Health Authority created a Non-Executive Director Network in November 1992 in response to 'Women in the NHS' – an initiative within the National Health Service aimed at promoting the goals of Opportunity 2000 the campaign to increase the number of women in senior management jobs.

The non-executive role was recognised at the outset as an important tool to keep the Opportunity 2000 initiative on board agendas, especially as money did not flow from the Department of Health after the campaign was launched, but rather was concentrated in the NHS Women's Unit created to lead and police the initiative and to act as a focal point for Trusts.

Originally, the network consisted of non-executive directors nominated by the boards to take lead responsibility for the Opportunity 2000 initiative. In July 1993, it was broadened to include NHS officers.

The network now consists of 25 non-executives and 32 officers from NHS Trusts, directly managed units (DMUs), Family Health Service Authorities (FHSAs) and District Health Authorities (DHAs).

In response to the goals set by the Women's Unit, a programme of action was drawn up by each participant in the Oxford region. This is closely monitored by the network and progress towards the goals recorded and disseminated to participants on a quarterly basis. In addition, participants enjoy a wide range of events relevant to their needs in furthering the goals. Events cover issues such as Equal Opportunities law, harassment policies, job sharing and management development for women.

One of the most useful results of the network has been to provide its participants with contacts in other organisations, often diverse in terms of size and sophistication, so that good practice can be shared and the re-invention of the wheel avoided.

It has also served to spur organisations on as non-executive directors have been able to demonstrate to their boards that others have already introduced, for example, job-sharing or a crèche. In this way, non-executives have been able to overcome objections from their own boards to similar proposals.

Visits to projects

Many voluntary organisations recognise that there is no better way for new trustees to learn about the organisation than by allowing them to see for themselves what it is trying to achieve on the ground. Many find, too, that an appreciation of the efforts and frustrations of people in the frontline makes trustees all the more diligent in executing their duties. The only danger in this approach is in ensuring that trustees do not become so enthused by what they see that they are tempted to meddle in the day-to-day running of the organisation. Rather, trustees must be clear that their role is one of directing strategy through the management committee and not trying to exercise authority that is not rightly theirs.

Whatever induction methods voluntary organisations choose to use, however, the starting point must be to educate trustees in their legal responsibilities and the current issues facing the organisation. Voluntary organisations must also find ways to support trustees by providing further training and identifying sources of information and expert professional advice. There is a danger otherwise that by making them aware of their onerous legal responsibilities large numbers of the people best able to perform the duties of trustees will be unwilling to take them on.

Writing in 'NGO Finance' Stephen Lloyd recounts the following cautionary tale:

"One hears stories of trustees resigning en bloc when their true responsibilities are explained to them! The writer has had the experience of being asked by a charity client to explain to a prospective trustee the duties of the role. He did so. This so impressed the prospective trustee that he refused to take up his trusteeship. This so incensed the charity client that he sacked the writer as his solicitor for having 'put off' the valuable new trustee!"

Training for trustees

Clearly, induction is a valuable first step towards ensuring that new trustees are effective in their role. But most new trustees will also require some level of training in their legal responsibilities and/or support in understanding particular aspects of their role such as financial control.

Some of the larger charities such as SCOPE and the British Red Cross provide a structured programme of training for their trustees. But most voluntary organisations lack the resources to offer this sort of support.

As a result, many trustees who are jointly responsible for organisations with turnovers of many thousands of pounds have little or no formal training. Nor are they required by law to have any. Indeed, many do not even know where to go for information.

The working party on trustee training set up by the NCVO and the Charity Commission in 1993 found a clear and pressing need for increased training for trustees. As the working party notes in its report ('On Trust', 1993):

"Many voluntary organisations have to grapple with the problems of managing growth and decline and with the emerging 'contract culture'. There is an increasing emphasis on making voluntary organisations accountable both to users and funders. Trustees have to function within a complex legal framework and new legislation affecting the work of charities and voluntary organisations.

"We believe therefore that the need for trustee training is greater than ever – and is likely to grow further. There are approximately one million trustees in the UK and up to three million members of management committees. Between them they are responsible for £17 billion per annum, over 200,000 paid staff and over 23 million volunteers. At present much of the training available for them is inaccessible, inappropriate or ignored."

The working party recommended that advice, support and training for trustees should cover eight subject areas:

♦ Organisational context.

♦ Legal responsibilities.

♦ Financial responsibilities.

♦ Personnel responsibilities, where relevant.

♦ Property responsibilities, where relevant.

♦ Strategic planning and evaluation.

♦ Strategic management and accountability.

♦ Working structures and relationships.

Appropriate training might usefully be provided by existing trustees – either through formal training sessions or as mentors. Alternatively, new trustees can attend external training courses such as those organised by The Directory of Social Change or the local council for voluntary service. The Trustee Service Unit at the NCVO also publishes a monthly diary of training courses, seminars and conferences for trustees. Another alternative is to ask one of the many consultants active in this area to organise a development day or residential weekend meeting for the entire board of trustees. (The NCVO's management development team can supply a list of consultants experienced in working with boards of trustees and offers advice on how to select a consultant to match the organisation's needs.)

In addition, the NCVO's Trustee Helpline and Good Trustee Guide is specifically aimed at charities too small to be able to afford extensive training for trustees.

Consultant Judy Welemensky observes that many trustees double as members of the Board of Management. Where that happens, she maintains: "they should have clear roles and job descriptions. They should be recruited and trained to fit those roles. What usually happens is that although the treasurer is brought in for specific skills, he is the only one. Where they don't have the skills, then they need specific training. Trustees also need training in corporate governance."

CASE STUDY ► The British Red Cross

In 1993, the British Red Cross introduced a comprehensive training programme for trustees of the Society and its 90 regional branches. The programme was initiated in response to the Charities Act 1992 which the foreword to the training materials states: 'refocused attention on and crystallised the significance of trustees' responsibilities'.

The mainstay of the programme is a one-day course held at different locations around the country which covers the roles, responsibilities and liabilities of charity trustees. This includes their:

♦ Legal responsibilities to see that the charity is fulfilling its objects, abiding by its constitution and operating within the constraints of the law.

♦ Financial responsibilities to see that any monies are properly used for the benefit of those whom the Red Cross exists to help and that all financial matters are effectively managed.

♦ Managerial responsibilities including the appointment of and contractual relationships with staff, volunteers and other authorities, ensuring accountability to funders, users and members.

The course also recognises that in order to carry out their role trustees need to be familiar with:

♦ The objects, mission, Governing Instruments and contents of the operating manual of the organisation.

♦ The relationship between branches and the society's council.

♦ The national strategy and other policies approved by the council for the whole society, which branches have responsibility for implementing in their own area.

♦ The fundamental principles of the International Red Cross and Red Crescent movement which guides the organisation's actions.

The course is divided into a number of sessions on trustees':

♦ Responsibilities – regarding money, property, staff and volunteers.

♦ Accountability – to the national council, to the Charity Commissioners and to the public.

♦ Liabilities.

♦ Insurance cover – with particular reference to indemnity.

♦ Qualification to be, and disqualification from being, a trustee.

♦ Duties – regarding the management of the branch including finance, staff, volunteers and property.

♦ Working effectively with others in the Red Cross – including branch members, director and staff, the finance subcommittee, the national council, national HQ and the international movement.

♦ Understanding accounts – including reasons for keeping them, their types and format, and how to read them.

♦ Knowing the sources of information and advice on which trustees can call.

The course also includes practical case study material of the sorts of problems trustees might be expected to deal with. These are discussed in small groups. All sessions are accompanied by fact sheets, with additional information provided on:

♦ Knowing the significant events shaping developments in Red Cross internationally and nationally.

♦ Knowing the principles guiding the work of the Red Cross internationally and how they are applied in UK policies and programmes.

♦ Understanding the functions of the Red Cross locally (in centres, districts and branches); regionally; nationally; and internationally.

♦ Understanding the legal framework for trustees.

The course concludes with a question and answer session a discussion of further opportunities for study and an evaluation of the course by participants.

CASE STUDY ➤ SCOPE

SCOPE developed an in-house training programme for its 24 main board trustees, then offered it to all its regional boards. According to an article in The Times: "An induction session explains the work of the charity and its committee, and trustees can choose from a range of skills workshops, including time management, media skills and – a special request – speed reading. Trustees are expected to spend three or four days a year on training. Says Alison Plant, the society's principal training adviser "The charity has to ensure that its trustees have all the resources and skills they need to make informed decisions."

Asking the right questions

Our research into the effectiveness of non-executive directors led us quickly to the conclusion that a clear framework would be very helpful in deciding what questions to ask and when. The following pages are an extract from a resulting manual for directors, which provides such a framework:

Director responsibilities: asking the right questions

Why didn't they ask the right questions?" is a criticism frequently directed at non-executives when things go wrong. But how do you decide what are the right questions? And to what depth is it reasonable to probe? The purposes of probing are to:

♦ Ensure that potential problems are exposed and explored.

♦ To test executive management's thinking and assumptions.

♦ To promote an atmosphere of vigour in the three areas of policy making, policy implementation and policy review/management.

Questions tend to fall into four natural levels:

Level 1

Do we have a policy/strategy on....?

Do we have procedures to implement the policy/strategy?

Do we have a process to review/measure performance against the policy/ strategy?

Level 2

a) Who is responsible for policy implementation/measurement?

b) What information would enable the board to exercise judgement over:

- the relevance/probity of the policy?

- the way in which the policy is implemented?

- the results/performance?

Is this information currently available in a form suitable for presentation to the trustees?

If not, what would be the cost of producing it in an acceptable form? If the cost is too high, by what alternative means could the board of trustees monitor this aspect?

Level 3

a) Quantitative data

- What do specific figures mean?

- What assumptions underlie them?

- Are the data and the assumptions behind them consistent?

- Is the source credible and reliable?

- Is more than one estimate required/prudent?

b) Qualitative data

- Is the data qualitative only because no-one can be bothered to produce comparative figures? (Or because someone wishes to obscure the issue?)

- Is the source credible and reliable?

Level 4

Major project management

♦ Is the project valid within the terms of the policy/strategy?

♦ Is it realistic?

♦ Does it have a clear and viable plan?

♦ How is it performing against budget and schedule?

The depth, to which questioning should normally go, depends on several factors. Among them:

♦ The strategic importance and level of risk involved.

♦ The degree of pressure from internal or external sources for demonstrated executive attention to a specific issue or activity.

The frequency with which each of these issues should be reviewed will obviously vary with circumstances. However, in general, levels 1 and 2 will typically be reviewed annually or bi-annually, level 3 from annual to ad hoc, and level 4 from quarterly to monthly.

Trustees and directors alike should seek external help whenever they are not sure what questions they should be asking. Equally, if they do not feel satisfied with the answers (or lack of answers) they receive; or the way information is presented.

Summary

The roles of trustees are undoubtedly evolving. More is being demanded of trustees and that in turn means there will be an increasing demand to enhance their competence through better recruitment and training. To date, the debates about non-executive directors and trustees have continued largely on separate tracks. There is so much commonality between the two, however, that it is high time the debates were brought together.

Questions about who should become trustees and what their precise function should be are at the heart of improving the effectiveness of the trustee role. The issue of self-advocacy is also growing in importance and is critical to the legitimacy of voluntary organisations. There is really little excuse for trustees who do not make consultation with beneficiaries an essential function.

At the same time, an important task faces the voluntary sector as a whole in ensuring that an adequate infrastructure exists to support trustees. This involves making training and professional advice available to those who need it – perhaps through national lead bodies – and individual organisations adopting best practice for recruitment and induction.

Checklist

1. Is the **role of trustee** in your organisation clearly defined?

2. Does the organisation have a **proper induction process** for trustees? Does it meet their real needs?

3. Are trustees aware of their **legal responsibilities** and do they know where to turn for **professional advice**?

4. Does the organisation provide **training** to help trustees contribute effectively?

5. How often do trustees **consult with beneficiaries**?

References

1. **A more detailed explanation of trustees liabilities is provided in Appendix 3**

2. Widget Finn, *'Experience that blooms from fresh pastures'*, The Times, April 8 1993.

3. Widget Finn, *'Training taken on trust'*, The Times 31 March 1994:

4. Stephen Lloyd, *'NGO Finance'*, Issue 9, Sept 1992.

5. *'On Trust: Increasing the effectiveness of charity trustees and management committees'*, Report of the NCVO/ Charity Commission working party on trustee training, 1992.

6. Charity Commissioners' pamphlet, Charity Commission (ref CC3).

7. *'The Good Trustee Guide'*, NCVO publications, 1994.

8. *'Training taken on trust'*, Widget Finn, The Times, 31 Mar 1994.

9. David Clutterbuck and Peter Waine, *'The Independent Board Director: Selecting and using the best non-executive directors to benefit your business'*, McGraw-Hill, 1993. (Plus Sunday Times articles).

10. *'Managing Urban Change'*, DOE 1988.

11. *'Training for Community Enterprises'*, ARC 1989.

Chapter 3

Facing up to competition

Key issues

♦ *To what extent is the voluntary sector a competitive marketplace? Should it be?*

♦ *Do voluntary sector organisations need to adopt private sector approaches to managing competition and collaboration or should they develop their own?*

There are few voluntary organisations which have not felt the blast of competition in recent years. Not only are voluntary organisations competing with one another, but the blurring of boundaries between the sectors has pushed voluntary organisations and private companies into bidding for the same contracts to provide services to the same clients.

Competition between voluntary organisations also exists for public giving. More recently, however, this has extended to corporate giving. Companies are increasingly choosing a small basket of charities (or even just one) on which to focus their activities and the fundraising by employees. Feed The Children, for example, often cannot even get to talk to community investment staff at companies which have allied themselves to the larger and more established Save The Children. The solution to FTC's problem has been to develop exclusive relationships of its own – which it is successfully doing. Most private sector organisations find it far more difficult to "lock out" competitors.

There are, at base, four major areas of competition within the voluntary sector. These are:

♦ Competition for **attention**.

♦ Competition for **funds**.

♦ Competition for **people**.

♦ Competition for **commercial contracts**.

We will consider each of these in turn. First, however, is competition justified? NCVO's Tim Dartington thinks it is. He argues the case in this way:

"What does competition in the voluntary sector mean? There is an essential paradox here. The voluntary sector is under tremendous pressure not to duplicate services. Funders ask questions if we do. But if you're

going to accept the principle of competition then it follows that there will be some duplication. That's the dilemma when you bring market forces into the social economy.

"In reality of course there's always been duplication in the voluntary sector. Some people argue that the Charity Commission should actually screen applications for new charities setting up so that they don't replicate what's already there. But I take the view that it's almost a British birthright to have the freedom to set up a charity of your choice. People like me can argue that an existing charity already covers a certain area. I've never won the rational argument, because someone setting up a new charity will always say they are going to do something different to what's already out there.

"There's always been competition of a kind. I have a name for the general principle at work. I call it the two pubs in a village principle. Basically, if you fall out with the landlord of one pub there is always another you can drink at. The idea is that there should always be a choice.

"If you look at the cancer charities, for example, or most other areas there's often at least two charities. Or take ME. There's the ME Association and Action for ME. They may have different policy priorities."

Competing for attention

In Chapter 5 we deal in more detail with issues of managing voluntary sector brands. Suffice it to say at this point that the strength of the brand will have a significant effect on the supply of all the resources a charity needs – volunteers and staff, money, goods in kind, clients, and opportunities to put its message across.

A number of factors appear to make the difference in gaining attention:

♦ The **size of the audience**(s) you need to reach.

♦ The **emotionality of the cause** (how good do people feel about doing something for your particular cause?).

♦ The **distinctness of the brand** and what it stands for.

♦ The **promotional resources** available.

♦ The **degree of innovation and creativity** shown by the organisation in attention-seeking.

It all comes down to effective marketing.

Voluntary organisations, like businesses, are all about supplying market demand. Quite simply, it is the job of a voluntary organisation to market its mission or cause to the widest possible audience of donors on the one hand and customers – clients or members – on the other.

To satisfy the needs of their customers all companies and voluntary organisations engage in a number of marketing activities. Some do so through formal marketing plans while others, particularly the smaller ones, tend to do it in a more ad hoc way. These activities include:

- **Market research** – to identify the real requirements of customers.
- **Market segmentation** – identifying and targeting key groupings of people with similar requirements from the organisation.
- **Promotion** – raising awareness about the organisation and what it does among targeted audiences either by advertising or promotional events.
- **Educating the market** – raising people's level of understanding about the work the organisation carries out and hopes to carry out in the future.

While it may seem unrealistic to suggest that a small voluntary organisation such as a mothers' support group works on these lines, it is nonetheless true. There may not be a written marketing plan, and many of those who engage in the organisation's marketing activities may never have heard of the concepts listed above, but they do them just the same.

Consumer marketing tends to view market segments in terms of customer profiles. So, for example, a company might define the characteristics of a particular segment of its customer base by looking at factors such as gender, disposable income, marital status, number of children or geographical location. A good illustration is the way that car manufacturers view the vehicle market. They see it as made up of several distinct market segments, such as prestige cars, medium-sized family cars, small cars and commercial vehicles (vans and trucks), and target and market their offerings accordingly. So, for example, if we look at advertising – one component of marketing – a car manufacturer's television advertising is made up of different commercials each aimed at a distinct market segment. Commercials are targeted to appear with programming that is likely to be watched by a large proportion of the market segment they are aimed at.

Voluntary organisations, too, have distinctive market segments. Take donors, for example. A person who has never made a donation to the organisation is clearly in a different market segment to a regular supporter of many years standing. The message the voluntary sends to these two different audiences should therefore reflect that difference. Typically, the message aimed at attracting potential donors will be short, snappy and aimed at getting their attention. It would explain what the organisation does in a concise way and try to elicit a small donation. The committed supporter, on the other hand, will already know something of what the organisation does. They will want to be brought up to date on recent achievements and to know something about the work their money has already assisted. It may be possible, too, to get them to increase their donation.

According to Peter Drucker, the American Heart Association divides the American public from which it raises its money into 41 different market segments and addresses each differently. Clearly not all voluntary organisations can afford to be so targeted but the principle involved is an important one.

Nor is marketing confined to just one group of stakeholders. In recent years companies have become increasingly aware of the need to market themselves not just to their customers and potential customers but also to their other key audiences including shareholders and their employees; as well as opinion formers such as members of the Press, City analysts and politicians. More enlightened companies now realise that they must communicate effectively with these often overlapping audiences using targeted marketing strategies.

Similarly, voluntary organisations need to market themselves to a range of key audiences. These include:

◆ **Customers and members** (beneficiaries).

◆ **Members of the public** (potential donors, volunteers, employees).

◆ **Companies** (potential donors, sponsors, partners).

◆ **Charitable trusts** (fund providers and potential fund providers).

◆ **Volunteers**.

◆ **Full-time employees**.

◆ **Civil servants** in government departments.

◆ **Politicians**.

◆ **Opinion formers** (such as journalists).

As a result, marketing techniques are becoming increasingly important. In particular, a number of recent developments offer important benefits for voluntary organisations. These include cause-related marketing; relationship marketing; and the use of mass media marketing to reach large audiences through events such as Red Nose Day and Children in Need. At the same time, a growing number of voluntary organisations now use advertising. All of these activities – which are discussed in Chapter 5 – require careful management.

Competing for funds

Competition for funds is becoming increasingly tough. According to Charity Trends, the annual survey by the Charities Aid Foundation, while 8% more people contributed to charities in 1993 than in 1992, the average monthly amount fell from £3.00 to £2.50. At the same time, while the top 200 charities' income rose by 4%, that of the next 200 fell by the same amount.

It's not just other voluntary organisations, who are competing for funds. Dr Henry Drucker, a University fundraiser, told The Times in December 1994 "Many small charities have seen well-financed campaigns on behalf of organisations such as universities and hospitals, which have other forms of support, as unwelcome competition. There is indeed a threat to these smaller charities".

Other new and competing demands on charitable giving have come from schools, which used to be totally self-funding, but which now require parental top-ups to provide non-essential equipment. Says Tim Dartington:

"It is now clear that many different organisations are chasing the same pots of money. This is already changing the way we do things.

"For example, we have always put the competition on our boards, recruiting trustees from organisations doing similar things. The old voluntary sector partnership idea was that everyone was on everyone else's boards. But now the conflict of interest over funding and the commercial sensitivity of board papers means that co-operation in that area will have to stop.

"The problem with competing for funds, too, is that there is no single distinctive feature that can convincingly be said to set charities apart from other sorts of organisations. You have to look at a cluster of factors to get some sense of why we are a special case. In a very real sense fundraising was the one truly functional specialism found only in the voluntary sector, but that's no longer the case.

"People are very wary of fundraising activities in what was formerly the public sector. The Wishing Well appeal was the first real example of that. The point is that there's only a limited amount of money available. If that is going into funding capital projects in what used to be the NHS it isn't going elsewhere. Small voluntary organisations, in particular, are going to suffer in terms of street collections. And it could get very dirty.

"At a recent public lecture organised by VOLPROF one of the speakers was a former marketing executive from Unilever who has joined one of the cancer charities. He said that he doesn't see himself in competition with other cancer charities so much as in competition with Sony and other consumer-goods companies for people's disposable income.

"The current row about the National Lottery is really about competition. Here's a private sector venture which will be in competition with every other fundraising activity for the voluntary sector. The Lottery is competing for the disposable income that would otherwise go into collection boxes, and as such it is an inefficient way to raise money for the voluntary sector.

"Nonetheless, I don't see Christian Aid and other large charities getting into a public wrangle over turf wars. It's very important that we maintain donor confidence. You come back to social and ethical values."

To cope with these challenges, voluntary sector organisations need to:

♦ Seek **new sources of funding** (for example, by trading or through alliances with companies).

♦ Make use of **alternative resources** wherever practical (people, donated premises and so on).

♦ Seek opportunities to **link consumable spending** directly with charitable giving (e.g. through cause-related marketing).

♦ Develop more **collaborative fundraising activities** within the sector.

The last item on this list raises the issue of how to make charities more capable of collaboration. Abandoning proprietorial attitudes towards clients is an essential first step. Equally important, however, is the development of distinct competencies and areas of activity, which others working in the same field will find more complementary than competitive. This is particularly important in positioning voluntary organisations to companies. The more distinct the contribution each voluntary organisation makes, the more likely companies are to give their support either to the individual voluntary organisation or, increasingly, to a coherent grouping of voluntary organisations attacking the same issue in different but complementary ways.

Evidence of a more mature attitude in this respect would be the growth of a sub-contractor culture in the voluntary sector. Private sector companies have by and large learned to concentrate on the activities they are good at and to encourage smaller companies in the sector to take on specialist niches as suppliers.

While charities do use outside help in all sorts of ways – from management consultants through to graphic designers – it is rare for a large voluntary organisation to sub-contract any of its activities to a smaller. Because the smaller voluntary organisation is seen to be in competition, it is regarded as a threat. If the business of the voluntary organisation is to administer to the homeless or elderly, then it should carry out all such activities in-house. Yet the dynamism, drive and creativity of new small voluntary organisations is what many established, large ones desperately need. And if global giant sector companies such as Ford, IBM or Nissan can actively encourage small companies in the same sector, recognising that this actually increases their competitive edge, then why can't voluntary organisations?

Some of the large private sector companies even provide the seed-corn and help new niche supplier companies start up. Rather than try to do everything in a sector itself, the large voluntary organisation could follow suit and help meet new needs by encouraging small organisations to set up in the same way. One of the benefits of doing so is that it avoids overstretching the resources of the larger organisation – both financial and managerial.

Competing for people

The consensus view within the voluntary sector appears to be that competing for people is not a significant problem, if only because high calibre people are in good supply. Tim Dartington again:

"The voluntary sector has tended to regard recruitment in terms of a process of self-selection. In other words, people who work in the voluntary sector usually are seen as less concerned about financial rewards, so people choose to work in the voluntary sector because of their personal

priorities. In the main, the level of commitment that voluntary organisations inspire from people means, too, that an adoption charity, for example, may well be able to attract very high calibre social workers because of its culture and the level of job satisfaction. Where causes are very strong – humanitarian projects in the old Yugoslavia, for example – voluntary organisations are able to recruit very good people. I don't see that changing."

Rachel Ball, who gained a first in Russian from Bristol University and now works for a charity that runs refugee camps in the former Soviet Union, is a case in point:

"Working in the voluntary sector offers me the chance to do something worthwhile at the same time as earn a living. The salary maybe a good deal lower and the perks maybe less but my job is to use my skills to help others and that is real job satisfaction."

Her commitment is such that even though Bristol University subsequently asked her to consider a lectureship she turned it down. People at the UN also spotted her talents but she told them to wait until she had worked for a few more years in her present post. To turn down such prestigious offers gives an insight into the depth of commitment that working for a voluntary organisation can engender.

How private sector organisations compete for people

As with much of what the private sector does, there is no great science to the way companies compete for people. In fact, most of it is simply common sense which has been tried and tested over many years. But there are three main areas that are particularly relevant to voluntary organisations. Typically:

1. Companies try to position themselves as good brand employers. For example by:

♦ Seeking Investors in People status and other forms of recognition.

♦ They provide mentors for new recruits.

♦ They offer salaries that are competitive in their sector (and monitor salary scales to remain competitive).

♦ They offer challenging working environments and create opportunities for personal growth – for example, by providing on-going training and management development programmes.

2. Companies use existing employees to identify people like themselves.

3. Companies develop centres of excellence – functions and areas of expertise that have such a strong reputation that they attract high-calibre people so that:

♦ People may only stay a few years, but they gain superb training.

♦ While they are with the organisation, they are motivated to perform exceptionally.

♦ When they leave, they open up opportunities for other talented young people to join.

Competition for business

Contracts from local or central government have become an important part of many voluntary organisations' funding and in some cases the majority of their funding. While there is some competition from within the sector, the majority comes from private sector organisations.

However, says John Williams of agency Fishburn, Hedges, Bays, Williams, which has helped numerous voluntary organisations communicate:

"The truth is that there has always been a contract culture. It is just more commercial nous."

It is also more intense, with more and more public sector provision being placed in private or voluntary sector hands. Some of the competitors for these contracts are however voluntary sector people who, instead of setting up their own charity, have decided instead to set up a business. Says NCVO's Tim Dartington:

"Some of these private sector providers put in a great deal of work for very little profit. Not all, of course, but they aren't all driven by profit maximisation alone."

On what basis do voluntary organisations compete in this market? The situation, say most observers, is very confused.

Research by the School for Advanced Urban Studies at Bristol suggests that there is little to choose between private and voluntary sector providers in quality of service. There are good and bad in both sectors.

Dartington points to three myths about the voluntary sector's advantages in this market. He explains:

"Voluntary organisations are supposed to be distinct from other organisations because of their:

1. Flexibility
2. Closeness to users
3. Innovation.

"Taking these in reverse order, there are some recent examples of innovation from the voluntary sector that stand out. For example, the emergence of voluntary organisations to tackle HIV and Aids, which introduced the idea of "buddying" and some other innovative approaches. But it isn't true to say that all voluntary organisations are highly innovative.

"If you say that voluntary organisations are closer to users, this may be true in some cases. Certainly they have the ability to put service users on

management committees, which can provide explicit ownership of the organisation. But if you're looking for leaders in the area of customer care, then the private sector is probably streets ahead at present.

"The flexibility of voluntary organisations has come largely through their use of volunteers. Meals on Wheels, for example, was originally a voluntary sector service innovation that was later adopted by the public sector. Voluntary organisations recognised too, that many existing services closed down over the Christmas period and were able to respond because they had a number of Jewish volunteers who were happy to work at that time of the year. But that sort of flexibility alone doesn't justify why voluntary organisations should get service contracts. So much then for the three myths.

"What you are left with then is that services provided by a voluntary organisation aren't necessarily better or worse than those that can be provided by the private sector.

"Where the voluntary sector can genuinely add value, however, is around campaigning for the needs of people. That's an area that a private sector residential home won't get into. So, for example, the added value part of voluntary organisations might be that they don't just see the market in terms of the current need or level of services, but take a wider view of their constituency to see what else needs to be done. I think that if voluntary organisations become too like businesses that element could be lost. That's the dilemma we face with competition.

"The voluntary sector has always seen itself as a developmental agency – identifying new services and issues – as well as a service provider. There's a danger that the purchaser-provider dimension could undermine that.

"The larger voluntary organisations are less at risk from the contract culture because they have a clear campaigning role as well as providing services. It is local voluntary organisations if they lose their grant status and become simply service providers that could be in trouble.

"One response might be to separate the campaigning role from the role of providing service. It may go that way, but if it does it will be with some regret from people like me who believe that the two activities feed off each other."

Dartington is not alone in this opinion. Says John Williams:

"It would be disastrous to separate fundraising and delivery. On the one hand, the opportunity to lobby and contribute to the public debate comes from being involved at the sharp end. On the other, to have fundraising capability, you have to be spending the money."

A critical issue for voluntary organisations seeking contracts is how active they should be in specifying the service. Says Dartington:

"If you see yourself as a voluntary organisation working with the needs of the elderly, for example, do you simply accept the day-care services set out by the local authority and tender for the contract, or do you negotiate with them about what actually should be provided? In other words, a voluntary organisation may know more about its constituency and their current and future requirements than the local authority.

"Ideally, there would be sufficient confidence from the purchaser side to want to consult the expertise of voluntary organisations. But there's a danger that won't happen as competition gets more and more entrenched.

"To put it another way, it's a bit like a brief for a management consultant; if the brief is too tight, then you might as well simply employ someone to carry out the task because you aren't giving the consultant the scope to contribute his or her expertise.

"My worry is that private sector providers will increasingly call foul against the voluntary sector providers unless they're in the same situation.

"Where the confidence could come from is the awareness that if you approach say Age Concern, you're not going to get advice that comes from what will give them the easiest way to maximise profits. Because of the nature of the organisation there will be some objectivity to what they say."

Another potential problem is what voluntary sector organisations may have to give up to compete. Says management consultant Shirley Otto:

"If you look at homes for the elderly, there's already competition between voluntary sector and private sector providers. There are some very good private sector suppliers in this market. The problem for voluntary organisations is that if they're offering the same service at the same price, how do they attach a value to the voluntary sector values they uphold.

"My worry is that when people think about contracting they think money, whereas other elements should be built into the equation. But how do we capture those other, less tangible, things?"

Among steps voluntary organisations can take (and to some extent are taking) are:

♦ Embarking on **customer education campaigns** (customers here being providers of funding and/or contract awarders). Raising the expectations of the customers should lead directly to contract specifications, which include more than simple service provision.

♦ Focusing on **quality** of provision rather than quantity.

♦ Helping **beneficiaries** have a greater input into service specifications.

♦ Seeking **alliances with commercial competitors**, to make maximum use of each other's strengths.

Even with all of these approaches, the challenge for voluntary organisations will still be significant in adapting to the new market environment without losing their essential values.

Keith Manley in his book 'Financial Management for Charities and Voluntary Organisations' says that some charities will decide not to compete in the new market:

"Many charities are jealous of their individuality and integrity to the extent that they will not contemplate getting involved in a competitive tendering situation. It could be argued that, unless a charity has something extra to offer, if it engages in trawling for contracts it is moving away from its charitable origins and in the long term will gradually erode its voluntary base."

He also plays down the idea that the voluntary sector and the private sector are competing for the same contracts:

"In many of the personal social services their very nature militates against commercial involvement and it is more likely that service agreements will be negotiated voluntarily although there will be instances where more than one charity may be capable of providing a service."

According to NCVO News in January 1995, local authorities view voluntary organisations as having a distinct advantage over private contractors:

"Research has shown that the majority of local authorities value voluntary organisations as potential contractors precisely because they can subsidise contract prices with donation and other income. 80 percent of authorities responding to the survey said this was either a very important or fairly important characteristic in encouraging them to contract with voluntary organisations rather than with private providers."

Again this dispels the idea that competition is hotting up between the voluntary and commercial sectors.

How private sector organisations compete for business

Again there are no great mysteries involved in the way companies compete for business. But three areas are particularly relevant to voluntary organisations. In general:

1. Companies identify and monitor their main competitors, gathering as much information as they can about:

♦ What competitors are offering.
♦ The price they are offering it at.
♦ How their value is perceived by customers.
♦ How they put together contracts.
♦ How they present themselves and their services.

2. They maintain close contact with customers, through:
♦ Market research.

♦ Establishing close personal relationships with key influencers and decision-makers.

3. They review every successful and unsuccessful bid to learn how to do it better in future, by:

♦ Identifying what determined the successful bid – i.e. was the contract awarded on the basis of price alone? Was it based on the quality of service offered? Or was it a combination of the two, and if so what was the winning mix?

♦ Obtaining feedback on unsuccessful tenders wherever possible.

Conclusion

Competition will increase within the voluntary sector and between it and the private sector. The challenge for voluntary organisations will be to adapt attitudes, structures and systems to:

♦ **Compete** more strongly.

♦ **Collaborate** more effectively.

♦ Provide clear **added-value** to partners in other sectors.

♦ Demonstrate the levels of **efficiency** and insight into client groups' needs that will inspire the **confidence** of all their partners.

♦ Ensure that they don't compromise their **integrity**.

This last point is an important one which merits a mention in its own right.

Ethical and practical dilemmas

The mindset of competition does not always come naturally to voluntary organisations. The increasingly competitive nature of the environment in which voluntary organisations will operate in future, however, means that voluntary organisations may face a number of practical and ethical dilemmas. These include the following:

♦ To what extent is it permissible to gather intelligence about competitors for contracts?

♦ Is it appropriate to use savings on one part of a contract to subsidise another?

♦ Should a voluntary organisation have a 'going rate' for consultancy and other services?

♦ Is it ethical to 'poach' key people from competitors (especially when they are likely to bring key contacts with them)?

It seems clear that such issues will have to be resolved by individual organisations according to their own sets of values, but in raising them we hope to encourage debate within the sector as a whole.

Summary

In any situation where different interest groups chase scarce resources, competition is inevitable. The fact that the voluntary sector has tended to tolerate some duplication of effort is, arguably, one of its strengths, but it is also an area that it has preferred to play down.

What is now happening is that the 'contract culture' is bringing many voluntary organisations into direct competition with private sector organisations, forcing them to take a hard look at what competition really means.

In the next few years, the debate is likely to centre on the issue of 'fair' competition across sectors. Voluntary organisations will be increasingly exposed to market forces, and will have to justify their 'privileged' existence.

There are four key areas where competition affects voluntary sector organisations. These are:

♦ Competition for **attention**.

♦ Competition for **funds**.

♦ Competition for **people**.

♦ Competition for **contracts**.

For voluntary organisations to ignore the challenges that face them in these areas would be like burying their heads in the sand.

Checklist

1. Do you know who your main **competitors** will be in the next few years? Have you identified the areas in which you will have to compete with them?

2. How does your organisation **compare with its rivals**? How should it be positioned to win?

3. Are you making the **best use of your brand**? In what areas can your organisation add value to its customers and funders?

4. Are there organisations – other voluntary organisations, public sector organisations, or companies – that would make useful **strategic partners**?

References

1. Keith Manley, *'Financial Management for Charities and Voluntary Organisations'*, ICSA Publishing, 1994, p.11.

2. NCVO News, *'Charities subsidise care services'*, December 1994/January 1995, p6.

Chapter 4

Managing people

Key issues

♦ *Do voluntary organisations make best use of their people?*

♦ *How do you provide professional quality of service through an army of "amateurs"?*

♦ *Are employees of voluntary organisations entitled to the same benefits and conditions as those in the private and public sectors? Should they be expected to make greater sacrifices?*

♦ *Should you use volunteers for what they are good at, or for what needs to be done?*

♦ *Can a voluntary organisation afford to spend income on developing its employees and volunteers instead of on its clients?*

People in voluntary organisations are usually motivated by something other than simply money and status. While this may of course be true of people working in the public and private sectors as well, on balance the aspirational content of the jobs of those in the voluntary sector is likely to be higher. This explains why people are prepared to work for salaries below the market rate for their level of expertise, and why others are prepared to work as unpaid volunteers.

The aspirational component of voluntary work can be summed up as a sense of personal satisfaction that comes from working towards some notion of a better world. Where it is effectively channelled, this aspiration is a very powerful motivator. Indeed, some would say that with the possible exception of fear, the desire to help others – emanating as it does from our empathy for our fellow human beings – is the strongest human emotion.

Cynics in the business world, on the other hand, might argue that money exerts a stronger pull. If that were so, however, then few of the people working in the voluntary sector would remain there for long; there are, after all, larger financial rewards to be had elsewhere. Yet the fact that many thousands of people prefer to contribute their skills and energy to voluntary organisations suggests that for these people the aspirational component of their work is extremely important.

This fact has two very important consequences for the way they are managed. The first is that voluntary organisations have a particular responsibility to ensure that the work their employees and volunteers are engaged in provides an effective outlet for their aspirations. The second is that if it is harnessed effectively to serve a worthwhile purpose there is little that these people cannot achieve.

To put it another way, voluntary organisations have at their disposal what is widely regarded in the business world as one of the most powerful resources around; namely a potentially highly motivated workforce. But there is also a downside. To remain highly motivated, people need to feel they are achieving something worthwhile, otherwise they will become frustrated. If that frustration leads to them becoming alienated from the organisation, then their energy is likely to come out in other ways such as indulging in dissent or in-fighting. The strength of commitment means, however, that in the short-run at least, voluntary organisations can often get away with managing people badly, especially their volunteers.

We have already discussed the need for leaders of voluntary organisations to create a meaningful mission. As in any organisation the ability of those further down the chain of command to secure results is directly affected by the quality of leadership at the top. There will always be exceptions to this rule, of course. There are no doubt instances where much has been achieved despite rather than because of the senior managers in an organisation. Like a badly organised army, parts of a voluntary sector organisation can sometimes operate successfully on the ground without good leadership from above. Such instances are relatively rare however, and are usually achieved by ignoring orders. In the long-run, it is difficult to sustain a battle, much less win a war on this basis. In any voluntary organisation the people in the frontline require adequate training, resources and support if they are to maintain morale and achieve their objectives. They also need discipline.

Managing jobs with high aspirational content

Organisational theory suggests that any individual's involvement in an organisation is based upon a psychological contract or agreement. In this unwritten contract the individual agrees to abide by certain terms and conditions laid down by the organisation and in return expects certain conditions of their own to be met. For example, a paid employee agrees to provide time and expertise in return for a bundle of benefits including pay and acceptable working conditions. When the expectations of the individual and the organisation meet, people are motivated to give their best. When the individual's expectations are disappointed they become demotivated and their performance tails off.

In the case of someone working in a voluntary organisation the psychological contract includes an expectation of a working environment which enables them to contribute visibly to the organisation's mission. This expectation is often reinforced by other characteristics. For example, people who work for voluntary organisations typically:

- Have **strong views** about the **direction** the organisation should be following.
- Expect to have greater **discretion** in their jobs.
- Are **not** in it primarily for the **money and status**.
- Expect a high degree of **job satisfaction**.
- Have a high demand for **information**.
- Want to **contribute ideas**.
- Are frequently **scattered** across the country in local or regional branches.
- Have higher expectations of **democratic decision making**.

All of these factors make the task of managing people in voluntary organisations potentially both more difficult and more rewarding. Julia Cleverdon expresses the point well when she says:

"The reason people work for less in the voluntary sector is to do with having a good cause. Certainly I find I can't get my people away when they get stuck in to work on projects. They say we can't come back to the office yet. The soup kitchen or whatever is really busy at the moment. We'll be back in a couple of hours when it slows down. It turns out to be a 24 hours a day operation."

Such enthusiasm and commitment among paid and unpaid workers can move mountains. However, it must be carefully handled or it can go off like an undirected firework.

Clear objectives

People in voluntary organisations need clear objectives. They perform well when expectations – their own and those of the organisation – are clear and realistic. However, setting objectives is no easy task.

According to Mike Hudson of consultants Compass Partnership, voluntary organisations face two problems in particular in agreeing realistic expectations with staff and volunteers:

"First: the very nature of voluntary organisations, often working for people in desperate situations or for highly ambitious objectives, makes setting specific targets extraordinarily difficult. The problem is exacerbated by everyone's commitment to the cause which sometimes blurs objectivity.

"Second: people ultimately need to set their own objectives. These should fit tightly into the organisation's overall plans. But because roles and tasks in voluntary organisations have to be flexible, the range of possible objectives people can set themselves is unusually wide."

In some areas of the voluntary sector, this is now changing. The spread of the contract culture – whereby voluntary organisations are contracted to provide certain services in line with agreed targets – means that objectives are more likely to be clearly defined in the terms of the contract. But in general Hudson's points remain valid, particularly in the area of staff development.

The challenge for voluntary sector managers, according to Hudson, is to cut through this uncertainty and put time and effort into helping people find stretching but achievable objectives which they will feel it rewarding to meet. This can best be achieved, he says, by providing adequate management support. For example by:

♦ Creating management structures in which between four and seven people report to one person (five or six is probably a better ratio).

♦ Setting aside a minimum of half an hour to an hour per week exclusively for supporting each staff member on an individual basis.

♦ Appraisal schemes which once a year allow a more formal setting for the review of performance, problems and job aspirations and the establishment of new patterns of behaviour.

Clearly, these goals are more easily attained when they are supported by a professional personnel function as they would be in the private sector. But even in the larger voluntary organisations which have full-time personnel managers, the task is often made more difficult by the highly decentralised manner in which the organisation operates. Organisations such as the British Red Cross and Barnardos, for example, have workers scattered across the country in many different branches. This places an enormous strain on the channels of communication and can create severe problems for applying personnel policies consistently across the organisation.

Moreover, many smaller community and regional organisations have no paid staff at all, relying entirely on trustees and volunteers to manage the people.

The wonder is that in so many organisations the enthusiasm of staff and volunteers is able to overcome these obstacles. But in the long-run, unless ways are found to support the aspirations of voluntary sector workers they are likely to become disillusioned and leave.

Ensuring the culture supports the mission

A key factor in retaining commitment is the culture of the organisation. As we have already noted, a motivated workforce is a voluntary sector organisation's greatest asset. The performance of its people is probably the single largest factor in determining how effective any organisation is. Many voluntary organisations spend a large proportion of their total income – often in excess of two thirds – on people. Yet many fail to create an environment in which people can do their jobs effectively.

Mike Hudson of Compass Partnership summarises some of the problems:

"Unrealistic expectations are placed on people, individual targets are unspecific or non-existent, praise is infrequent, time for feedback is extremely limited and working conditions are less than adequate."

These problems are compounded by the way in which employees of voluntary organisations think of themselves. Personal sacrifice is an important value in a voluntary sector organisation. So people are constrained from complaining about poor working conditions, unreasonable demands on their time or other impositions which would be resisted in other sectors. It's hard to resist arguments such as "but it's for the children!".

Where these problems are rife the internal culture of the organisation – made up of a set of assumptions and beliefs about the way things are done – can easily become out of step with what the organisation is trying to achieve.

There may even be more fundamental problems with the internal culture. An obvious example would be a charity dedicated to campaigning for the rights of disabled people that had no equal opportunities policy or had no provision to provide access for wheelchair users.

In most cases, however, a mismatch between the culture and the mission is more subtle. For example, an organisation that sees itself as a pioneer in its field but has an autocratic management style and which fails to empower employees to try out new ideas for doing their jobs. Or an organisation that says it values volunteers but uses them only as envelope stuffers. Or one that claims to be participative and democratic but is run on orders issued from on high. Regrettably, as unlikely as these examples seem, there are many cases of voluntary organisations with similar sorts of problems.

A useful exercise for any voluntary sector manager is to sit down with a piece of paper and write on one side of the page the qualities and philosophy that the organisation champions in its mission; and on the other the internal management culture it deploys to achieve its objectives. They should match. If they don't then it is unlikely that the people working there will remain motivated for long. A good way to check is to compare the organisation's staff turnover rate against other voluntary organisations. If it is substantially higher then there is probably a cultural problem.

The issues of equal opportunities policies and empowerment are of particular importance to voluntary sector cultures and are examined in their own right in Chapter 6.

Recruitment

For all its negative connotations the recession has had at least one positive effect on voluntary organisations; it has led to an upsurge of interest in job vacancies in the voluntary sector.

A recent report by VOLPROF showed that 53 per cent of voluntary sector managers are currently recruited from outside the voluntary sector. This also indicates that voluntary organisations have a high regard for management skills from other sectors.

Much of the new interest in voluntary sector positions comes from people formerly employed in the private and public sectors, especially at senior management level. This is not surprising since down-sizing among companies and cutbacks in the public sector have left many managers in their late 40s and early 50s stranded.

As Olga Johnson, director of Charity Recruitment told Third Sector' magazine recently:

"Two or three years ago, of the applicants at the chief executive or executive level half would be from people in the voluntary sector and half from people outside. Now its more like 75 per cent from outside."

Overall, the effect has been to increase competition among applicants for voluntary sector jobs. For example, estimates suggest that in the last few years general management positions advertised in voluntary organisations have attracted two or three times as many applicants as they did in the late 1980s. But as Susan Woodison of the National Trust, one of many personnel directors in the voluntary sector who report a large increase in the number of job applicants, points out it is the quality not quantity of candidates that counts. Many voluntary organisations still find it difficult to recruit suitably skilled people with expertise in specialised fields.

Positions in areas such as conservation and social work remain particularly difficult to fill, with the number of qualified applicants limited by the availability of training opportunities in the voluntary sector itself. Not surprisingly, too, the recession has also meant that good fundraisers are in short supply.

At the same time, although many in the voluntary sector agree that the overall standard of applicants has risen in the last few years, voluntary organisations are becoming tougher in their demands. Many are also wary of recruiting outsiders fearing what will happen when the effects of the recession wear off.

Stuart Ball, director of personnel at Barnardos, confirms that many of the new job-seekers are fleeing the fear of redundancy in the private sector or cutbacks in the public sector rather than pursuing a career in the voluntary sector.

In the long-run this raises the spectre of a migration in the opposite direction when the economy picks up and the better-paid jobs return.

There is also concern among voluntary organisations that a lack of real commitment among these private and public sector refugees can cause problems when fitting into voluntary sector cultures.

David Wickert of Charities Aid Foundation UK and now of CAF America, has his own methods of separating the job applicant wheat from the chaff. He explains:

"One very rough way is to tell them how much we are going to pay and see if they still turn up for the job interview!

"At interview stage I prefer people who say 'I have the following skills and this is how my expertise can help you', rather than the approach 'I've been working in the private sector for a while and now I want to do some good'. My attitude to that is that if someone works in insurance or for an oil

company even, they are contributing to the needs of society. If they apply for a job here what I want to know is how their skills can help CAF."

Most large voluntary organisations now use similar recruitment procedures to the private sector and may buy in specialist external support. David Wickert explains the CAF approach:

"We require the right people and a high level of commitment. We have a Human Resources department here that uses whatever agency services it needs. We advertise vacancies and short list just like companies."

With a high premium on teamwork, Wickert prefers to build in an additional check to determine whether a job applicant will fit into the CAF culture.

"In my division, we also ask people to do presentations to us about why they believe they are the best person for the job."

As the effects of the recession fade, and the glut of professional managers begins to evaporate it is likely that voluntary organisations will find recruiting the calibre of people they need more difficult. Skills shortages – much talked about in the 1980s but largely masked by the recession – are likely to return with a vengeance, requiring voluntary organisations to make employment prospects and working conditions more attractive if they are to recruit new talent and retain what they already have.

In the private sector, a number of more far-sighted companies are already taking steps to prepare for a tighter skills market in the future by positioning themselves as 'good brand employers'. For example, these companies now use recruitment advertising which carries a message about the sort of organisation they aspire to be.

Voluntary organisations could learn from the techniques these companies are deploying, in particular ways to get added value from the money they spend on recruitment advertising.

Tom Redman and Brian Mathews of the Teesside Business School, who have been researching recruitment advertising for the last four years, say there is now a growing trend for companies to view corporate advertising – which aims to promote the image of the company among key audiences such as customers, shareholders, analysts and the wider public – and recruitment advertising as complementary.

In part this reflects changes in the way that recruitment advertising itself is seen. Back in 1960, C N Parkinson suggested in his book 'Parkinson's Law', that the perfect recruitment advertisement would be one that "would attract only one reply and that from the right man". But as Redman and Mathews point out, quite apart from the outdated notion of the right applicant being male, most companies realise today that the effectiveness of the recruitment process relies on attracting a wide field of suitable applicants from which the best can be selected. To do so, the advertisement itself must attract attention, generate interest and stimulate action.

However, say Redman and Mathews, in the past advertisements too often put potential applicants off by listing criteria they were expected to meet without providing them with sufficient information about the values and aspirations of the organisation concerned. In short, ads were seen as lacking in the informational content their target audience wanted.

Corporate advertising, meanwhile, was increasingly aimed at informing audiences about the values and expertise embodied by the organisation. When you consider, too, that in a single year some very large companies such as British Airways may spend in excess of £1 million on recruitment advertising, against a total advertising and promotion spend of around £40 million, it makes sense to use the one to reinforce the other. Redman says:

"Several organisations are now trying to obtain synergy and coherence between corporate advertising and recruitment advertising."

Particularly prominent in this area are the award-winning advertisements of the Apple computer company and car manufacturer Ford. Both use recruitment advertisements which contain a message about new products, new techniques or product performance and which promote the employer as an innovator at the leading edge of their industries to attract top talent.

In both these cases, too, techniques to measure the effectiveness of recruitment advertisements, including the ratio of successful appointments to applicants, have shown that the advertisements attracted not simply high numbers of candidates, but the right calibre of applicants for the jobs.

Another approach is that of professional services group Price Waterhouse which uses recruitment advertisements as part of the company's general marketing strategy, reasoning that those executives who flick through the appointments pages are also potential users of their services.

According to Hamish Davidson, managing consultant at the executive search and selection arm of Price Waterhouse:

"We see recruitment advertising as an opportunity to gain more clients. We try to make the ads a hook that will generate interest even from people who aren't actively looking for a job. Sometimes we pick up new assignments directly from ads that an executive sees flicking through the paper."

Similarly, voluntary organisations could use recruitment advertising to reach beyond potential job applicants to other key audiences including business leaders and donors.

EXAMPLE: National Westminster Bank recruitment-corporate advertising

A recent TV campaign by National Westminster Bank shows how the recruitment-corporate advertising process can also be operated in reverse. In the advertisements a series of young Nat West employees are depicted talking about their jobs. The aim is to project to the public an image of a friendly, happy bank. But the ads also contains a more subtle message for school leavers who may be choosing a future employer. They enhance the bank's brand as an attractive employer, a development that prompted one human resources manager to say:

"I am suffering from jealousy. Why have I never worked for an organisation where the brand managers see an advantage in advertisements that praise the people as well as the product? It would save so much effort in the recruitment process. I am enjoying the Nat West addictive vision of nurture, equal opportunities and careers being fun. I think the charm of those life stories will last longer than any suggestion of redundancies."

Other techniques could greatly relieve the pressure on voluntary organisations to constantly recruit new people by avoiding the burn-out of existing staff. By managing the people it already has better, in particular by ensuring they have the support they need to maintain pride in their work, voluntary organisations in America have found they can drastically reduce staff turnover.

CASE STUDY ➤ El Camino Hospital Mountain View California

Voluntary sector El Camino Hospital in Mountain View, California, was able to avoid the recent national nursing shortage in America because of the way it was managed. In fact, it reported waiting lists of applicants for nursing posts at a time when the nursing shortage was already causing staffing problems in other hospitals.

A study by the American Nurses' Association in 1983 which looked at what allowed El Camino and other 'magnet hospitals' to remain well staffed found that the secret was not higher salaries and benefits. Rather, the study concluded, one of the most important factors was the high ratio of registered nurses to patients almost 21% higher at magnet hospitals than the national average.

Other factors included: visibility and accessibility of administrators; a participatory management style; quality nursing leadership; and decentralised organisational structures.

As the nursing shortage deepened in the mid to late 80s, El Camino took a holistic view of the problem by not overloading nurses with more patients than they could care for. With a licence for 464 beds, the hospital operated only 380 beds.

"Nothing will make nurses leave faster than being placed in situations where they feel compromised in delivering quality patient care", says El Camino's chief executive officer Neilson Buchanan.

Management training and development

While many voluntary organisations now acknowledge the need for training in administrative tasks such as word processing they have been less quick to recognise the importance of on-going training to prepare staff for management roles. In fact, management training and development were almost unknown in the voluntary sector a few years ago, with managers expected to acquire the necessary skills in the job. Today, the situation appears to be improving. However it will probably be some time before the sorts of management development programmes that exist in the private sector are established in voluntary organisations. In the meantime, many ambitious voluntary sector workers will continue to find their routes to top management jobs blocked by a lack of formal management training.

This view is supported by the VOLPROF report referred to earlier which showed that 53 per cent of voluntary sector managers are currently recruited from outside the voluntary sector. The report noted that many voluntary organisations are wasting their own resources by failing to grow their own people. While it seems likely that the high take-up of managers from other sectors could be due in part to a temporary glut of experienced managers from the private and public sectors, we nevertheless agree with the report's authors.

However, as voluntary sector staff discover that senior management levels are likely to remain closed to them unless they acquire management training and qualifications, the pressure on voluntary organisations to address this issue is likely to increase.

Our own research found signs that the picture may already be changing. A survey we conducted among top voluntary organisations showed many were investing widely in training – an important signal of the trend to become more business-like and to develop their own people. When asked what areas they trained staff in the responses were:

◆ Communications/ public relations   79%

◆ Project management   41%

◆ Financial management   50%

◆ Fundraising   63%

◆ Information technology   71%

◆ Marketing   49%

Other areas specified were: Total Quality Management (TQM), time management, teamwork, systematic approach to general management skills, service delivery, research, business management, law/contracts, counselling, relationships – external and internal, running corporate and community events.

Yet, a fundamental problem remains. Many voluntary organisations still find it difficult to balance their short-term aims and commitments to support projects and provide services, with the longer term needs of the organisation and the developmental needs of their people. As Sandra Greaves, former editor of 'Third Sector' magazine, puts it:

"How do you justify a training budget if it diverts money away from recipients? There is now a big move towards training, particularly among the larger voluntary organisations. But it's more difficult for smaller voluntary groups. Once again, it's like the difference between a large and a small company. If you're a small campaigning local environmental group, chances are you run on high-energy, high burn-out, just like a small business. Until you hit critical mass, you're not going to be sending people away on management training courses."

In reality, of course, this is a problem of managing short-term objectives and long-term needs – something professional managers have to do all the time. CAF's David Wickert expresses the changing mood among the larger voluntary organisations:

"I think most people accept now that it is necessary to develop people to ensure the long-term performance of charities."

Mike Tuffrey goes further:

"Both employees and volunteers want personal growth through their involvement with the organisation. Having selected and recruited the right people no organisation can afford to keep them static. You will retain and motivate people as employees or as volunteers if they have a sense of going somewhere and acquiring skills. There is something of a tradition in the voluntary sector of not doing that – of using people and then spitting them out. It's actually true across all areas of British life.

"There is a clear effort now in the private sector to do something about it through training and personal development. But the real problem for voluntary organisations comes from the need to divert resources away from the frontline to achieve it. At l'Arche for example, a training and development budget could employ someone. It is true, of course, that once trained there is nothing to stop someone leaving and taking the investment with them. But that is no justification for not developing people.

"In the end it comes down to the hierarchy of purpose; for instance, if you say we are here to serve the homeless, you have to make the connection that this purpose is best served by paying your people well and training and developing them."

That recognition does not necessarily extend to keeping pace with private sector developments in training. Nevertheless three voluntary sector organisations have achieved the distinction of winning the National Training Award; the Scouts some years ago, the Women's Royal Voluntary service (WRVS) and the National Trust in 1994. Few voluntary organisations have yet defined competencies for their employees and volunteers and used these as a basis for training. Looking at the issue from a different angle, out of over 11,000 companies committed to Investors in People, only just over 1,000 have actually achieved it. Yet the Children's Foundation has achieved Investors in People status and 11 voluntary organisations are committed to the standard. This is as many as one could surely expect considering the size of the voluntary sector.

Nonetheless, says Tom Jennings, who runs IBM's courses for voluntary sector managers:

"Most large voluntary organisations have now got to grips with the formal procedures associated with staff and employees -for example, appraisal systems and performance assessments, writing job specifications and recruiting people to fill them – so the need for training in these areas is beginning to tail off."

In putting in these potentially bureaucratic approaches, however, voluntary organisations have tended to accept the successes of the private sector without asking what didn't work. Says Jennings:

"I think some voluntary organisations are destined to repeat the mistakes that businesses have made in recent years. When putting in performance assessment processes for example a lot of businesses made mistakes. At IBM, for example, a lot of effort went into performance appraisal. It seemed to work well and to be motivating staff, but after a while it was clear that mistakes had been made. I think some voluntary organisations are in danger of repeating those mistakes."

Some of the larger voluntary organisations are already well-equipped to provide their own in-house training. For example, the RNIB provides comprehensive training for junior and middle managers which includes the option of taking a certificate of management studies. The programme has been running since 1989, with an average of 12 people participating each year.

In-house training

The majority of the RNIB £397,000 training budget is devolved to RNIB's various management cost centres. Each of the organisation's 2,000 members of staff – around 150 of them managers – undergoes a two-day induction and the individual needs are determined as part of the appraisal system which covers most staff. In addition, everyone who carries out appraisals or recruitment interviewing must undertake special training.

"We find it more cost-effective to do most of our training in-house", corporate training manager Howard Platt told 'Third Sector' magazine recently. "Often you can't get the right courses outside, and a spin-off from in-house training is that you can foster better relations within the organisation. There's such a diverse range of cultures and working environments here that it's important to build bridges."

"For an organisation of our size, the provision of training is very substantial", says external relations manager Mike Lancaster, who came to RNIB with an MBA (Masters in Business Administration) acquired while at British Rail. Lancaster accepts that even the best management development opportunities will not keep managers if there is no clear career path for them, but he believes the RNIB programme benefits the voluntary sector as a whole. "If we train people and they stay within the voluntary sector, we'll grow the whole of the skills base within the voluntary sector."

The National Trust won a National Training Award for its scheme to develop school leavers as potential head gardeners. In 1991 the management board approved the introduction of a quality apprenticeship for young people called 'careership'. The objectives behind the careership programme were to provide a BTEC National Diploma (the equivalent of NVQ Level 3) to successful trainees at the same time as give them an understanding of the specific methods and approaches adopted by the Trust.

Initially 12 head gardeners were selected to act as mentors to trainees over a three year period. In the following two years 24 more trainees were recruited at different gardens and training now extends to the Trust's 16 regions. Training was evaluated by a series of regular reviews and trainees elected a spokesperson to raise issues they felt were important. Head gardeners were consulted each quarter and an annual review was held with everyone involved. One major modification resulting from this was the introduction of formal NVQs and work-based assessment. One of the main benefits for the National Trust has been the introduction of assessment in the workplace for NVQs. Head gardeners inadvertently acted as pilot NVQ assessors and internal verifiers in Amenity Horticulture and other staff at the Trust have now registered for this award. As a result, it is now proposed to offer NVQs throughout the Trust's gardens and some head gardeners involved in the pilot have asked to work towards NVQ Level 4 and 5.

The introduction of NVQs has, in general, raised staff morale, offering a clear career path that was not there before.

Training opportunities, and particularly management training, for people in smaller voluntary organisations are thinner on the ground. Mike Hudson of Compass Partnership believes the time has come for the voluntary sector as a whole to take senior management training seriously.

"My proposition is that the sector needs to grow its own senior management training programme organically, focusing primarily on chief executives and their senior managers", says Hudson. "It might start with a pilot programme, consisting of one day a month for a group of say 20 managers. This could then be expanded to include more subjects over time. In ten year's time there would be a range of programmes available to suit the different needs of individuals. At one end of the spectrum it might include a one week intensive course for newly appointed chief executives, and at the other an MBA in not-for-profit management."

Others, including Ian Bruce and Diana Leat of VOLPROF, believe that the voluntary sector should develop a competencies approach to management training by identifying key skills for voluntary sector managers to create a framework of competencies similar to that developed in the private sector by the Management Charter Initiative (MCI).

In the near future, however, the sticking point for both schemes seems likely to be lack of funding. An alternative way forward would be for voluntary organisations with good links to the business world to negotiate places on the many private sector management development programmes. Some companies such as IBM already offer a limited number of places on existing programmes to voluntary organisations.

Others sponsor voluntary sector managers on external courses. For example, Business in the Arts runs a scheme whereby companies such as English Properties sponsor managers from Arts organisations to attend a management course of their choice.

Courses available include those provided by leading management training providers such as Sundridge Park and Cranfield University School of Management.

Alternatively, there are courses at South Bank University and a growing number of specialist voluntary sector consultancies including the Compass Partnership which offer tailored programmes for voluntary organisations.

In addition, large national organisations, umbrella bodies or networks can also help. For example, organisations such as The National Federation of Housing Associations might usefully take advantage of economies of scale to provide training programmes for members.

The following organisations also organise short management training courses and provide information on other courses and freelance trainers:

♦ London Voluntary Service Council's Training Unit.

♦ The Local Development Team at the NCVO.

♦ The Directory of Social Change.

Addresses and telephone numbers for these organisations are given at the back of this book.

What should voluntary organisations do with incompetent people?

Just because staff can be trained, however, doesn't mean that all staff are capable of doing the jobs assigned to them. Staff competence is a problem of increasing frequency for voluntary organisations – an issue they have tended to avoid, wherever possible.

A degree of toughness in tackling such problems is recommended by consultants such as John Williams of Fishburn, Hedges, Bays & Williams:

"Voluntary organisations have every right – even more than large companies – to ensure that they spend their money wisely and efficiently. So they must have competent people and the right to redeploy incompetent people."

But there is a dilemma for any cause-led organisation. Is Mencap's primary responsibility, for example, to have a highly efficient receptionist or to demonstrate the employability of mentally handicapped people by reserving such jobs for them? Or should Friends of the Earth prefer a more competent researcher to someone demonstrably committed to the environment? There is no right answer to such dilemmas. The issue will depend in each circumstance upon the importance of the task and the importance of supporting a strong value.

Experience in the private sector indicates that there does not have to be a dilemma in such circumstances. The Body Shop, for example, spends a great deal of time and money selecting people who have both the talent and the commitment to deliver high levels of service and relate closely to customers. The retailer maintains that its hiring policy is a major part of its success story.

Moreover, the assumption that voluntary organisations need to adopt business practice in employee management may hide misconceptions of what actually happens in business. Says Tom Jennings:

"The voluntary sector thinks that managers in the private sector are hard and are able to make very tough decisions, especially about people. In reality many of the tough decisions were avoided by the private sector until the recession really bit. They often got rid of people simply by transferring them to a different department. But I find that voluntary sector managers are very capable of making tough decisions because they have to due to the scarcity of resources. They make hard decisions about whether someone fits into the organisation, for example."

Best employment practice would dictate, for example, investing in trying to help an under-performing employee to improve. But trustees of voluntary organisations may feel a stronger duty to remove such employees, on the grounds that supporting incompetent staff is a misuse of beneficiaries' funds.

The answers are not straightforward and decisions will often need to be made on a case by case basis. Key questions to help decision-making will include:

♦ What is the **impact** of this job on the organisation's purpose?

♦ How severely will it affect **efficiency**?

♦ What would the general public think was **the right decision**?

♦ What would the voluntary organisation's **clients** think?

♦ How does it affect **general morale** and pride in the workforce?

Reward and recognition

The issue of the size of salaries paid to voluntary sector staff, particularly senior management, remains a touchy subject. The perception that voluntary work is its own reward will not completely disappear, while others welcome moves to reward voluntary sector managers with pay packets more in keeping with their expertise.

However, despite increasing professionalism in the sector there is often still a considerable gap between pay and benefits received by voluntary sector staff and their private and public sector counterparts. Research suggests, however, that this gap may be narrowing.

Recent estimates by recruitment agencies put the average salary differential between voluntary sector workers and nationally agreed public sector pay for similar positions at between 5 and 10 per cent. Compared to commercial rates the gap is estimated to be between 20 and 30 per cent. As might be expected, however, the gap is often much greater with very small voluntary organisations and Third World aid groups.

Perks such as company cars are also less common in the voluntary sector. Motivational tools such as share options or profit sharing are simply not available.

The 1993 Charity Recruitment Salary Survey found that on average the gap between the salary of senior executives in the voluntary and private sectors was relatively unchanged on previous years at 23 per cent, but that the salaries paid to chief executives and fundraising directors in middle income voluntary organisations had risen substantially in the preceding 18 months. For example, the survey found that the chief executive of a voluntary organisation with an income of £1-3 million earned a median figure of £34,800 in 1993 compared with £29,540 in 1992, representing an increase of 15 per cent. Similarly the pay of fundraising directors had increased by 17 per cent from £23,203 to £27,784.

This is probably the result of the realisation that running a voluntary sector organisation can be just as challenging as managing a major private company or a local authority.

According to Peter Brown, chairman of the specialist recruiters Charity Appointments:

"There's an understanding now that if you want to have well-managed voluntary organisations you've got to have properly paid managers. The voluntary sector is now established as a sector for high-flying professionals."

Some in the voluntary sector disagree, however, especially those working in the area of overseas aid. Tim Moulds, head of personnel at Christian Aid, told Andrew Cornwell of 'Third Sector' magazine recently:

"The argument that if you want good people you have to pay high salaries has a superficial logic which doesn't actually hold. We are quite tough about pay at the top end."

Christian Aid tries to maintain no more than a 3:1 differential between its lowest paid and highest paid staff, while paying slightly above the market rate for its lowest paid clerical staff. It claims that paying managers salaries 30 per cent below the prevailing rate in the voluntary sector has not created problems in attracting motivated staff. Many people in the sector feel that high salaries are inappropriate for organisations whose beneficiaries are very poor.

However, the issue that many voluntary organisations have still to address is what the public thinks about them paying large salaries to managers when they know that those salaries are funded by donations. Yet much would be gained if more voluntary organisations were prepared to confront this issue head-on instead of fudging it by being coy. At present, many still prefer to avoid giving details of the salaries they pay their top managers. This lack of transparency leaves the door open to abuse.

In the long-run, a much better approach for voluntary organisations would be to nail their colours to the mast. If the organisation believes its aims are best served by paying staff at market rates why then not explain its position? The number of donations that might be lost as a result would be small beer compared to the potential damage to public trust caused by the information being leaked.

What people are less likely to accept is that voluntary organisations want to have their cake and eat it. Besides, it is by no means clear that the public would object. As David Wickert of CAF points out, there are varying attitudes among the general population:

"Public opinion varies from surprise that voluntary sector employees are actually paid at all, to surprise that they are paid so little.

"There is a line voluntary organisations have to hold. We have to pay a salary around the median to get people who are capable of doing the job. Every member of my staff could command a higher salary in the commercial sector – perhaps as much as twice their salary here. The voluntary sector has to realise that people need to live, they need to be able to afford to dress appropriately for meetings and to get into work each day.

"Also, other organisations we deal with expect our services and systems to be efficient, and that requires capable people. I've just come back from New York – yes we do need to travel like other managers – where I was negotiating with the information services company Bloomburgs for them to distribute information for us around the globe. They have sophisticated systems and they need us to get the relevant data to them very quickly; they take it for granted that we're the sort of organisation that can do that and we have to make sure we are by attracting people with the right expertise."

Mike Tuffrey agrees:

"People in the voluntary sector are motivated by something other than money, but you can't grossly underpay someone and expect them to be happy. It's a myth that people in the voluntary sector don't need money. You have to understand why people are there. Employees are there to earn a living and to do something more immediately good than they would be able to in the private sector."

Based on current trends it seems likely that in the next few years pay differentials in the public, private and voluntary sectors will continue to narrow. At one level, this is to be welcomed as the requirements of professionalism on voluntary sector managers are likely to be raised in the process. However, there is clearly a question mark over how voluntary organisations will be able to fund higher salaries with their limited resources. The most likely outcome is that the larger voluntary organisations will pay salaries closer to those of the larger companies, while smaller voluntary organisations like smaller companies will pay less.

At the same time, it seems likely that the political and social landscape of the latter part of the 1990s will involve much greater overlap between the three sectors, making it easier for individual careers to span private, public and voluntary organisations. In particular, we can expect managers to be more mobile between the voluntary sector and private sector. As the recession comes to an end and the skills shortages become more evident this may create a very real problem of poaching as the private sector looks to expand its management pool by raiding the voluntary sector.

To avoid an expensive upward spiral of salary increases, the voluntary sector will have to find ways to retain staff that do not involve competing on pay and benefits alone. Reward and recognition strategies to ensure that the aspirational component of jobs is met will become more critical.

Performance-Related Pay

Performance-related pay schemes – whereby a proportion of salary is determined by an assessment of the individual's job performance, or that of the team in which they work – are much in the news at present. A number of companies have introduced these schemes and they are now being introduced in areas of the public sector. In principle, at least, PRP schemes would appear to have much to recommend them to the voluntary sector, too.

However, many commentators have pointed out that PRP has not yet delivered the benefits it was supposed to in the private sector. Indeed, it has been claimed that by placing too much emphasis on the individual, or the performance of small teams, such schemes are divisive and counterproductive. Certainly less scrupulous employers have used the introduction of PRP as a means to achieve cost cutting objectives at the expense of employees. For this reason, until such time as clearer evidence of real benefits can be seen, we do not believe PRP will provide the answers to the voluntary sector's problems.

A more profitable avenue for many voluntary organisations may be to find internal reward and recognition mechanisms which are inexpensive to operate and yet fit with the culture of the organisation and support its mission. A range of recent developments in human resources could help. For example:

◆ Employee award schemes to recognise outstanding performance.

◆ One-on-one career counselling to support the individual.

◆ Job-sharing and crèche facilities to make it easier for women returners.

◆ Sabbaticals – allowing employees to take a year off to fulfil personal aspirations.

◆ Personal development plans.

Alternatively, voluntary organisations which lack the resources to provide support on this scale can develop highly individual approaches to reward and recognition at a low cost. For example, an idea used at the Downtown Pittsburgh YMCA in America which was reported in the American management publication 'On Achieving Excellence' has an elegant simplicity.

CASE STUDY ➤ Downtown Pittsburgh YMCA's ROSE programme

The Downtown Pittsburgh YMCA has an employee recognition programme called ROSE, which stands for Recognition of Superior or Special Efforts.

The programme allows 'anyone at any time' to recognise an exceptional contribution by a member of staff. A rose emblem is hung on the notice board with a card explaining the reason for the award. Everyone who receives an award gets a real rose in a box at the annual rose banquet. The person with the randomly placed odd-colour rose wins a trip to the Rose Bowl football final.

One member of staff won a rose by noticing that the washing machine was broken, taking the dirty laundry to a launderette on her own initiative (paying for it out of her own pocket) and then folding and returning the clothes. Another received a rose for telephoning a disabled YMCA member who had missed several workout sessions to check that everything was alright. When he found out that the reason she was staying away was because the pavement was too icy to manoeuvre her wheelchair, he made sure the pavements were kept clear so she could get into the building.

According to executive director George Babish, the ROSE awards are a way of recognising the small things that take an extra effort.

Volunteers

From its earliest origins, the voluntary sector has always been heavily dependent on the efforts of unpaid workers or volunteers. Despite the growing numbers of full-time paid employees who work within the voluntary sector, many smaller voluntary organisations continue to rely on volunteers in order to operate.

According to the 1991 National Survey of Volunteering, as many as 23 million people – over half of the adult population of Britain – were involved in volunteering that year.

So just who are these volunteers? A 1993 report by CAF suggests that the profile of a typical volunteer is a middle class professional (man or woman), aged about 48, who has children, is a committed church member and gives an average of 40 minutes a month to a voluntary organisation, probably by raising money or organising an event.

However, the report, based on a survey of 1,032 respondents, also found that the number of volunteers appears to have fallen since the first CAF survey in 1987. If this trend continues it could have dire consequence for many voluntary organisations. What is already clear is that voluntary organisations must make every effort to manage volunteers well if they are to retain this valuable resource.

In the future, a combination of factors is likely to alter the pattern of volunteering in the UK. One important factor will be the changing demographic profile of Britain. Increased life expectancy and fewer births mean that the make-up of the population is altering. In the next few years, there will be a increase in the ratio of older people to younger people which is likely to have a number of effects.

In the short term, this will favour volunteering. The higher proportion of older people, boosted by greater numbers taking early retirement or displaced from the workforce by redundancy, will create a larger pool of potential volunteers for voluntary organisations. In the medium-term, however, as the number of older people dependent on a smaller number of young people active in the workforce increases, there could be serious shortages of volunteers.

Fortunately, other changes are moving in the opposite direction. One significant factor is likely to be the shift in the number of people becoming involved in volunteering through the workplace as a consequence of employee volunteering schemes.

Employee volunteering schemes

By getting more employees involved in community work such as caring for the elderly, crime prevention and urban regeneration, employee volunteering schemes could dramatically expand the pool of volunteers available to help the voluntary sector in the future.

Employee volunteering schemes began in America in the mid-1980s. Companies found that many employees were willing in principle to become volunteers but lacked information about how to get started. By recognising and encouraging these aspirations, companies discovered they could release enormous energy among the workforce, simultaneously boosting staff morale, increasing employee loyalty and enhancing the company's local reputation.

Since then the idea has crossed the Atlantic with pioneering initiatives in British companies such as Allied Dunbar, Whitbread and Grand Metropolitan. Through their employee volunteering schemes, these companies provide information and resources to support staff volunteers. In doing so, they send an important message that voluntary work outside of office hours is valued within the organisation.

There are three basic strands to employee volunteering schemes. Companies may support and recognise volunteers by:

♦ **Providing help-in-kind.**
  For example, by providing offices for meetings or making design and printing facilities available free of charge. Senior managers can also help by taking an interest in volunteer projects and sending personal letters to those involved.

♦ **Matching employee volunteers with local community needs**.
  For example, Whitbread Plc has appointed a full-time employee volunteering programme manager to co-ordinate activities, and Allied Dunbar maintains a skills bank – an inventory of willing employees whose technical and professional skills can be matched with requests from voluntary organisations for help in areas such as advising on computer systems and preparation of accounts.

♦ **Developing their own community projects**
  Either on a one-off or on-going basis – involving a group of employees working on specific goals or events. For example, employees at Royal

Mail in Leicester planted a tree for each member of their family in a new national forest in Leicestershire.

Most companies opt for a mix of these three components. But whatever the mix, the key is to make volunteering more accessible to staff. And the roll-call of companies committed to employee volunteering schemes is growing. Two recent developments are also likely to accelerate the trend.

On 28 February 1994, the Home Secretary Michael Howard announced a government-backed initiative, 'Make a Difference', which aims to tap what Mr Howard described as a potential "army of volunteers available to help others." One of its key objectives is to promote employee volunteering schemes to business.

Under its auspices, a team of senior executives from the private, public and voluntary sectors will map out a national volunteering strategy; and grants of up to £20,000 will be made available to assist in setting up partnerships between business and voluntary organisations.

On the same day, a new organisation to help companies get started was launched. Action: Employees in the Community, created out of a merger between Action Resource Centre (ARC) – the organisation which specialises in secondments to the voluntary sector – and the Employees in the Community campaign run by Business in the Community, offers a one-stop-shop for employers and voluntary organisations, acting as a broker, facilitator and manager to develop employee volunteering schemes.

Unlike secondments, which typically involve managers in assignments of at least 100 days, employee volunteering does not require a great commitment of time – often just a few hours is sufficient to be of value. This makes it accessible to a larger proportion of the workforce. The wide range of activities employees engage in – anything from fundraising events to professional advice – also means that employees at all levels can participate.

In the words of David Hemsworth, information manager at Action: Employees in the Community:

"Employee volunteering is an idea whose time has come. When employee volunteering is done well everyone benefits. Employees – typically people who have never volunteered before – tell us they get a lot of pleasure and satisfaction from their involvement. Companies get good local PR and a raised profile leading to better community relations. Voluntary organisations get a valuable source of volunteers. We also find that morale among employees is raised and loyalty to the company increases. People are generally very proud to work for a company that does these sorts of things."

Julia Cleverdon agrees:

"The biggest growth in the 1990s in our view will be in the area of getting employees into community action. That's why we have joined forces with

ARC (Action Resource Centre) to create Action: Employees in the Community.

"In the future companies will increasingly make their contributions through their employees. There are some excellent example of this already. The people who work for the Royal Mail in Leicester understand about the voluntary sector because they're really involved. I think volunteering is one of the areas where the shibboleths between voluntary and private sectors are breaking down now."

Indeed, we would argue that the growth of employee volunteering is a clear indication of the shape of things to come. Such schemes provide an excellent example of how the two sectors can best be harnessed to each others' needs as employees take their skills to voluntary organisations and bring their enthusiasm back into the workplace. In some organisations, volunteering is becoming an important part of the corporate culture.

The Body Shop International, for example, encourages all employees in its head office to spend half a day each month on voluntary work of their choice. The company also requires all staff to do at least one day of volunteer activity within their first six months of employment. Activities include the 40 members of the head office finance department taking residents of a local Cheshire home out for day trips, and a three-year commitment by the company to send staff to help in Romanian orphanages.

At Royal Mail in Leicester a staff member organises the Christmas party for Leicestershire's orphans and a number of management staff are school governors and JPs. Allied Dunbar's 'Volunteers at Work' is supported by a quarterly bulletin to staff which features volunteer opportunities and successfully recruited 800 volunteers in its first three years.

Nick Temple, chief executive of IBM UK and the first chairman of Action: Employees in the Community puts the case succinctly:

"I approach this as a businessman not a philanthropist. Whatever their size, employers who encourage employee community involvement usually find themselves in a win, win, win situation.

"The employer gains a way to unlock the potential and enthusiasm of employees and to develop solid durable links with their local community. The employee gains a chance to develop business skills in a new and challenging environment and a sense of fulfilment from contributing to the community. The voluntary sector gains practical support in essential business skills which would otherwise be unobtainable or unaffordable."

Companies with established employee volunteering schemes such as Allied Dunbar and Whitbread also claim they improve communications within and across company departments through internal networks of volunteers. Where projects are shared with other employers in the area – as in two pilot schemes in Leeds and Leicester – it can also help with networking between companies.

Policies for managing volunteers

At present the management of volunteers in the voluntary sector is patchy. As Julia Cleverdon points out:

"In general, the voluntary sector does well on volunteers and many manage volunteers very well. But others manage them very poorly. They get away with it because the cause is so strong in itself."

Sandra Greaves, former editor of 'Third Sector', agrees:

"A lot of voluntary organisations still use volunteers as envelope-stuffers and ditch-diggers. Maybe if you've got hundreds of people turning up as Greenpeace has, for instance, then it's a valid response to use volunteers as bodies at demos to lie in front of bulldozers. But I think you've got to be very careful that you don't lose the enthusiasm of volunteers."

However, according to Diana Leat:

"In some organisations there is a real problem with unpaid volunteers. In some way they have to say we'll treat volunteers as equals. But the whole thing can become something of a charade.

"Really, you have to come clean whatever sort of organisation it is. For example, the managing director would probably make a complete mess of washing the dishes and similarly you can't expect or pretend that the people washing the dishes can do the MD's job."

NCVO's Tim Dartington says:

"The distinction between managing staff and managing volunteers isn't as clear as it might be."

Our own findings suggest that those voluntary organisations which manage volunteers well have a formal policy on volunteers which includes guidelines on their recruitment, training and support. At present, good practice in this area includes:

♦ A formal **recruitment process**, including vetting procedures to protect clients and the reputation of the organisation

♦ **Induction packs** providing background information and history of the organisation as well as details of current projects

♦ **Written job descriptions**, clearly setting out roles and responsibilities.

♦ **Disciplinary procedures** similar to those for paid staff.

♦ The **opportunity to apply** for paid staff vacancies when they arise.

♦ The **opportunity to discuss** issues through suggestion schemes and other two-way channels of communication.

♦ **Support and training** from paid staff as required.

♦ **Good internal communications** via volunteer newsletters, magazines etc.

♦ **Formal recognition** via volunteer awards or personal letters from senior managers or trustees.

A recent article in 'Third Sector' found that volunteer policies in four voluntary organisations varied greatly but displayed many of these elements.

London Lighthouse

The London Lighthouse provides care and support for people with HIV and Aids. It has clear recruitment procedures for volunteers and gives all voluntary staff a written contract, job description and manual. It also uses a vetting procedure and gives compulsory training. Volunteers have the same disciplinary and grievance procedure as their paid colleagues and are given appraisals and support throughout their involvement with the charity.

There are currently about 200 volunteers organised into 19 neighbourhood teams, providing emotional and practical support to about 100 people with HIV and Aids across London. A further 160 volunteers are based at the centre, working in areas such as the cafe and residential centre.

Carol Gibbons, group head of community services, which runs the home support programme and organises the centre volunteers, believes that making volunteers a central part of a team effort has contributed to a very low turnover rate among volunteers.

"I don't think we could exist without them", she says. "One of the things that people with HIV and Aids have always faced is stigma. The fact that volunteers are helping gives acceptance. They have a commitment to what they do and that is something you can't buy."

People interested in becoming volunteers attend an information session, fill in an application form and are interviewed. They then have to provide references and those interested in working in the playgroup subject to checks with the police.

Volunteers working in the neighbourhood teams out in the community undergo 80 hours of training which helps them identify their own support needs and develop a non-judgmental approach to their work. A team development officer provides volunteers with support and assistance on the ground and everyone receiving services who has HIV or Aids is appointed a key worker. Volunteers who work at the centre have a three-day induction period and on-the-job training.

"We are very fortunate in normally having more people than we need", says Gibbons. "We have a great diversity in terms of sexuality, gender and age, and our volunteers give a richness of opinion we wouldn't otherwise get."

Age Concern England

Age Concern England has a network of about a quarter of a million volunteers throughout the country. Each of its 1,400 branches is run autonomously, but there are national guidelines on the way volunteers are managed. These are supported by a director of operations and a staff of 15 field officers on the ground to advise the branches.

The guidelines include vetting procedures for potential volunteers who will come into contact with elderly and sometimes vulnerable people. The vetting procedure is seen as essential to protecting clients and can involve talking to the police. References are required for all jobs which may involve visiting elderly people in their homes.

The charity has the same disciplinary procedures for all staff – paid and volunteers alike, and many branches have a job description and personnel file for volunteers who are often encouraged to apply for paid staff jobs as they become available.

Most volunteer activities are run by a paid team leader who heads a group of volunteers which can range in number from six to sixty. Team leaders provide guidance, training and support for all those involved, and a volunteer coordinator meets with all prospective volunteers for an informal interview followed an introduction to the appropriate team leader.

"The system is more or less the same for volunteers as it is for paid staff", says Pat Cusack, manager of Leicester Age Concern. "We couldn't really cope without the help of volunteers. They make things work at every level."

Save the Children Fund

At Save the Children, volunteers are organised into regional networks which enable them to have a real input into fundraising initiatives. The vast majority of the charity's 20,000 volunteers help out in one of the 800 local branches or 162 shops throughout the UK. There are few opportunities for volunteers to work on overseas projects, however, as the charity takes on local help in the countries concerned.

Michael Cowcher, volunteer development manager at the charity's London headquarters explains that all volunteers are supported by a network of 90 staff who work in regional fundraising, with ten staff in the regional management team. Staff are divided into seven regions which in turn are split into 40 areas, with a paid area organiser and an area representative who is elected by the volunteers. The representatives meet regularly as a national committee and receive training and skill sharing from the paid staff in their region, and discuss issues central to fundraising work on the ground.

The charity also makes use of voluntary help and expertise on committees which give investment and financial advice as well as input on overseas issues. Other projects such as family centres work closely with the communities they serve and often co-opt parents onto the local management committee, while paid expert staff provide care.

"The work of the volunteers forms the backbone of the organisation", says Cowcher. "Volunteers have been completely crucial from day one. We couldn't have an organisation and continue our work without the support of volunteers."

Feed the Children

Says FTC's chief executive David Grubb:

"It was a flag nailed to our post from the first day that we would involve a much wider variety of volunteers than usual – everyone from truckers and warehouse operators to computer people. We wanted their ideas, their imagination and their skills. Quite a few of our staff have joined us originally as specialist volunteers. At the moment, we have 86 volunteers working at our warehouse and offices in Reading and a total of about 600 fundraisers around the country. We bring them together for an annual celebration to thank them for their efforts.

The problems we experience with volunteers are classic:

♦ They hear us saying we believe they are important, but they may get offended if we insist they come in at regular times.

♦ They often overdo it and burn out.

♦ Because they really do want to be involved, keeping them up to date about what we are doing is important. They have to change with us, but of course not everyone is prepared to do that.

♦ Some salaried staff tend to give volunteers less important tasks, because they are not quite sure when they are going to be available. There is a danger here that you devalue the qualities of the volunteers by, say, giving them the filing to do. I've just discovered someone packing shoes who has good experience of corporate management, which we can use.

We try to deal with these problems by interviewing all our volunteers about their skills and trying to get to know as much as possible about them. It's important to assess what they want to do – for some people, part of the attraction in being involved is doing something different than their normal job; for others, it's using their work skills for a more rewarding cause.

Greenpeace

Environmental pressure group Greenpeace employs up to 200 volunteers to help it with routine administrative tasks at its London headquarters. However, like all campaigning organisations it relies on a voluntary membership to work up and down the country on fundraising and campaign projects. Greenpeace has about 412,000 'supporters' in the UK and an estimated five million supporters worldwide.

The group has a high media and public profile and relies on paid consultants for most of its specialist work and environmental research, with few opportunities for volunteers in these areas.

"Occasionally we have people who want to work for us and can offer knowledge of a particular field", says a Greenpeace spokesperson. "They might be able to work with a campaign team but it is fairly rare because we now employ very highly qualified experts."

There is a rigorous vetting procedure for those who do get to work at head office, even though most of the demand is for general administrative work such as answering telephones and stuffing and addressing envelopes.

According to personnel manager Jean Goodland all prospective volunteers are sent an information pack and attend an interview where they are given a presentation about the organisation. Those still interested are then interviewed by personnel staff before being put to work initially in the public information office.

All volunteers are asked to commit themselves for a minimum of three days per week for three months. They are encouraged to apply for temporary paid work which is advertised internally. Following a period of dealing with public enquiries and correspondence, volunteers may be given the opportunity to branch out into other departments including campaigns, finance or fundraising depending on the need.

"We do try to target older people", says Goodland. "Sometimes volunteers do not stay very long, particularly if they are students or young people looking for work experience, and older people are very reliable although they are not always attracted to us as we might seem a bit radical."

As with many other aspects of management in the voluntary sector, recent developments are creating new demands on the way voluntary organisations view volunteers. In the very near future many of them will have to face up to new challenges.

Diana Leat suggests that the new contract culture in particular will pose new dilemmas for managing volunteers:

"There are issues of competency and accountability. If you are not paid or work on short-term contracts, what does that do to your accountability? This is critical in the context of contracting. What happens when a voluntary

sector organisation is contracted to provide a service which is delivered by volunteers? Who is accountable? The move towards contracting will force voluntary organisations to face up to these sorts of issues.

"Put another way, if you are legally contracted to provide X amount of care, can you rely on volunteers to provide it? Some people would argue that volunteers are just as reliable (and unreliable) as paid staff, but where do you stand in law if it goes wrong? Is it negligence to rely on volunteers with whom you have no legally binding contract? If so, do you then need a legal contract with volunteers? These are pressing issues that the voluntary sector must explore.

"Take a recent example. A private agency providing care services did not employ care workers but used instead self-employed care workers. However, the contract was between the agency and the social services. One of the care workers murdered a social services client. This actually happened and threw up the whole issue of responsibility. Where do self-employed people fit in this case?

"Clearly this needs clarifying. If that can happen with self-employed care workers, what would be the position with volunteers?"

In the next few years we expect to see new techniques for managing volunteers emerge as the contract culture becomes more established and voluntary sector service providers begin to face up to the issues raised by Diana Leat and others. In particular, we suggest that there should be clear delineation between professional contract service providers and volunteers, or where volunteers are used to deliver contracted services the use of legally binding contracts either between volunteers and the voluntary sector organisation or between the volunteers and the statutory authority.

These developments will not be welcomed by everyone. Will volunteers feel exploited by the system? Will it seem less like voluntary work if it is formalised in this way? The likelihood is that voluntary organisations will evolve cultures that operate well in partnership with the public sector (and tend more and more towards professional employment) and those that maintain the all-volunteer state-independent tradition.

Managing secondees

Secondments or temporary loans of professional managers to the voluntary sector are an increasingly popular way for companies and public sector organisations to support the voluntary sector.

Often, the secondee brings specialist expertise to the voluntary organisation, carrying out an assignment which produces a report with valuable recommendations for improvement in systems or processes in a particular area.

Since the cost to the voluntary sector host is only that of providing management direction and support, secondees represent an excellent resource for voluntary organisations.

David Hemsworth, Communications Director with Action: Employees in the Community points out that secondment is a two way street with enormous benefits in staff development for companies who place secondees:

"Organisations are increasingly viewing secondment as a good way of developing management skills. Secondees are learning a real situation. Employees' communication skills are rapidly developed because they have been put into this new environment.

"Project-based secondments which take a day a week over three months are becoming increasingly popular. The two year full time secondments are in decline – it is very expensive for a company to pay an executive's salary for up to two years while he or she works elsewhere."

We believe that as the benefits on both sides become better known, secondments will provide an increasingly valuable technique to transfer expertise between the three sectors.

However, to achieve the potential benefits, better management is required on allh sides. In particular, there are a number of issues that need to be thought through by companies and voluntary organisations. These include the following:

♦ How do you manage someone from a **different culture**?

♦ Will the **salary scale** of secondees cause resentment among other members of staff doing similar work? (This is particularly important with longer term secondees.)

♦ Are secondees' personal **career objectives** clearly defined? Is there a proper system in place to manage their re-entry into their home organisation?

♦ What happens if the secondee's job becomes **redundant** while they are on secondment?

And on a more positive note:

♦ How can voluntary organisations make **best use** of the secondee as a link to build a deeper partnership with the company? What resources within the company can be accessed in this way – for example specialist skills in IT, or marketing?

♦ What can the voluntary organisation **learn** from the culture and skills of the secondee? How can those lessons be passed on to its own people and retained by the organisation?

Summary

In general, the aspirational content of jobs in the voluntary sector is high. Where employees and volunteers feel that their efforts are well directed they are likely to be extremely committed. To manage them effectively, voluntary organisations need to provide:

♦ Clear **objectives**.

♦ A **culture** that supports its mission.

At present, too many voluntary organisations take it for granted that they are 'good brand employers', paying insufficient attention to issues such as equal opportunities and career development. In fact, much still needs to be done in terms of developing effective personnel policies which truly meet the needs of their people. Volunteers in particular are still poorly managed in many voluntary organisations.

Our research suggests, too, that although important progress has been made in recruitment and training in recent years, there is still considerable scope for improvement, particularly in the area of management development. Best practice in the private sector provides managers with personal development plans, leading to a wide variety of individualised opportunities for learning skills and behaviours. People are expected to take increasing responsibility for their own development and supported in doing so.

The current debate on the future of the voluntary sector means that questions about the legitimacy of using donations to fund training and to pay professional managers, which many voluntary organisations have preferred to 'fudge' in the past, are now beginning to surface. This we believe is a good thing as it will lead to wider discussion about how needs can be met in the future.

It is to be hoped, too, that greater awareness among companies of the learning opportunities presented by the voluntary sector will encourage cross-fertilisation, with important benefits for both sides.

Checklist

1. Does the internal culture of your organisation match the **aspirations of its people** (in other words does it walk the walk as well as talk the talk)?

2. Does your organisation have **clear recruitment procedures**? Does it specify what skills and characteristics are required for specific jobs?

3. How well does it **manage its volunteers**? Are they seen as envelope stuffers and ditch diggers? Does the organisation audit the skills volunteers bring with them? Could better use be made of them?

4. Does the organisation have a **formal equal opportunities policy**? Who is responsible for it?

5. Are there **proper disciplinary and complaints procedures** in place? Do employees and volunteers have 'safe' channels to raise ethical concerns?

Chapter 5

Is the image right?

Key issues

♦ *Should a voluntary sector organisation's image be an accurate reflection of its work and its values, or an image that will attract greatest sympathy and support?*

♦ *How careful do voluntary organisations have to be about who they associate with?*

♦ *How can they balance spend on image and on service delivery?*

Managing a voluntary image

If a voluntary organisation's greatest asset is its people, its public image or *brand* understandably comes a close second. Indeed, you might argue that the brand is most important because it attracts the right people to the organisation.

Indeed, it is often because voluntary organisations are held in such high esteem by the public that any whiff of scandal attracts so much media attention.

What is increasingly clear is that at a time when competition for funds in the voluntary sector is intensifying, organisations of all sizes require additional checks and balances to safeguard their image. This has important implications for the use of techniques such as Cause Related Marketing – discussed later in this chapter – and for managing the ethical climate – discussed in more detail in Chapter 7.

What is the brand?

Brands are about perception rather than reality, although they need an underpinning of reality to sustain them. The Royal National Lifeboat Institution has managed its brand perception well, according to NCVO's Tim Dartington: "The public image is of small communities of volunteers around the coastline, but RNLI is mainly a major shipbuilding organisation." The brand image needs to reinforce not what a voluntary organisation does, but the value of the cause it serves.

A great many voluntary organisations are fortunate enough to have a long and distinguished history of service to the community. The fact that they are seen as agents for good endears them to the general public and provides an excellent platform from which to canvas support.

In marketing terms a good image is invaluable. The goodwill it generates is often what allows a voluntary organisation to function effectively – but a good image should not be taken for granted. All voluntary organisations should guard their reputations jealously because once they become tarnished it can take a very long time to regain the moral high ground, if ever.

In the 1990s, there are a number of indications that voluntary organisations need to be more conscious of the need to safeguard their image.

For example, SCOPE (among others) was recently dragged into the Asil Nadir scandal via fundraising. The Cancer Research Campaign and the Imperial Cancer Research Fund were severely criticised by the Charity Commission for funding the fundamentally flawed Bristol Study which unjustly dealt a devastating blow to alternative medicine.

Nonetheless, for most organisations, the strength of the brand is reinforced (or not) by the way people in the organisation behave, how the organisation interacts with others and by its culture.

Effective management of the brand, then, requires the voluntary organisation to consider issues such as:

♦ What kind of **identity** do we have and do we need?

♦ What **impression** do our people make?

♦ Are we keeping **the right company**?

♦ Are we **communicating effectively** to all our audiences?

What kind of identity do we have and need?

In recent years a growing number of voluntary organisations have recognised the need to reposition themselves in the public eye by changing their image. Often, the most visible sign of this is an organisation's decision to alter its name and corporate identity.

However, while the trend has accelerated in the last few years, the influence of marketing people on voluntary organisations has been apparent much longer. As Bill Cater reported in The Times in September 1993:

"In 1970, when he was a manager marketing soap products for Unilever, 25-year old Ian Bruce walked into the office of an old people's charity and made an announcement: "I'll help you sell the problems of old people using techniques I've learnt in marketing." He was given a job.

"On his first day, Bruce wrote a memo declaring that his new employer, the National Old People's Welfare Council, should alter its uninspiring name. Just under a year later the council was re-launched as Age Concern." It has gone on to become a household name. Says Bruce: "I think it was the first charity to use market research to choose its name. We took 100 names and put them each out to market research. Then we told the committee 'that's what the public wants'."

More recently, Bruce has been instrumental in launching a sharper image for The Royal National Institute for the Blind. The re-launch followed market research surveys commissioned by the charity which found that although people thought of the RNIB as doing good work and as honest, solid and reliable, they also perceived it as old-fashioned, inaccessible, boring and bureaucratic. Worse still, they often confused the RNIB initials with RNLI (lifeboats) or the RSPB (birds).

After much agonising, the charity decided to keep the same name because it was well-established with the public and a new title could have taken a long time to register, but that other changes should be made. In particular, it decided to alter the symbol of a man with a stick used in its logo. The charity felt that while it was an instantly recognisable emblem, the figure depicted was too hesitant and presented a rather pathetic impression of blind people. He was therefore replaced by an altogether more jaunty and purposeful figure with his head held high. The words 'challenging blindness' were also added to make the RNIB instantly distinguishable from other charities with similar initials.

What makes the re-launch more likely to succeed is that the charity has also taken the theme of challenging blindness to heart in its new thinking. In particular, it has launched a new campaign to improve access to information and reduce the dependency of blind people on others. Official government forms such as those for tax, and electoral registration which in the past have made no allowance for visually impaired people have been targeted. The charity wants public bodies and businesses to follow the example of the big four banks, which provide Braille or large-type statements on request; or of British Telecom which sends out bills in Braille; or Boots which publishes Braille catalogues.

In the past few years, other voluntary sector organisations have also taken steps to revitalise their images. For example, The National Federation of Community Organisations was re-launched as Community Matters; The Church of England Children's Society is now The Children's Society; and the National Marriage Guidance Council switched to the altogether snappier name Relate.

But while the name change decision at Age Concern and these others was prompted by the need to have a more easily recognisable identity in the marketplace, some voluntary organisations have been influenced by other concerns.

For example, at the centre of the long-running debate about whether the SCOPE should change its name was the question of its appropriateness in the modern context. Like other voluntary organisations working with disabled people, the society had faced mounting pressure against negative stereotyping which forced it to reappraise its public image. The charity's own market research indicated that its name had become a barrier to potential supporters of its work for people with cerebral palsy. It found that many people believe that the word spastic has become degraded to the level of a playground taunt. In November 1992, the society's members voted 4:1 in favour of a name change and re-launch as SCOPE. People at the charity chose Scope because it was short, easy to remember and offered a blank canvas which could be invested in meaning. Another alternative, the Cerebral Palsy Association was rejected as too specific and therefore limiting. John Williams, who was involved in the name change, explains: 'We wanted a name that could evolve as the organisation evolved.'

Mencap, too, has tried to re-cast its image. In October 1992 it dropped its Little Tommy logo because it was felt to have negative connotations for people with learning disabilities. It was replaced with a series of positive images. However, the charity has so far resisted pressure to change its name, which is derived from the term 'mentally handicapped'.

Yet, the dilemma for all these organisations is that by re-launching themselves under a new title they risk losing existing supporters who may not recognise the changed name. In the increasingly noisy voluntary marketplace, where old and new organisations compete for donations, giving up an established name – or brand – is potentially costly. It is hard, for example, to imagine any company renaming a successful product which it has spent many years building into a brand offering. Any decision to revamp the Mars bar, for instance, takes it as read that as market leader the name is non-negotiable.

NCH: Action for Children opted for continuity when it changed its name. As John Williams, consultant at Fishburn, Hedges, Bays & Williams explains:

"NCH came to us at the beginning of 1992 and asked us to sort out the inconsistencies in their name. Since the mid Eighties the organisation had gone by the initials 'NCH', but the change had caused confusion about who it was. The people at NCH wanted to change the name because it had moved out of funding children's homes into working with children in the community and in their homes. The name no longer represented what it did.

"After consultation, the charity decided to retain the NCH for continuity. There was risk that if we lost the 'NCH' part, then people wouldn't recognise what is an old established organisation. One suggestion was 'NCH for children and families' but the public couldn't understand the concept of working for families. We looked at various other descriptors with a core element of children and finally decided on NCH: Action for children. We kept the logo for visual continuity. The name was launched in 1994, the 125th anniversary of the organisation. After just one year, it is used widely and seems to be accepted as the new name."

Several years after it changed its title, Relate, on the other hand, is only now reaching the point where it no longer needs to add 'formerly the National Marriage Guidance Council' after its name.

For a voluntary organisation, the benefits of a new organisational identity must therefore be weighed against not only the obvious design, printing, and other administrative costs, but also the potential loss of donations – hopefully short-lived – and the need to mount a large-scale marketing awareness campaign to support the new identity.

Voluntary organisations have found, however, that wherever possible it pays to retain at least a link with the old identity. For example, when Barnardo's decided to update its image in 1988 it decided that dropping anything more than the 'Dr' from its famous name was not an option. As Alan Booth, Barnardo's head of publicity explained to 'Investors Chronicle' in March 1993, with its brand-leader position in the charity world it would be counterproductive to go further. Nevertheless, the charity's relaunch under a new logo was seen as a significant move to distance itself from its Victorian 'orphan' image. The charity estimates that the initial cost of implementing the change was £100,000, but increased donations following the relaunch recouped the outlay.

Other voluntary organisations, too, have tinkered with their names to make them more politically correct. For example, The Royal National Institute for the Deaf has become the Royal National Institute for Deaf *People*.

However there is a danger in all this that voluntary organisations focus too much of their attention on the visible elements of image. Giving the organisation's identity a new coat of paint instead of addressing more fundamental areas where changes are required is unlikely to improve its image in the long-run. The public is generally very good at making up its own mind about whether changes have had any real effect or are simply cosmetic. It is that perception that will ultimately determine the image of any organisation.

As Joe Saxton, director of fundraising at Brann Direct Marketing, observed in 'Investors Chronicle', voluntary organisations should not see massaging the organisation's name or logo as a panacea for repositioning it:

"Typically, trustees are obsessed by letterheads and logos and see changing them as the route to repositioning their charity in the market. In fact, these things only go skin-deep as far as the public is concerned."

What impression do our people make?

For many charities, the only time their people meet the public is when they make collections, or in providing services to clients. Others, such as the St John's Ambulance or Salvation Army have a more substantial public presence. In both cases, however, the people who represent the organisation become inextricably linked in the public mind with the organisation itself.

It is difficult to think of Mencap, for example, without thinking of Lord (Brian) Rix. His sometimes controversial views attracted many public supporters and alienated others. Whether people visiting Oxfam shops will return depends upon how they perceive the staff to have treated them.

Visitors to a RSPB bird sanctuary may be influenced by the friendliness and knowledge of the warden. Purchasers of *Big Issue* may be influenced by the appearance and behaviour of the vendor.

The key factors in these impressions appear to be:

♦ **Manner** – is it appropriate to the cause and the circumstances? Does it fit the image?

♦ **Values** – do other people accept or agree with them? (People with strong pro or anti views on abortion may tend by extension to assume that anyone of the opposite view must be immoral, corrupt and/or uncaring.)

♦ **Appearance** – is it appropriate to the image and the circumstances?

The last of these points deserves a fuller discussion. Many companies have strict dress codes, but this is rare in the voluntary sector (the main exceptions being the uniformed charities – St John's, Salvation Army, Red Cross, Scouts etc). Charity shop workers are usually indistinguishable from their customers.

Some observers, such as IBM adviser to voluntary organisations, Tom Jennings, are strongly against dress codes. They argue that over-formalisation of behaviours and appearance can make a voluntary organisation look *too* business-like and therefore make volunteers and donors uncomfortable. On the other hand, too casual or scruffy an appearance can also have a detrimental effect.

There is no doubt that uniformed charities, such as the Salvation Army or the St John Ambulance, gain from being readily recognisable. But would charity shops find that the benefits from imposing a standard form of dress on its sales volunteers (making staff easily recognisable, for example) were outweighed by a reduction in the number of volunteers coming forward? In many instances, this is an issue of clients versus volunteers. Meals on wheels recipients, being elderly and often scared of unfamiliar callers, would probably be reassured by a consistent uniform; volunteers might find it an unwelcome intrusion.

There is no generic answer to this dilemma. Each voluntary sector organisation needs to work out its own best solution. However, useful guidelines might include the following:

♦ Most volunteers will accept some standardisation of **dress code** if they understand how this will benefit the recipients of the service.

♦ **Impressions** are more important in some instances than in others. Relatively few voluntary organisations pay much attention to the impression made by their reception staff, for example, yet this initial encounter can colour the perceptions of visitors sufficiently to make the difference between whether they do or don't become volunteers, and whether companies do or don't decide that the voluntary sector organisation is a viable partner.

♦ In the end, it is how people **talk and behave** that makes the more lasting impression; but inappropriate dress may mean you never get over the barrier of first impressions.

It is interesting that the private sector is gradually moving towards less formalisation in dress codes. For example, electrical goods chain Comet has "casual dress" days at its headquarters, to encourage informality and teamwork. Some City financial firms have "Dress Down Fridays" for the same reasons. Although the suit and tie remain dominant in male office environments, "smart casual" is increasingly becoming the norm in many companies and this seems to be a practical compromise for many voluntary organisations, too.

Appearance applies equally to offices and buildings, vehicles and other capital assets. While few voluntary organisations would wish to be seen to spend their money on top of the range luxury office suites (and most have to take what accommodation they can afford or scrounge), what counts is how that space is made to work. Frugality does not need to extend to failure to paint or maintain an office, for example. From the point of view of a visiting manager from a potential partner company, the critical questions regarding appearance are likely to include:

♦ Do these people c**are about the environment** they are in? (are they trying to make the most of it?)

♦ What does **the environment** say about the way this organisation regards its volunteers and people?

♦ Does it **look organised and professional**? (are there piles of paper everywhere? are safety regulations being adhered to?)

♦ Does the **appearance** of the people and the offices give me confidence that this organisation can do what it promises?

A walk through the offices, trying to look through the eyes of a visitor, may provide a whole new perspective!

Also important is the presentation of documentation and correspondence. Comments from community investment managers suggest that poorly presented proposals, with misspellings and incoherent arguments are depressingly common from voluntary organisations. While such failings may not in themselves be sufficient to preclude a positive response from the company, they give an impression of lack of professionalism and inattention to detail.

Are we keeping the right company?

In 1989, Asil Nadir offered SCOPE (then The Spastics Society) £5 million for a specific project in Milton Keynes. But the charity had only received £125,000 seed money for the project before the Polly Peck empire collapsed. The society abandoned the project in early 1991 but the donation received press coverage linked to Nadir's alleged attempt to buy himself a knighthood.

James Rye, head of public relations at Scope, told Tom O'Sullivan of 'PR Week' in July 1993:

"There is no evidence at this time that the issue has damaged the charity. Charities have to be vigilant because the income stream is so very important but the image of the charity cannot be sacrificed to short-term financial needs."

The Nadir case is just one of a number of dubious associations that have caused questions from stakeholders. In this case, the decision as to what should have been done is relatively clear. But other decisions are more difficult.

♦ Should health charities take money or other assistance from subsidiaries of tobacco companies? (And is it Allied Dunbar's fault it was taken over by BAT?)

♦ Should the National Childbirth Trust have taken the decision to endorse Pampers nappies in return for an estimated £300,000 over three years? Wrote Lucy Williams in The Guardian on the 10th April 1994, 'Many members feel that the NCT has been naive in allowing this multinational company to use its good name to recommend one particular brand. That the product in question is a disposable nappy has caused a rash of objection on environmental, ethical, financial and health grounds.'

If the ethical questions can be satisfactorily answered, then the voluntary organisation can safely seek private sector partners. When it does so, it must be aware of what it is trading, because it is the voluntary organisation's *brand* which commercial partners will be looking to make use of.

One of the fastest-growing forms of alliance between private and voluntary sector organisations starts from the premise that the two brands can support each other. Cause-related marketing has the potential to revitalise fundraising and develop great collaboration and understanding between the sectors. But it also has its dangers.

Another form of collaboration which voluntary organisations are increasingly adopting is relationship marketing. Whether the term alone has been imported from the private sector, or the practice as well, is irrelevant. This is a powerful networking tool for expanding influence where it matters.

Cause-related marketing (CRM)

Cause-related marketing became popular in the United States during the 1980s and has since spread to other countries. It involves a company and a voluntary organisation in a joint promotional campaign in which consumers are encouraged to buy the company's products or services because they know that a percentage of each sale will go to the voluntary organisation the promotion is linked with. Typically, CRM works by the company making a donation of a fixed amount for each sale the promotion generates.

The concept took off in America in 1983 after the spectacular success of a campaign linking American Express with the project to restore the Statue of Liberty.

Since then, thousands of similar partnerships have been created across America between consumer-oriented companies and voluntary organisations. Partners have included large national organisations such as The Red Cross and MasterCard, as well as many local social service agencies working with local retailers. In some cases, voluntary organisations have approached companies to develop a campaign jointly. But more often companies have targeted and approached voluntary organisations.

However, in the UK CRM has been slower to take off. A 1993 survey by NCH: Action for Children, for example, found that although businesses are increasingly aware of the symbiotic relationship which exists between business and the community, less than 12 per cent of a sample of 100 major plcs had a company policy about the marketing of their voluntary sector link up. This suggests, the survey concludes, "that many companies are not taking maximum advantage of opportunities with their corporate and marketing strategies.

Yet the survey also found that 63 per cent of the companies that had used CRM consider it as or more effective than advertising for enhancing the company image, 61 per cent for improving brand image.

A CRM campaign with the right voluntary partner seems to offer a dream ticket for the marketing department of any company. The idea is deceptively simple. By tapping consumer interest in a popular cause the company is able to increase its sales whilst at the same time creating goodwill and enhancing its image among customers. Moreover, the voluntary organisation which lends its name to such a campaign is rewarded by a higher profile with the public – through advertising and promotional materials – and cash from the company donations. With a well-managed CRM campaign everybody wins.

In fact, so popular has CRM become in America that some of the larger, better known voluntary organisations have created full-time staff positions to handle the many requests to form CRM partnerships and to develop and manage these programmes.

Such campaigns have already proved an extremely lucrative form of marketing both for companies and voluntary organisations. For example, voluntary organisations such as the American Cancer Society, the Special Olympics, the American Heart Association and Big Brothers Big Sisters have all raised millions of dollars through CRM campaigns. Nor are the benefits confined to just the larger organisations. Smaller voluntary organisations have raised smaller amounts – generally less than 10 per cent of their annual income – but the secondary benefits of raised public awareness and attracting volunteers and new donors create added-value beyond the cash sums generated.

The experience of business has been equally positive. A CRM campaign by Scott Paper Company with Ronald McDonald Houses was the most successful sales promotion in Scott's history and Johnson & Johnson described its Shelter Aid CRM campaign as the company's most successful promotion ever. Smaller companies have also benefited from local CRM campaigns, which have boosted sales and consumer interest and strengthened their image in local communities. Many claim, too, that there is a lingering effect of improved morale among employees.

As Dr Richard Steckel and Robin Simons put it in their book 'Doing Best by Doing Good':

"If there is such a thing as a win-win proposition, cause-related marketing is it. Companies earn money and goodwill. Voluntary organisations gain money and exposure. And consumers get to spend money and feel good about it. In cause-related marketing, capitalism has actually become a philanthropic tool."

Steckel and Simons are right, but there is an important caveat to cause-related marketing. When it works to the advantage of all three groups, it is an extremely effective technique. But the cost of getting it wrong can also be high.

Managing a CRM campaign

A degree of caution is clearly required when considering any CRM opportunity. Shelter, for example, recently took a behind the scenes decision to reject money from a donor on the basis that it would be bad for its image.

The charity was approached by a tobacco company with the offer of an on-pack promotional link up which would have netted it an estimated £50,000.

Fiona Hesselden, Shelter's manager of major gifts, confirmed to Tom O'Sullivan of 'PR Week':

"We were approached. The deal was worth a lot of money, we researched it and decided to go ahead.

"But after further research we decided the deal would be detrimental to Shelter's long-term position. It is very difficult because smoking does not cause homelessness – there is no direct conflict involved. We pulled out because of the damage it would have done to Shelter's image."

It is a very healthy sign that such considerations were placed before the financial concerns of fundraisers. What concerns many in the voluntary sector is that in the future Shelter's example may prove the exception among voluntary organisations rather than the rule.

It is essential for a voluntary organisation considering CRM to understand the motivation of the company it will be linked with. The outcome of the campaign may well be one with benefits for all, but the primary purpose from the perspective of the company is to increase sales.

As long as the voluntary partner is clear on that one critical point, and is comfortable with the implications of its name being linked to the company for that purpose, then benefits are likely to accrue on both sides. However, there are pitfalls for the unwary, not least the temptation to leap into CRM because its impressive track record makes it seem a dead-cert.

Nor are the risks all on the side of the voluntary partner. Companies have to be extremely careful when becoming involved with CRM campaigns that they do not appear to the public to be cashing in on the plight of disadvantaged people or peddling their wares by exploiting convenient causes.

As Steckel and Simons point out: "The danger in cause-related marketing is that it looks so easy. So easy to look good. So easy to make money. So easy to get in and out fast. The trouble with that attitude is that it makes it so easy to *fail*. It is so easy for a campaign to backfire because it is perceived not as *helping* a voluntary, but as *using* a voluntary to sell a product.

The key to managing CRM campaigns on both sides is honesty. Both partners must be honest and up-front about their reasons for becoming involved in such a promotion. If they are not, CRM can quickly become an embarrassing entanglement with a potentially devastating impact on the image of both partners. As Mike Tuffrey points out:

"A voluntary organisation has to ask whether it is valid to lend its brand and therefore its bundle of values to a company. It must be clear that both parties can gain from the arrangement; i.e. the voluntary organisation gets money and a higher profile, and the company increases sales.

"But you have to look at the long-term – it's a particular hobbyhorse of mine. Voluntary organisations and companies should be managed for the long-term, so there is an incentive to make sure the fit is good on both sides.

"My doubts come from the fact that it may be a cynical exercise on the part of the company. But I'm a great believer in the notion that the truth will out. If the company doesn't genuinely share the values of the voluntary organisation then it will end in tears. The pragmatic side of me says you have to err on the side of 'don't do it if it's clearly wrong'. If on balance you are comfortable with the areas of uncertainty – the grey areas – then go ahead. At the end of the day, you have to make a value judgement."

David Wickert, the former director of company services at CAF, now director of CAF America, also believes that both partners should exercise caution:

"I think the dangers lie in either the company taking the voluntary organisation for a ride or the voluntary organisation taking the company for a ride, either is possible. One side or the other can easily over-sell itself and then fail to deliver on promises.

"There are danger signals that voluntary organisations in particular should watch out for. If the company is only involved in this one action,

i.e. it doesn't have a community programme to speak of, then that is a sign that it simply wants to maximise its profit. At the same time, I have nothing against companies maximising their profit, especially if it enables them to give more to the voluntary sector. But the voluntary organisation should be aware of the motivation before agreeing to get involved. **"**

It is important to realise, too, that when marketing promotions backfire there can be disastrous consequences for those involved. And the higher the public profile of the campaign, the more egg on the faces of all concerned.

There are a number of basic questions that voluntary organisations should ask themselves before becoming involved in any CRM campaign. These include:

♦ Are we comfortable with **what this business does**?

♦ Are we comfortable with the idea of **boosting its profits**?

♦ Are **our stakeholders** – including beneficiaries, donors, volunteers and employees – comfortable with this arrangement?

♦ Is the campaign sufficiently **well defined** that we know:
   (a) how long it will last?
   (b) the tone of its message?
   (c) approximately how much money it will raise for us?

♦ Is the relationship a **genuine partnership**, allowing for input from both sides, or will the company be calling all the shots?

♦ Do we have **sufficient control** over the management of the campaign?

♦ Do we have **access to information** on sales figures?

♦ Do we **know enough about this company** to trust it with our reputation?

Clearly, whether all of these questions can be answered satisfactorily or not, voluntary organisations must still exercise a degree of judgement about any CRM campaign. The risks can be greatly reduced, however, by starting small.

By resisting the temptation of a single large windfall in favour of a step by step approach, voluntary organisations can build a sound working relationship with a business partner. A good partner will actually welcome the chance to test the synergy of their product with the voluntary's cause on a small scale before launching a national campaign. For example, a series of local or regional campaigns could provide a good basis to assess the effectiveness of a wider campaign later. Voluntary organisations should remember, too, that if a campaign doesn't work at a local level it is unlikely to work at a national level and will most likely cause them only embarrassment. A company that insists on an all or nothing opportunity – through a one-off national campaign – is probably best avoided anyway.

CASE STUDY ➤ American Express and the Statue of Liberty-Ellis Island Restoration Fund

The first cause-related marketing campaign to draw widespread attention was that run by American Express in 1983. This linked purchases made using the American Express credit card, and sales of American Express products such as travellers cheques, with donations from the company to the Statue of Liberty-Ellis Island Restoration Fund. American Express spent $6 million on an advertising campaign to support the promotion and the results were spectacular. Over the three month duration of the campaign American Express card use jumped 28 per cent; new card applications increased by 17 per cent; and the campaign raised $1.7 million to help restore the Statue of Liberty and Ellis Island. So successful was the campaign that most people thought American Express was an official sponsor of the project to restore the national monument, although the company had never paid to be one.

The campaign made marketing history and sent shivers up the spine of marketing executives all over America. But American Express had actually been practising CRM campaigns in local communities since 1981.

The concept was developed to meet three clearly defined marketing goals. First, to convince consumers to acquire and use Am Ex charge cards. Second, to persuade more businesses to accept the cards as a method of payment. And third, to do so in a newsworthy way which would attract media interest.

At the same time, the company was aware of the increasing onus on American businesses to act in a socially responsible manner. Marketing executives at American Express calculated that the company's marketing goals and the wider demand to give something back to the communities in which it operated could be linked. They quickly realised, too, that the company's marketing budget could be used to lend muscle to voluntary organisations with small budgets but big messages to put across.

In earlier CRM experiments the company had successfully linked its products with an arts group – a theatre, a museum and an orchestra – all involved in activities that would interest the company's target audience, and all located in communities where the company wanted to expand its services. Advertising campaigns urged card holders to shop, dine and travel in the knowledge that every purchase with their Am Ex cards would benefit the selected organisation. Ads also raised the profile of the voluntary organisations.

In every one of these campaigns card use increased and local media picked up the story, generating the publicity the company wanted. For their part, the arts groups received unrestricted income and the exposure of a high profile advertising campaign. They also received additional benefits such as donations from people who saw the ads.

By 1983, American Express was ready to take its CRM strategy onto the national stage. With the Statue of Liberty promotion the company spawned a new marketing phenomenon.

CASE STUDY ➤ RNLI and Life Boat Tea Bags

The RNLI has a marketing alliance with the Warnford Tea Company which produces the Life Boat brand of tea bags. Under the arrangement, the company uses the RNLI logo on its packaging and marketing materials and 4p from every sale goes to the RNLI.

CASE STUDY ➤ Doc Martens and The Prince's Youth Business Trust

Explains a spokesman for Doc Martens' manufacturers, the R Griggs Group:

"The Prince's Youth Business Trust is a charitable trust that provides finance, business advice and marketing opportunities for unemployed 18-29 year olds to set up their own business. It provides help to those unable to get all the support they need elsewhere – often the PYBT is the course of last resort. The sponsorship with The Prince's Youth Business Trust was a perfect fit as The Prince's Youth Business Trust was looking for a commercial organisation that was appropriate for their profile group from 18 to 29. Also from the Dr Martens point of view, it was an ideal situation as Dr Martens have primarily made their money from this age group as well.

"Because of this ideal profile, the R Griggs Group were the first company to use the Crown "C" logo in a £100,000 campaign targeted towards the consumer through shoe retail outlets. The slogan 'Putting the Bounce Back in British Youth' was used with one million pairs of special Limited Edition of Dr Martens boots and shoes.

"A point of sale campaign provided materials to the retailers to promote The Prince's Youth Business Trust and Dr Martens brands. For every pair of Dr Martens footwear sold, 25 pence was given, up to £250,000. The campaign was supported by London Underground posters on the escalator panels, as well as trade advertising.

"We have felt that the brand has increased in value, due to our support to The Prince's Youth Business Trust. We know, through feedback from The Prince's Youth Business Trust itself, that it has raised their profile – to the point that the general public does not confuse The Prince's Trust (which assists with community based projects in the inner cities) with The Prince's Youth Business Trust."

CASE STUDY ➤ NCH: Action for Children and Bisto

NCH: Action for Children have a mutually beneficial alliance with Rank Hovis MacDougall's (RHM) Bisto. RHM has integrated the charity into Bisto's marketing strategy by printing the NCH name and logo on all the Bisto products. NCH's fundraising manager, Paul Amardi, explains, 'This type of alliance has nothing but benefits for us. The chief benefit is guaranteed funds. This is critical because we make decisions three or four years in advance. Companies gain greatly from this type of relationship; we undertake annual surveys of companies to gauge how they perceive involvement in the voluntary sector and over 76 per cent of companies believe it will enhance their image.

Relationship marketing

The term relationship marketing refers to the benefits that on-going relationships with key audiences can bring to an organisation. The idea behind relationship marketing is probably as old as business itself, but the expression entered the vocabulary of management during the 1980s when management writers observed it at work within the high-tech business community of California's Silicon Valley. At that time, commentators noticed that many of the small highly innovative companies in the region didn't market new products to the larger computer companies on an individual basis. Instead they formed strategic relationships with them, which allowed the smaller company to work almost as part of the customer's organisation. In a very fast moving industry the closeness of these relationships was critical to the ability of the smaller firms to develop solutions that met the needs of their customers. It became apparent that their success often depended on personal relationships which had developed into close friendships.

The logic of relationship marketing is simple; rather than communicate intermittently with key customers, it often makes more sense to develop a relationship of trust so that the dialogue is continuous. The technique depends on getting close to, and forming personal relationships with, key individuals.

The idea is that if you are constantly aware of what customers or partners require and keep them informed of developments within your own organisation, then the customer-supplier link becomes a seamless web. In relationship marketing the details of the products or services become subservient to the trust that has been established. Why, after all, would a customer go elsewhere if you constantly monitor and adjust what you are doing to meet their needs now and in the future? The advantage of such an arrangement is that problems can be averted before they become crises. The only reason then that you would lose that customer is if the relationship breaks down.

The real strength of relationship marketing lies in its ability to tap the power of human interaction. For example, it is one thing to read a proposal from a potential supplier, it is quite another to hear it from someone you have known for a long time whom you trust and respect. At the same time, allowing key individuals to get to know your organisation means they have a much better appreciation of what it is capable of.

There is no stronger form of marketing for voluntary organisations than involving people in their work. It is a technique that Business in the Community has used to great effect.

Since 1989, for example, BITC's 'Seeing is Believing' initiative has allowed over 400 very senior executives from the private and public sector – many of them chief executives, chairmen and main board directors – to spend half a day or more visiting schools and projects to see the voluntary sector at work. As Julia Cleverdon explains:

"The reports from business leaders who we arranged to visit voluntary projects indicate that when they see what is going on at the sharp-end in the voluntary sector they are absolutely staggered by the grip and passion and commitment of the people on the ground. For example, we sent the chief executive of the courier company DHL to the Family First project in Nottingham. He was so impressed at what they were doing he said look if you need something delivered from one place to another just call us and we'll do it. That's what often happens when you bring business leaders into contact with voluntary sector projects.

"I think the other thing private sector managers get from contact with the voluntary sector is a very humbling experience when they see what these organisations are trying to achieve with the limited resources they have. By comparison, the private sector is incredibly well resourced. When we send chief executives into schools, for instance, it makes them realise the size of the budgets these organisations are working with. Often they are awed."

Don Sloan, marketing director of Woolworths, had this to say after one such experience:

"My visit left me with an overwhelming sense of admiration and respect for the people involved in the projects we visited, not to say a personal sense of inadequacy with regard to my own contribution in this sphere."

Once again, however, relationship marketing should be tempered with caution. There are instances where business leaders see that poor management in voluntary organisations obstructs the achievement of objectives. As Julia Cleverdon notes:

"In the voluntary sector there can be a tendency to put the people before the task. That can be a danger when, for example, the volume of need varies at certain times of the day. Your people have to fit their work hours around the demand. For example, as soon as the supermarkets announced they would stay open later at night, immediately the off-licences had to follow suit. Business people understand those sorts of market pressures, but the voluntary sector doesn't always."

But another story illustrates the power of human interaction. A senior manager in a large British charity wanted to get the ear of a very prominent business leader. He discussed his aim with a friend in the private sector who knew the target well and who offered the information that it was the habit of the man in question to lunch at the Ritz. "In fact", he said, "I'm having lunch with him on Thursday, why don't you just happen to be at another table and I'll introduce you." The following Thursday, the charity manager arranged to lunch at the Ritz as planned. When his friend and the target arrived he was introduced with the line 'This is the chap I've been telling you about, you should listen to what they're doing, it's just the sort of thing your company should be getting involved with'. Naturally, the charity manager was invited to join their party and put his case over lunch. It was the beginning of a very productive relationship for all concerned.

It's a good story and all the better for being true, but it also points up the value of existing relationships as a means to facilitate new contacts. It is likely that to arrange a meeting with the business leader concerned – who spends a large part of his time jetting around the globe – would have been extremely difficult. But in a social setting he was both approachable and extremely interested in what the charity was doing. Nor was it an imposition because the man could have easily and politely declined to involve his company using any one of a hundred valid excuses.

Do we know who our audiences are?

It may seem an obvious question to ask, but one of the most common reasons for marketing failure is inadequate definition and understanding of the target audiences. Best practice, whatever the sector, involves:

♦ **Listing** *all* relevant audiences.

♦ **Prioritising** them on clear criteria.

♦ Gaining a deep **understanding** of the views and perceptions they hold and how these views are influenced and derived.

♦ Using these insights to design **targeted communications**, audience by audience.

Are we communicating effectively to all our audiences?

All organisations have problems with their communications – the only real difference is that better-run organisations have a better idea what the problems are and a systematic approach to improving them. The competences and techniques to develop external communications – particularly campaigns – are well documented for both the private and voluntary sectors. Internal communications is a much younger discipline. Although the private sector has long had individuals responsible for discrete internal communications activities, such as editions of the staff newspaper, it is only in recent years that responsibility for managing internal communications as a whole has been assigned within organisations. One of the drivers behind this change is a recognition by top management that the most brilliant strategies are worthless if people are not aware of them and committed to making them work – and that effective communications is therefore a *strategic* rather than operational issue.

Against this background, the informed observers we interviewed put forward four significant arguments about how communications in voluntary organisations should best be managed.

Argument 1: Internal and external communications have to reflect each other.

On the face of it, this seems obvious. The organisation that puts out a different message to staff and customers is inviting problems. Communications schizophrenia can eventually give rise to a variety of negative reactions from clients and staff alike, from open dissent to whistle blowing.

However, voluntary organisations do sometimes produce promotional campaigns, to which their staff and volunteers cannot relate. Staff do sometimes hear about important decisions that affect them from external media before they hear internally.

Planned management of communications aims to prevent misalignments. It will normally involve careful segmentation and understanding the communication needs of each audience and their receptivity to types and topics of communication. It will also involve a consideration of where communications should sit in the organisation. At present, it is often located in the strongest department – for example, in lobbying or fundraising; or it is located centrally, pulled in several directions by the various functions.

The issue of location needs to be decided at a strategic level, along with the precise remit. Among questions to be considered are:

♦ Should internal and external communications be in the same department?

♦ To what extent should we (and do we) differentiate and manage differently strategic and operational communications?

Argument 2: Internal communications to staff and volunteers make them feel involved and wanted.

Again, the point seems beyond argument. However, the reality is that different audiences need different treatment. For most voluntary organisations, staff and volunteers are spread throughout the country – and in some cases across the world, in highly inaccessible places with poor communications. Information starvation is a frequent complaint from staff and volunteers. Feed the Children, for example, publishes a simple, but well-produced newsletter keeping staff, volunteers and advisers up to date with progress on its projects. Among the objectives of the newsletter is to give volunteers a reason for continuing their commitment.

Some voluntary organisations argue that it is inappropriate to produce expensive, professional news sheets for their people, and in many cases this may be true. On the other hand, for some people, this may be virtually the only communications they receive. A highly professional newspaper need not be seen as an indication of money-wasting – rather, it should be seen as a recognition of the importance of communicating well.

The role of internal communications manager has yet to be properly defined in most private sector organisations and the same is true of the voluntary sector. To make the role effective requires a strong and experienced manager capable of exerting influence across the organisation – and that usually means substantially upgrading the status of the post.

Argument 3: Press and other key influencers need an opportunity to ask questions, to understand the organisation and its aims.

Christian Aid and a number of other charities chartered a British Airways jet and took a press party round Africa. It stopped at major destinations and took the journalists on a tour of local aid projects. The writers gained a real insight into what these charities did and the charities took the chance to educate some influential people into their work, aims and needs.

Christian Mission Aid, a small international charity, raises money for relief and development in East Africa. Its office in the UK approached a number of colleges and asked whether any journalism or PR students would like to volunteer to be press officer in their free time. Some enthusiastic students took up the challenge and successfully raised CMA's profile in the local media.

Argument 4: Advertising pays.

The Advertising Association spends a good deal of money researching the benefits of advertising to commercial companies. It claims that there is a very clear difference in the fortunes of companies which increase their advertising spend in recessionary times, versus those who decrease it. On average, the former significantly outperform the latter.

The same principles probably apply to voluntary sector advertising. Even the Church of England is now advertising as an effective means of promotion and fundraising following a recent report, entitled 'Paying the Piper: Advertising and the Church'.

The report, by a Church working party, said that the Church should drop its aversion to advertising and use more sophisticated approaches to get its message across. Published in February 1994, it found that there was no ethical bar to advertising as long as it was used in a unified fashion within the Church of England, and in close co-operation with other churches. The report even went so far as to urge different denominations to act together to hire an advertising agency for large-scale campaigns.

Canon Colin Semper, treasurer of Westminster Abbey and chairman of the working party, said he was aware that some people might feel that for a church to advertise "was somehow supping with the devil". But, he observed, this was a strange piece of theology given that Jesus came into a world that was hugely corrupt.

Whatever this might suggest about Canon Semper's view of the secular world of advertising, a growing number of voluntary organisations appear to agree with his sentiments. Many of the larger organisations now use highly professional national advertising campaigns to get their message across to the public. And although the high costs associated with producing ads for television (typically between £10,000 and £30,000 for a short commercial) and the buying of airtime have limited the number of voluntary organisations able use this medium, those which have tried it have been impressed with the results.

For example, the Samaritans have funded three television advertising campaigns and claim they have been effective in reaching a very wide audience. The first ad in 1991 was aired in the Tyne-Tees area to improve the level of awareness of the charity. The Samaritans found that once the adverts were shown the level of awareness increased substantially.

In a recent issue of 'Charity' magazine, Paul Farmer, the Samaritans' communications officer, told Alan Jabez that there were also highly positive results from the second and third campaigns which were aimed at promoting a new national telephone number in Scotland and to help recruit new volunteers.

One of the reasons for their success, Farmer said, was their careful timing. The volunteers' campaign, for example, was aired during daytime programmes when people with free time would be watching. In other words, it was targeted at what the charity saw as a key market segment.

But while most of the voluntary organisations which can afford to use it view broadcasting as a medium for raising public awareness about important issues and their work, some have begun to see it as direct means to raise funds.

For example, the NSPCC has used television advertising to increase its database of donors. The charity reports that it now regards the medium as simply an extension of its direct marketing campaign. Commercials carry a free phone 0800 number which is linked to a specialist direct marketing company, and a freepost address is shown on the screen. Ads aim to prompt potential donors into making a contribution by explaining how a £15 donation would be spent. The charity has also benefited from the generosity of production companies whose help reduces the costs of making the commercials.

The Multiple Sclerosis Society has also received generous support from production companies for advertisements aimed at raising public awareness. But as Rebecca Porter, the charity's fundraising manager, told Alan Jabez, it is essential to consider the sensitivity of the illness when designing the advertisement.

According to Porter, although the MS Society tries to make a big impact on viewers it places equal importance on ensuring that adverts will not distress or offend anybody with the disease.

Other charities, however, take a different view. For example, the RSPCA has deliberately used shock tactics, opting for a hard-hitting approach to advertising containing harrowing images depicting cruelty to animals. By being controversial the charity has also been able to boost the impact of advertising campaigns by attracting editorial coverage in the media.

Clearly, however, the threshold of good taste and sensitivity is an issue that requires very careful management.

Fundraising vs the dignity of beneficiaries

A number of voluntary organisations have come under attack from civil rights campaigners for using inappropriate images in their marketing.

Disabilities charities in particular have been criticised for reinforcing negative stereotypes about the position of disabled people within society. The use of emotive images of children in Africa and elderly people in the UK by organisations such as Comic Relief has also been questioned.

The dilemma for these voluntary organisations is that while images which present their beneficiaries as deserving of 'pity' or 'charity' may be effective in tugging at the heart strings of potential donors, they may do so at the expense of the dignity of the beneficiaries. In the case of disabilities charities, for example, fundraising activities may actually do more harm than good to the interests of disabled people if they present them as less than equals.

What these voluntary organisations have to manage better in the future is the conflict between the simplistic view that they exist to raise funds to help their beneficiaries, and the wider issue of what is really in the best interests of those people. Conflict between fundraising and the dignity of beneficiaries can best be resolved by focusing on the real mission of the organisation – which in most cases will be to support the aspirations of beneficiaries, rather than simply to raise funds to provide services. In this way the longer-term aims of the organisation will usually prevail.

In fact, it seems likely that the disabilities charities which break away from the negative stereotyping and present their cause to the public using images explaining how their work supports the positive aspirations of those they serve will clean up in more ways than one. The Shaftsbury Society, for example, has successfully run a campaign with a picture of a disabled man and the slogan 'It's your problem, not his'. The message attacks the barriers that society puts up against disabled people, and is supportive of their right to be treated equally. Voluntary organisations should also find effective ways to carry out market research among sensitive stakeholders to ensure that the tone of advertising fits with their mission.

Sensitivity is one of the main considerations featured in the Independent Television Commission's code of practice on charity advertising. The code also states that charities:

♦ Must not address any fundraising matters specifically to children.

♦ Must not make any comparisons with other charities.

♦ Must not suggest that any one who does not support a charity either lacks proper feeling or fails in any responsibility.

According to Rebecca Porter of the MS Society, a number of factors contribute to the success of the charity's advertising campaigns. In particular, she emphasises the importance of:

♦ Presenting a **clear message**.

♦ Undertaking **extensive market research** before beginning each campaign.

♦ Ensuring there is **no ambiguity** by displaying the organisation's logo clearly on the screen.

Smaller voluntary organisations which want to take advantage of more lively mediums for putting across their message might consider the use of video or audio cassettes. Although quality video production is far from cheap, it is usually less expensive to produce a short documentary style information film than to produce a commercial for broadcast. Distribution through branches or local groups is also much less costly than buying air-time. There is no reason either why newsworthy films should not be distributed among specialist journalists who may then pick up on the story and provide wider coverage.

Professional audio productions, on the other hand, are generally much less expensive and can be used in connection with a local radio advertising campaign which is an extremely effective and under utilised medium.

A number of big and small voluntary organisations now distribute videos and audio formats to raise awareness. For example, a recent schools appeal pack to help raise money for the Red Cross food parcels included video and audio tapes. The video uses pictures from Sky and ITN news crews to provide a clear summary of why the disintegration of Yugoslavia has created so much suffering. Also, in 1993, Tear Fund commissioned a video entitled 'Out of the Shadow' focusing on developments undertaken by evangelical Christians in Croatia, Bosnia, Romania and Russia.

CASE STUDY ➤ RSPCA advertising

A full-page photograph of dead dogs in a national newspaper does not fit with the cosy image of animal charities. Nor do advertisements highlighting the distress of lambs being transported. But public awareness advertisements carrying disturbing images and hard-hitting messages are part of the RSPCA's approach to its fight against cruelty to animals.

The RSPCA claims to be Britain's best known charity. With an annual income of £27 million it is the eleventh largest charity in the country. Since it was formed in 1824 it has been dedicated to preventing cruelty and promoting kindness to animals. According to director general Peter Davies, one of the important methods of achieving its aim is through education.

"An informed public is the best insurance against cruelty", says Davies. "The society allocates a significant budget to education services and our officers visit schools, teaching centres and colleges to get the message across."

In addition, the RSPCA spends approximately £1 million a year on advertising. Its campaigns have provoked protest, controversy and even criticism from the Advertising Standards Authority. In other words the ads are working.

Jerry Lloyd, the RSPCA's campaign director, is unrepentant. "We use graphic advertisements to bring home the message that cruelty to animals is shocking", he told Widget Finn of the Times in December 1993. "We need to make the public aware of issues such as the export of animals for slaughter, or the misleading label on eggs from battery hens."

The advertising strategy is carefully planned. The prohibitive cost of buying air time on ITV channels has meant that the charity has limited its television campaigns to the satellite channels. But by clever marketing it has also managed to get its ads onto mainstream television at no additional cost.

The strategy is to make controversial, and therefore newsworthy, public information' ads relating to issues such as not leaving dogs in cars and not giving pets as presents. It works because major press campaigns are timed to coincide with the launch of advertising campaigns. In this way the charity receives news coverage on terrestrial television channels and in national, regional and local newspapers which help get the message across.

Mass media events

The early success of mass-media events such as Live Aid and Comic Relief's Red Nose Day revolutionised voluntary fundraising appeals. In more recent years, however, many people have begun to question whether such events are sustainable over time.

For one thing, the money raised by these events has dipped. For example, the televised Children in Need appeal has been going for 13 years and while pledges from viewers on the night rose through the 1980s to peak at £17.5 million in 1992, in 1993 the total fell by £5.7 million to £11.8 million. Red Nose Day, a two-yearly event, raised £27 million in 1989, but dropped to £21 million in 1991. The total for Telethon, also two-yearly, dropped from £24 million in 1990 to £15 million in 1992.

Telethon also attracted protests from civil rights campaigners who criticised the appeal for reinforcing negative stereotypes of disabled people. The format was subsequently changed. Again, a more clearly focused mission could have avoided this adverse publicity.

Concern has also been expressed about whether large-scale media blitzes actually de-sensitise the public or encourage them to make donations to large appeals at the expense of smaller local voluntary organisations.

But as Jane Tewson, chief executive at Charity Projects and one of the dynamos behind Comic Relief's Red Nose Day explains:

"The approach of the event is very different to other appeals. We started from the premise that we wanted to ask people to get involved. That's an important difference to past approaches. For example, the film footage we put out isn't simply 'here's a poor person, give us some money; it's 'here are the issues, do you want to get involved?'

"Interestingly, our approach means that unlike other appeals, money keeps rolling in after the event is over. We are trying to educate people. So people who've never given to a charity before will give to us. Also, it allows them to go away and think about the issues. I'm always pleased to hear that someone has been sufficiently engaged to find out more and give to other causes as well."

But while many of the larger voluntary organisations feel there is room for the 'mega events', some smaller organisations are less sure. As Val Howarth, Childline's director, explained to the Guardian's Lynn Eaton in 1993:

"There is only a finite amount of money available. Many people are out of work and thinking twice about giving their money."

The larger child care societies such as the National Society for the Prevention of Cruelty to Children, Save the Children and SCOPE gain directly from the events. Although there may be grumbles about the difficulties of meeting the changing criteria for the appeals – which often target small, local voluntary groups – many of the larger voluntary organisations take the view that it is money that they would not otherwise receive.

Charles Holden, appeals director at Barnardo's summed up the feelings of many of the larger voluntary organisations towards the media appeals when he told The Guardian: "It's good news and has to be encouraged. It would be very churlish to say that they are taking money away from us."

But Holden, too, suggests that the days of the mega appeals may be numbered:

"I don't believe Telethon or Red Nose Day have an infinite life. They should be reviewed or people will get bored. There's a limit to how many red noses you can put on your car."

Charity Projects, which runs Red Nose Day, is very aware of the danger of the appeal losing its appeal. In 1993 it revamped the format injecting spoof B-movie melodrama with 'the invasion of the comic tomatoes'.

Since then, says Jane Tewson, the organisation has been rethinking its role altogether, recognising that the real challenge is how to sustain the freshness and originality that are critical to the campaign's success.

In many ways the challenge facing the 'mega appeals' is the same as that for all voluntary marketing: how to sustain interest in the message without desensitising the public. However, although the future of the existing mega appeals is uncertain, it is clear that a new force in fundraising has been established.

Whether these sorts of mass-media events continue to be run as on-going campaigns with a consistent identity or are re-launched periodically in a new guise, the phenomenon is unlikely to go way. The power of these events to harness new information technology which is already enhancing the immediacy of the electronic media to reach people in their living rooms, seems to assure them of a place in the voluntary armoury.

The logical next step would seem to be for smaller voluntary organisations to find ways to enhance the benefits they derive from the publicity and goodwill generated. Why not, for example, add street collections by authorised local voluntary groups timed to coincide with these media events? In this way local voluntary organisations would ensure that donations go to projects in the local area of the donor. By calling in person they would also remove the last obstacle to giving – that of picking up the telephone and waiting to get through on busy pledge lines. Clearly such a scheme would require very careful management to ensure that funds were not misplaced, but this is not beyond the many talented people within the voluntary sector.

Managing the brand

The wealth of promotional options and the subtlety of some of the decisions, which need to be made, demand close management. That means, in practice, a well-considered, well-constructed and well-informed marketing plan.

There is no shortage of advice and guidance on how to develop and implement a marketing plan and it is not the purpose of this book to duplicate what is readily available elsewhere. However, the following checklist may provide a useful foundation, against which to assess a voluntary sector organisation's current practice.

- **What are you doing to promote the brand?**
  What are you doing that might undermine the brand?

- **What are the purposes of marketing for your organisation?**
  What are the relative importance of achieving influence, raising funds, attracting and informing clients, and so on? Does the resource allocation roughly match the priorities?

- Have you defined clearly, all the audiences you need to market to? Do you fully understand the differences in their motivation, perceptions about your organisation, perceptions about your cause?

- **What has changed or might well change in terms of:**
  (a) the needs of your clients/ beneficiaries?
  (b) the circumstances of your sponsors and volunteers?
  (c) the attitudes of your sponsors and volunteers?
  (d) the arrival/ departure of competing organisations?
  (e) the nature of your relationship with strategic alliances or partners (e.g. government)?

- How effective have your marketing activities been in the past year? How does this compare with the sector in general? With best practice? What lessons can you learn from your experience? What good ideas can you borrow and adapt from elsewhere?

- **How realistic are the targets set for this year?**
  Do you have the resources to achieve them?

- What resources do you need?
  To what extent can you "borrow" resources from sponsors and elsewhere? Can you expand the resources available by collaborating with other organisations, in or outside the sector?

- **Are your marketing activities sufficiently focused to achieve maximum impact?**
  Is there sufficient balance between not putting too many eggs into too few baskets and not spreading resources too thinly?

- **Are there clear and effective systems in place to measure the success of each marketing activity?**
  Are they being used? Is the information being acted upon, as a means of driving continuous improvement?

- **Are you tapping all the sources of creativity available to you?**
  Do you at least have a marketing advisory panel?

Summary

The public image or 'brand' of a voluntary organisation is one of its most valuable assets. As such, it should not be left to chance. Brand management techniques used in the private sector can be usefully adopted by voluntary organisations to safeguard and enhance their image over time.

New opportunities such as cause-related marketing will also make it essential for voluntary organisations to manage their image carefully.

To some extent, too, it is already necessary to present different images to different audiences. So, for example, the impression that a charity seeks to create with a potential corporate sponsor – one of business-like efficiency – may not be appropriate for its end-users. A greater awareness of the issues, however, should enable the organisation to maximise its impact.

The need to periodically review and update a voluntary organisation's image is also already apparent in a number of areas. The decision by several charities to change their names in recent years, for example, is an indication of the growing importance they attach to the issue.

The current debate about whether fundraising campaigns which reinforce negative stereotypes about end-users are morally acceptable goes to the very heart of brand management and is one which we believe will grow in intensity.

Checklist

1. What image does your organisation present to its key audiences?

2. What image of its end-users does it seek to promote? Do images undermine the **dignity of beneficiaries**? Are beneficiaries consulted about images presented in advertising campaigns etc?

3. Does the organisation have a **dress code** which specifies situations where formal attire is required?

4. What are the organisation's **brand values**? What does its brand mean to the public, its end users, companies etc?

5. **Who manages the brand**? Are there safeguards to protect it from damaging activities or associations?

References

1. Tom O'Sullivan, *'Public image an invaluable asset'*, 'PR Week', 8 July 1993.

2. *'What's in a name?'*, Investors Chronicle, 26 March 1993.

3. Lucy Williams, *'Disposable Income'*, Parents section, The Guardian, April 10th, p12

4. Bill Cater, *'Giving the RNIB a sharper identity'*, The Times, 17 September 1993.

5. Widget Finn, *'Shock tactics to conquer cruelty'*, The Times, 11 December 1993.

6. Lynn Eaton, *'Losing Appeal'*, The Guardian, Wednesday 10 March 1993.

Chapter 6

Ethical management

Key issues

♦ *Do voluntary organisations set an example for other sectors to follow? If not, how can they do so?*

♦ *How can they balance the interests of their clients against those of other stakeholders?*

A glance at recent newspaper headlines is enough to confirm the fascination that scandals involving voluntary organisations have for the public (and for newspaper editors). The following outraged headlines all appeared in the past few months:

'Charity fund swindler is jailed', 'Woman set up fake charity' '£2 million charity fraud men flee London', 'Cancer charities attacked for lack of fund control', 'The fund-erasers', 'Charity ignored warning about £7 million deal'.

Behind each story, of course, is a unique set of circumstances that led ultimately to maladministration or malpractice or plain and simple fraud. A casual observer might assume from the column inches and air-time devoted to these cases that the incidence of voluntary sector scandal is disproportionately high. However, this is not so.

In fact, given the size of the voluntary sector and the unwieldy governance structures that many of the organisations within it have to operate by, the number of incidents of maladministration and malpractice is actually very low compared to the number of similar cases involving companies.

However, the simple truth is that newspapers and the media in general make much of the relatively small number of voluntary sector scandals that come to light. Many people would argue, too, that they are right to do so. The position of trust that voluntary organisations enjoy is such that the public has a right to know when something goes wrong. Sandra Greaves, former editor of 'Third Sector' magazine says:

"The tabloids love scandals involving voluntary organisations. It's probably because they see a charity fall off its pedestal, and perhaps it seems more heinous because it's the public's money instead of shareholders'. But no way is it more rife in the voluntary sector than in the other sectors. It doesn't mean that the financial controls aren't there,

especially with the big charities. On the other hand, with the recent problems with the Salvation Army, clearly the checks and balances weren't there any more than they were with the Maxwell companies.

"Really, you can divide voluntary organisations into layers just the same as you can companies. Big charities – say the top 400 – are much more likely to be managed professionally than small charities. It's the same with companies. Small charities suffer from the same problems and weaknesses as small businesses. People from outside lump charities together as if they're homogenous, which they aren't any more than a multinational corporation and a one-man-and-his-dog company. But overall you'd be hard pushed to say large charities are managed unprofessionally."

Fraud, on the other hand, is an entirely different matter. Fraudulent activities by organisations or individuals out to line their own pockets under the cloak of charitable work is an abuse of our caring society which deserves to be exposed for what it is, and met with the full force of the law.

Unfortunately, the tendency for some newspapers in particular to tar all voluntary sector scandals with the same brush can have negative side-effects. It has led to a vicious circle with many voluntary organisations being overly secretive because they know that the slightest whiff of a scandal can have a disastrous effect on fundraising. The effect is that simple mistakes and transgressions are allowed to snowball because they are not corrected early enough.

Many of the problems in the voluntary sector that make the headlines could be avoided if the organisations concerned adopted more transparent reporting procedures. In our experience there are almost always enough people in any voluntary organisation prepared to ask the right questions to avoid a scandal, if they have sufficient information to do so. Sandra Greaves agrees:

"Charities could improve their openness and transparency of reporting. For example, they are often unwilling to acknowledge how much money goes on administration. The traditional response is to massage the figures in the annual report. It's curious that charities with widely different ways of operating show a low administration cost, typically somewhere around 10 per cent. But really, different sorts of charities should have different administrative costs.

"Take a charity whose main function is to operate help-lines, for example. The bulk of what they do is telephone based, so their money is spent on what in other organisations would be administrative costs – the 'phone bill. There shouldn't be any problem with the charity stating that because that's what it does."

In some cases, of course, the lines of accountability are ignored or require clarification and the level of competence of the people taking decisions is inadequate. However, these sorts of problems would almost always come to light earlier if the organisation was more open about internal difficulties, including costs and ethical concerns.

Clearly, too, this is not a problem confined to the voluntary sector. A great many companies come to grief for exactly the same reasons. Where actual wrong-doing occurs, it is also often the result of an internal culture that regards openness as potentially dangerous.

Some years ago, for example, a research project in the United States investigated what it called 'corporate deviance'. The research showed that senior managers who stray from the straight and narrow are frequently otherwise remarkably law-abiding citizens and often pillars of the local community. However, they have built up a wall between the morality that applies in their personal life and that which applies in business. What appears to happen is that the company becomes such a dominant part of the manager's life that his or her sense of moral values becomes distorted. If it is right for the company, it must be right for the community, becomes the logic underpinning decisions.

What the study also showed was that few of these managers act in isolation. They usually gather round them a coterie of equally committed people within the organisation who reinforce each others' values. People who would not approve, or who might blow the whistle, are excluded from the club – where the action is – making those within it feel even more close-knit. The club then develops a momentum of its own, becoming difficult or even impossible to stop. There are a number of recent examples of this phenomenon among very prominent British companies.

For voluntary organisations, the dangers are equally real. In the recent inquiry into the financial transactions, which led to the alleged fraud of Salvation Army funds totalling £6.2 million, it came to light that the advice of the charity's investment board had apparently been ignored by senior officers. On a number of occasions the board – made up of three lay experts from the investment world – expressed concerns about the deal, which involved investing large sums of money in standby letters of credit. They also expressed doubts about the credentials of the investment consultants proposing the deal, who were said to be promising returns of between 50 and 100 per cent in one year. A source within the charity later told 'The Independent':

"The advisory board said the scheme would not work; if making money was that simple, then we would all be millionaires. Mr Padovan [a member of the advisory board] later warned that the investment company was not registered. But the whole thing went ahead without anyone telling the committee. We were suffering financial difficulties... and Colonel Burn [one of the senior officers from the Salvation Army at the centre of the transaction, who was later fired by the charity] seemed mesmerised by the scheme."

When questioned about why the charity was not given a receipt for cash paid on expenses totalling several thousand pounds, one of the investment consultants involved with the alleged fraud told a High Court inquiry: "They didn't ask for a receipt. They were only interested in the profits, not in how we got them."

In this case it would appear that the motivation of Colonel Burn to raise money, not for himself but for the well being of the charity, blinded him to the risks involved. Here too, then, a wall appears to have been erected between the charity's interests and the correct procedures to monitor the means that were being deployed.

Managing the ethical climate

The cases mentioned above point up the need for voluntary organisations to manage the internal ethical climate. So what can voluntary sector trustees and senior managers do to ensure that the organisation behaves ethically? There is no simple answer, nor is it likely that an organisation from any of the three sectors can totally eradicate the possibility of wrong-doing – either deliberate or by error.

The Charities Act and the Act's new statement of recommended practice for financial reporting (Sorp 2) will help tighten standards and improve disclosure. The Act gives the public the power to ask for any charity's detailed accounts, the provision of which is already established as good practice. In this respect, well informed and suitably trained trustees and voluntary sector accountants hold the key to improving the ethical climate within the voluntary sector at large. However, the management committee of any voluntary organisation has a duty to take what practical steps it can to maintain an open and ethical climate among all those involved with the organisation. These should normally include the following:

♦ Setting a clear **example**.
♦ Publishing a **code of ethics**.
♦ Monitoring **performance**.
♦ Appointing **ethical champions**.
♦ Creating **effective channels** for registering concern.
♦ Supporting the ethical climate with **training**.

Setting a clear example

Our work advising organisations on communications has shown time and time again that messages from on high are rarely taken seriously by those further down unless senior managers set a clear example. The common assumption by top management that simply saying something is important will be enough to make everyone within the organisation treat it as such is often a naive one. People, particularly those who have little contact with senior managers, are much more likely to take their cue not from what they are told are the organisation's values but what they see acted upon. The key, then, to setting an example on ethical issues is visibility and practice. Among actions the management committee can take are:

♦ Include ethical considerations on the **committee agenda** every time the committee meets.

♦ Make much of ethical issues in the **annual report** and elsewhere particularly in **employee and volunteer magazines** and communications.

♦ Create opportunities to **demonstrate ethical commitments**. For example, by standing on principle when making fundraising decisions.

♦ Ensure that the message delivered to internal and external audiences is **consistent**. Nothing will undermine the integrity of an organisation more quickly than insiders believing the organisation says one thing in public and quite another in private.

Publishing a code of ethics

A formal code of ethics serves a number of functions. For example:

♦ It provides **guidelines** for managers and workers to follow when making decisions based on value judgements.

♦ It creates a **formal obligation** for everyone within the organisation to take ethical issues into consideration in the course of their job. They know they have a formal duty to assess their actions and the actions of others against what is right in the eyes of the organisation as stated in the code.

♦ It provides a **basis for on-going discussions** about the nature of ethical behaviour.

The very existence of an ethical code is a partial protection for an employee or volunteer who observes unethical behaviour, because he or she can demonstrate conformance to the code. It also legitimises taking the issue outside of the immediate work team if the individual cannot resolve their doubts with their immediate boss. For example, the Coca Cola Company tells its employees in its code of business conduct: "The guidelines contained in the code are of necessity broad principles. As a result, employees may from time to time need assistance in determining how the code applies to situations which confront them. Questions about the code's application to specific circumstances should be directed at an employee's supervisor or to the company's general counsel." In other words, if you can't resolve the problem satisfactorily with your immediate boss, there is an outside source to talk it over with and you have an obligation to do so.

A code of conduct should include:

1. An explanation of the need for guidelines and how to use them

2. The role of individuals in maintaining the ethical climate of the organisation in the following areas:

Behaviour towards people outside the organisation:
- (a) clients
- (b) suppliers
- (c) funders
- (d) the general public
- (e) the media

Behaviour towards colleagues at work.

Behaviour towards the organisation and its:
- (a) property
- (b) time
- (c) assets
- (d) intellectual property and copyright

Confidentiality.

Activities outside of working hours.

Conflicts of interest.

3. What individuals should do if they are concerned about other people's behaviour or the organisation's policy in a certain area.

4. What the organisation owes individuals in terms of its ethical behaviour towards them.

The code should be distributed to every employee and volunteer and discussion groups held to clarify its meaning and explore issues.

Valuable as it may be, however, a code of ethics is only part of the answer. Unless it is supported by an infrastructure that reinforces the values it expresses it is likely to be regarded as no more than another memo from on high.

Monitoring performance

An ethical code is only of value to the extent that people take notice of it. Monitoring the performance of managers and staff against the code is therefore essential. The organisation has to take active steps to police the policy.

Companies use a variety of means to do this. For example, the American firm Perkin Elmer requires all managers to confirm that they have not deviated from the ethical guidelines. The company conducts sample audits to check that these statements are true.

Others – about one in four of Britain's top companies – make ethical monitoring a specific responsibility of non-executive directors; in some cases, this involves setting up an ethical sub-committee of the board. Among the danger signals that non-executives or trustees should look for are the establishment of secretive cabals where a small group of key individuals withhold information that would normally be more widely available; or an employee who consistently refuses to take a holiday. Another sign that should set the alarm bells ringing is when the formal decision-making process involving professional expertise is being short-circuited for any reason. This appears to be what happened in the recent Salvation Army affair.

Appointing ethical champions

A number of companies have ethical committees which are often sub-committees of the main board and are made up predominantly of non-executive directors. The role of the ethical committee is to monitor the ethical climate of the organisation and to consult with managers to establish ethical guidelines. The members of the ethical committee also provide a focal point for employees who have ethical concerns to consult with. As such they have an important part to play in the system of checks and balances that are essential to maintain an ethical climate.

Voluntary organisations could also create ethical committees as sub-committees of the management committee. Trustees appointed to the ethical committee would provide an effective force to champion ethical issues and training, as well as monitoring the performance of the organisation against the ethical code.

Creating effective channels for registering concern

Monitoring and training will still not necessarily bring all wrong-doing and incompetence to light, particularly if senior managers are implicated. Voluntary organisations therefore need mechanisms which encourage people who feel disquiet about activities to register their concern. Chief among these is to provide 'safe' channels by which an employee or volunteer can raise concerns with the management committee without fear of reprisals.

Until very recently organisations which failed to provide these safeguards often presented concerned insiders with only one alternative – to go public by blowing the whistle on the organisation. Experience shows, however, that in almost every case where an employee feels compelled to blow the whistle publicly, both the organisation and the whistle-blower suffer. (Often the individual suffers most, because once his or her identity becomes known they become virtually unemployable.)

Help for whistle-blowers

Potential whistle-blowers now have another option. Public Concern at Work, a new charity established in October 1993 offers confidential independent advice for employees who feel a public duty to reveal malpractice at work but are unsure what to do. In particular, it helps them review internal channels rather than resorting to the so-called 'brown envelope' method whereby information is leaked anonymously to a newspaper or another outside party. Its first report, published in January 1994, provided a unique insight not only into the secretive world of whistle-blowers, but also into the ethical concerns that exist within voluntary organisations.

The charity received seven calls in its first four weeks from employees working in voluntary organisations – a figure only exceeded by callers from the health service, local authorities and the education sector.

One of the calls from the voluntary sector concerned a part-time worker at a national charity who was convinced that local managers were diverting money meant for the charity to their own personal accounts. When she confronted them about her suspicions they invited her to make bogus expenses claims herself. The concern was investigated internally and reported to the Charity Commission.

Taking all three sectors – private, public and voluntary – into account, the report showed that a third of all the calls dealt with by the charity's help-line in the first month of operation concerned corruption and potential fraud, with public and consumer safety a close second. It also revealed that people at all levels – including senior managers – sought confidential advice.

Support the ethical climate with training

An increasing number of business schools now have ethics on the curriculum. However, in North America, where there are now over 500 business ethics courses taught on campuses, no fewer than 16 business ethics research centres and at least three journals dedicated to the subject, there are signs that managers are no clearer about the real issues than their British counterparts.

The problem for voluntary sector managers is much the same as that for their private sector counterparts; namely that while most have a very strong desire to behave ethically, they are given little preparation to help them deal with the sorts of ethical dilemmas they are likely to face. Ethical training can help them in two critical areas by:

1. Enabling them to identify when an ethical dilemma is present. For example, they need to be able to:

   ♦ Determine where and how conflicts of interest might arise.

   ♦ Establish whether the dilemma is real or potential.

   ♦ Understand and examine their own attitudes and motivations.

   ♦ Become sensitised to the nuances of ethical issues.

Role playing exercises where a number of hypothetical situations are analysed and discussed by a group of voluntary sector managers, for example, allow the ethical dimensions of a decision to be better understood. Such exercises can also provide an excellent vehicle to lead into discussing real situations that people face in their jobs.

2. Providing a decision-making framework – something they can refer to, to help think through what is ethically correct, or to put conflicts of interest between stakeholders into context.

Writing in the Harvard Business Review (3), Andrew Stark, an assistant professor at Toronto University, suggests that despite considerable interest in the subject, US managers remain largely bewildered by it. It is not that managers dislike doing the right thing, he observes, simply that they lack practical advice on coping with the grey areas where competitive pressures can easily lead to unethical decisions.

According to Jack Mahoney, director of Kings College Business Ethics Centre:

"The aim of business ethics is to integrate business and economic values into a wider view of the significance of and quality of human living at both individual and social levels." A more practical interpretation from Stanley Kaier, director of the Institute of Business Ethics is: "Business ethics are ordinary ethics applied to business. For a rule of thumb, anything you want to hide is probably not ethical."

Equal opportunities and managing diversity

Founded as they are on principles of social justice, the issue of equal opportunities has particular ethical resonance for voluntary organisations. Yet it is one that continues to be a stumbling block for many. The simple fact is that because voluntary organisations are seen as championing the cause of social equality they are expected to be paragons of virtue in the area of equal opportunities.

Furthermore, voluntary organisations are often expected to ensure equality of opportunities in areas that go beyond those normally covered by companies. An equal opportunities policy for a voluntary organisation might include:

♦ Services that are **accessible and sensitive** to the needs of clients and members.

♦ **Fair employment** practices.

♦ Proper **representation** in terms of staff, management and volunteers.

♦ Commitment to the development and **empowerment** of client groups.

♦ Overall concern with **social justice** and other ethical issues within the organisation.

Where there is a clear link between equal opportunities and what the organisation does the pressure is even greater. For example, it is taken as read that a charity which exists to support people with disabilities should have the necessary procedures in place to cater for disabled job-applicants. Employment, after all, is one way of empowering disabled people in society, so how can the organisation expect others to heed its message if it doesn't practice what it preaches?

Unfortunately, a lack of resources often means that voluntary organisations view equal opportunities as a non-core area activity. They are reluctant to divert resources that could otherwise be used to provide services for beneficiaries.

As a result, the issue frequently does not receive the attention it deserves. The effectiveness of equal opportunities policies is not monitored, and the organisation fails to keep up with best practice. In a recent book on the subject – 'Equality in Action: Introducing equal opportunities in voluntary organisations' (4) – the authors Mee-Yan Cheung-Judge and Alix Henley observe that despite great and often painful effort there has been little real progress towards equal opportunities among voluntary organisations. They note:

"Diverse user groups are still rarely represented, especially on management committees; the profiles of members, volunteers and staff, particularly at senior levels, have changed little; services are still mainly available to the 'traditional' pool of clients; the cultures of most voluntary organisations do not incorporate equality. Even those organisations that have made some progress are often still struggling with equal opportunities intentions rather than actions. And most people in the voluntary sector are still asking 'Why equal opportunities?' rather than 'When?' or 'How?'"

Although equal opportunities principles are enshrined in law and all employers are obliged to develop and implement a clear equal opportunities policy, the reality is often very different. Action among voluntary organisations ranges widely from an actual policy statement to a dusty file marked draft consultation. In addition, many voluntary organisations have tried to take short cuts presumably aimed at reducing the time and administrative costs involved with putting such policies in place. Others are simply not aware of how recruitment procedures and criteria embody unintentional discrimination. For example, according to Mee-Yan Cheung-Judge:

"Many [voluntary] organisations have tried to implement equal opportunities simply by borrowing another organisation's policy, or have introduced rigid selection and recruitment procedures. Despite good intentions such partial measures are bound to fail, often leaving a bitter legacy of dashed hopes, disillusionment and suspicion."

Yet, even where a policy is specifically designed to meet the needs of the organisation, its existence is not enough to ensure success. The only way that the principle of equality of opportunity will become a reality in any organisation is if it seen as a core value. The aim of an effective approach to equal opportunities should therefore be to reach a point where it is integral to the culture of the organisation and becomes a fundamental element of 'the way we do things here' rather than simply a policy document. But it takes time for the types of behaviour that will support such a 'living' policy to become ingrained.

At SCOPE for example, a recognition of the charity's inadequate record of employing disabled people has led to a review of policy and an active campaign to remove barriers to access for both physically and psychologically handicapped people.

Scope also faced a difficult ethical dilemma over a factory it ran for the disabled, and which was losing money. Should the charity fund the deficit or close the factory? The trustees eventually opted for closure.

The first hurdle to tackling the issue of equal opportunities is the acceptance that there is an issue to be tackled. In the first instance leadership can only come from the management committee.

Moreover, we would argue that a priority for voluntary organisations should be to widen the pool of potential trustees to include groups that are currently under-represented. In particular, more people from less privileged groups, ethnic minorities and disabled groups could make a valuable contribution by serving on management committees.

Figures published by 'Third Sector' magazine in 1993 show that only about 2 per cent of voluntary organisations in England and Wales have black trustees. A study of voluntary health groups by Liverpool University in 1990 found that 95 per cent of management committees had no black members – in an area where the black population was 8 per cent. Part of the problem appears to be that black professionals with the skills and background to make good trustees often do not move in the same professional or social circles as their white counterparts. The situation is compounded by the clubbish recruitment tactics of many voluntary organisations. According to Peter Brown, chairman of Charity Appointments:

"If a trustee board only uses the old boy network to recruit, then the chances are that it will end up with middle class white candidates."

Danger of excess

Charities' desire to be seen to be equal opportunity employers has led in some cases to "politically correct" policies and behaviours that undermine the good intentions. One community investment manager points with exasperation to a charity, where managers are not permitted to interview potential direct reports, in case they exert any bias in the selection process.

Accessibility of services

Access to services is another important equal opportunities issue for voluntary organisations. In practical terms, what the organisation actually does is usually more important than who it employs. The critical question then is whether the way the organisation operates creates barriers to certain groups who might otherwise be beneficiaries.

For example, if a Citizens Advice Bureau were to be located in a very affluent area, would it be accessible to people who are less well off, or would its position act as a barrier which effectively discriminates against them?

Another dimension to this issue is the question of special needs versus mainstream services. In one case, for example, plans for much needed toilet facilities in the streets of New York were eventually dropped because disabilities activists insisted that all would have to be accessible to people with disabilities, something that increased the costs beyond the budget available. A better solution might have been to create some facilities for those with special needs rather than making it a matter of principle.

The problem in such cases is that special needs can override economic and practical considerations with the result that services are not provided at all. Voluntary organisations are particularly vulnerable to this sort of problem.

Clear policies on how the concerns of special needs groups are to be balanced with mainstream services would help voluntary organisations which face these sorts of dilemmas. But ultimately the decision-making process must differentiate between *consultation* with special needs groups and giving them what amounts to an effective veto.

Making equal opportunities policies work

There are a number of key steps an organisation can take to develop and strengthen its commitment to equal opportunities. Among them:

- ◆ **Establish an equal opportunities task force** – the task force should have a wide spectrum of members including representatives from key minority groups and wherever feasible user groups. The task force should have clear terms of reference and authority to examine internal practices and procedures.

- ◆ **Carry out an equal opportunities audit** – the task force should spend time examining current practices in critical areas such as recruitment, promotion, and the procedures for appointing trustees, and accessibility of services. For example, a very simple test of how equal promotion opportunities really are is to analyse how many people from minority groups are represented in each tier of management. Where an equal opportunities policy is effective there will be a good spread of people from minority groups across the management levels, or at least signs that people are beginning to work their way through the tiers towards senior roles. But where members of the task force are told that poor representation is the result of the poor calibre of candidates then there is almost certainly something wrong with the procedures. Either the promotion criteria are biased in some way or the recruitment process itself is failing to attract good candidates and requires scrutiny.

- ◆ **Recommendations of the task force should be presented to the management committee** and action taken, including necessary changes to the existing policy if one exists and the setting of clear objectives. For example, a thorough review and re-design of recruitment procedures within the next six months.

- ◆ **Equal opportunities training** should be provided for those involved in critical processes identified as susceptible to unconscious discrimination.

- ◆ **Equal opportunities champions** should be appointed from among the trustees and at all levels within the organisation to ensure that problems are brought to light. Where appropriate equal opportunities champions should consult staff before recommendations are finalised. The Equal Opportunities Commission observes for instance that 'employers are often surprised that after introducing measures such as a workplace nursery or crèche places are not taken up. If they had asked staff they might have found that childcare vouchers would have been more appropriate'.

♦ The **equal opportunities audit** should be repeated periodically to ensure progress is being made and that the policy is effective.

Another useful technique is an annual equal opportunities report which evaluates progress. At Oxfam, for example, the equal opportunities working group measures performance in relation to previous years and studies the staff profile to produce a yearly report. Says a spokesman:

"*We realise that we are still predominantly an organisation with white males at the top and that's a challenge for us. We want more equality because it makes for a better organisation.***"**

CASE STUDY ➤ Friends of the Earth

Friends of the Earth set up its equal opportunity policy in 1988. All job candidates now receive a summary of the policy, the interviewing panel receives special training and all interviews are attended by personnel staff. Applications are monitored and senior FoE managers recently reviewed the policy to take account of the lessons learned over the past five years.

Managing diversity

Programmes to manage diversity arose from the observation in the United States that equal opportunities were failing to deliver results. Grand Metropolitan's US operation, Pillsbury Inc describes it as seeking "to create a climate whereby those involved want to move beyond the achievement of a more statistical goal. People really begin to accept the values of differences between individuals (and groups) and recognise the benefits that multiculturalism can bring to an organisation".

Pillsbury, which has a vice-president of cultural diversity, sees it as a means of "making us more effective with each other and with our customers". It invests heavily in training people at all levels to seek opportunities to capitalise on the fresh perspectives that diversity brings. Managers' bonuses are tied to achievement of diversity goals. A cultural diversity council, made up of representatives from all areas of the business, provides an additional impetus to the programme, which has resulted in significant changes to the cultural make-up of the management cadre.

Another US company, Armco Steel, uses a system of "consulting pairs" to educate colleagues on cultural diversity issues. These are employees, who have undergone extensive training in cultural diversity issues, whose role is to help managers become aware of actual or potential discriminatory practices and (more positively) to help them take advantage of inputs from more than one culture.

Cultural diversity schemes have not taken strong root in the UK, and may never do so. There is likely to be (initially at least) fierce resistance from managers who see the approach as one of "thought police". However, a programme that emphasises the benefits of cultural diversity in management, as opposed to one that focuses on penalties, has much to recommend it.

Summary

Their special position of trust makes voluntary organisations particularly vulnerable to scandals. Not only are they expected to be paragons of virtue, many are encumbered with unwieldy governance structures which actually make it more difficult for them to monitor ethical behaviour. Indeed, some are accidents just waiting to happen.

There is little doubt in our minds that the current debates about corporate governance in the private sector and standards of probity in public life could usefully be extended to the voluntary sector. That aside, there are a number of measures that voluntary organisations can adopt to strengthen their internal checks and balances.

A code of ethics, for example, requires little in the way of investment. Appointing ethical champions and introducing measures to encourage staff and employees to voice their concerns are also relatively inexpensive.

Acting before a problem occurs will also enable voluntary organisations to lead the debate about probity in British public life, something many in Britain would thank them for.

Checklist

1. Does your organisation have a written **code of ethics**? Does it provide guidelines for how employees and volunteers can recognise and handle ethical issues?

2. Does the organisation encourage staff to **discuss their concerns**?

3. Who could they go to if they were **worried about unethical behaviour**?

4. Does the organisation have a clear policy on equal opportunities? Does it provide **training to support its values**?

References

1. Steve Boggan, *'Charity ignored warning about £7m deal'*, The Independent, 26 February 1993.

2. Andrew Stark, *'Harvard Business Review'*, May–June 1993.

3. Mee-Yan Cheung-Judge and Alix Henley, *'Equality in Action: Introducing equal opportunities in voluntary organisations'*, NCVO, 1994.

4. Sandra Greaves and David Obaze, *'The great, the good and the white'*, Third Sector, 18 November 1993.

5. Greenslade, Malcolm, *'Managing diversity: lessons from the United States'*.

Chapter 7

Does charitable money work hard enough?

Key issues

♦ *Would better long-term financial planning lead to more effective service provision and more effective use of funds?*

♦ *How can voluntary organisations manage their financial image?*

This chapter is *not* about the most commonly debated issue of financial management by voluntary organisations – the proportion of total funds spent on administration. This is an irrelevant issue despite problems with some voluntary organisations. The amount a voluntary organisation will need to spend on administration will depend substantially on what it does.

At one extreme, straightforward fundraisers, such as the Rotary Club, can be expected to spend very little on telephone lines, office rental and paid employees. But at the other extreme, a charity such as Childline rightly spends most of its income on premises, telephones and staff costs. The point here is that for the Rotary Club these items constitute administrative costs but for Childline they are service delivery costs.

If anything, voluntary organisations are over-sensitive about this issue, sometimes to the detriment of what they do. Expenditure that might significantly improve service provision – for example, staff training and development – can easily be shelved in the name of maintaining low overheads.

In fact, the Charity Commission has said that money spent on administration can be a good thing. The questions voluntary organisations should be asking themselves are not:

♦ How can we **minimise administration** to keep the costs down?

♦ How can we fudge the issue with the public so that **expenditure doesn't look too high**?

But rather:

♦ Are we **appropriately administered**?

♦ How can we **present the figures** in our annual report so that funders and the public recognise that money is being spent in the right areas?

The new guidelines for charities recommend that costs are broken down to show what has been achieved with the money spent and should help voluntary organisations focus more on the critical issues of **administrative efficiency** and **value for money**.

Keith Manley in his book, 'Financial Management for Charities and Voluntary Organisations' makes an important point about administrative overheads:

"Very often whether an administrative overhead is regarded as 'administration' or attributed to the charity's primary object or to 'fundraising' is an accident depending on how the charity is structured.

"Many charities in recent years have tackled this problem by analysing all their central overheads and arriving at a formula for charging to charitable activities and/or fundraising costs such proportion of each overhead as may be appropriate. This approach has now been endorsed by the current thinking behind the revised (1993) Draft Statement of Recommended Practice for Charity Accounts (Sorp 2) which supports strongly the principle behind such forms of apportionment.

"For most charities the main cost in administrative overheads will be salaries and salary-related expenses, often accounting for as much as 80-85 per cent of the total. In the smaller charity, where the manager and clerical staff may be engaged in a wide range of duties, it may be necessary to apportion an individual's time between charitable, fundraising and administrative activities. In more complex organisations there may be whole units devoted to an aspect of administration such as personnel, salaries and pensions or information technology. Senior management will need to decide an appropriate method of apportionment bearing in mind the characteristics of each function."

The critical financial questions for voluntary organisations seem to revolve around the twin issues of long-term financial planning and investment.

John Williams, a consultant at Fishburn, Hedges, Bays & Williams, points out two common problems:

"People in the voluntary sector don't understand that it is acceptable to run a planned deficit. They think if you have a deficit you should cut back, even if it means abandoning a service that took five years to build up. They need to understand how to smooth funding over a period.

"Unfortunately, there's a prejudice against large surpluses. One company has banned its staff from collecting on its premises for Guide Dogs for the Blind, because the charity is perceived to be cash-rich already."

This misperception can also apply to reserves. Being uncapitalised, voluntary organisations tend to require higher levels of reserves than would usually be the case in the private or public sectors. Clearly there is an educational job to do in both companies and charities.

Financial planning for the long-term

How voluntary organisations generally plan their finances

There is such a wide spectrum across the voluntary sector, both in the nature of activity and the scale of operations, that it is impossible to generalise about how voluntary organisations plan their finances. Endowed grant-making foundations, for example, are able to plan with the knowledge of assured income within a narrow range and can make their grant decisions accordingly.

At the opposite end of the spectrum is the service-providing voluntary organisation, which has to balance available resources with the needs of both current and future clients, where the total demand may far exceed the resources available. Both the timing and volume of cash generation is of vital importance in ensuring that existing commitments can be met, after which decisions on further expansion of activity can be made on the basis of what funds are available or can be raised.

The voluntary organisation's primary management control mechanism is the agreed annual budget. In well-run voluntary organisations, staff at all levels are encouraged to participate in the budget-setting process to ensure they are fully committed to making it work. The final budget statements and commentary are the prime responsibility of one person, usually the director of finance or the chief executive. A detailed annual budget enables a full system of financial control to be operated. Individual budgets are set for each project, each cost centre, each capital project and any other activity included within the annual business plan. Senior management agree upon the method and the frequency of the financial reports which compare the actual results with the planned expenditure as agreed in the budget. According to Keith Manley, who was Barnardo's finance director and secretary for 19 years:

"Most medium and large voluntary organisations usually adopt a monthly system as this usually fits in with other accounting cycles (invoicing fees, accounts payments and payroll management). Many grants are paid and received quarterly and for smaller organisations quarterly reports may be sufficient if supplemented by other information such as regular cash-in-hand/bank reporting. For some functions or at certain times of the year, more intensive reporting is required. Voluntary organisations operating shops selling donated goods usually take weekly or daily reports of cash takings to compare with budget expectations.

"Where there is a large volume of cash and cheque transactions, the bank position may need to be monitored daily to take the best advantage of surplus cash, which may be placed in the overnight or very short term money market. There may also be a seasonal activity (a Christmas donor appeal, or a Christmas catalogue) where daily monitoring may again be appropriate so that remedial action can be taken at an early stage if there are urgent requirements, such as stock reordering during a limited season."

Reserves

'If you do not know what your reserves are or why you have got them, then they are too high.' This provocative comment made at the April meeting of the Charity Internal Auditors Group made the point that reserves should not be built up by default nor without justifiable reasons. Addressing the same meeting, Ray Edwards, Head of the Monitoring Unit at the Charity Commission pointed out that reserves were necessary for a variety of legal and operational reasons. The Commission's main areas of concern centred on the level of what he described as 'free reserves', which were unrestricted reserves after taking account of operational needs, such as the organisation's working capital commitments, the need to maintain a fundraising base and, in certain cases, redundancy, maternity and similar contingencies.

The Charity Commission is currently drawing up guidelines for reserves. These will aim to produce:

♦ A clear understanding within the voluntary sector, and between the Charity Commission and the sector on **acceptable reasons** for reserves.

♦ Recognition that it is the **needs of beneficiaries** which should dictate policies on the application of income.

♦ **Common standards** in fundraising appeals and other public statements.

♦ Assurance that trustees are making **proper use of funds**.

The fact is that voluntary organisations need sensible policies on reserves and contingency finance if they are to be sure of meeting their future commitments.

The Cancer Research Campaign writes off all its grant allocations as soon as it makes commitments. So, for example, if it commits £100,000 a year to an organisation for 10 years then it writes off £1,000,000 in its accounts.

But there is also the matter of 'goodwill' which should be taken into account. Most voluntary organisations know that the goodwill of donors means that money will continue to come in providing a certain income each year.

A sensible reserves policy should take a balanced view on monies already committed and the probable income that will accrue. At the same time, the best way to guarantee income is maintained in future is by spending money in the current period to achieve the organisation's stated aims.

Some degree of contingency planning is clearly desirable for any organisation, but the level of reserves that a voluntary organisation can justify to its constituencies is likely to vary.

Probably donors and beneficiaries would agree that two year's reserves is a reasonable level. But many voluntary organisations feel uncomfortable asking people to make donations when they are sitting on what may be quite large piles of cash. Until very recently, for example, the Directory of Social Change had less than two months' reserves. Other voluntary organisations, on the other hand, have been criticised for allowing reserves to accumulate without a proper system to monitor what is happening.

In general, the key to managing reserves is twofold. Voluntary organisations need:

♦ Adequate **financial reporting and accounting procedures** which ensure the management board has accurate and up to date financial data on the current running costs, future commitments and projected income.

♦ A clearly defined **reserves policy** which can be publicly justified and includes sufficient regard for contingency finance, which should be regularly reviewed by trustees.

From a practical point of view, there are four fundamental questions that should be answered for any charity:

1. What do we mean by reserves?
The dictionary definition of reserves is something kept back or set aside for future use or contingency. In practice, reserves are needed for a variety of reasons both current and future. By and large, the intricacies of the reserves are a mystery to most members, yet they can easily be explained. Making it clear what is meant by reserves helps focus the attention of staff on what is important for the organisation.

2. Is there a need for a sector-wide policy?
Because voluntary organisations are so different, it is impossible to come up with one simple rule which will be fair to all of them. For example, voluntary organisations without permanent endowment may need far greater reserves than those with because their future incomes may be less secure. There are also certain circumstances where particular attention to reserves is needed. For example: Voluntary organisations with committed future expenditure (e.g. looking after the elderly in residential care). Voluntary organisations with trading operations where there is a measure of risk (e.g. contracts). Voluntary organisations with hidden contingency costs (e.g. provision for redundancies of operation have to be closed down or lease commitments).

3. Why should charities have a reserve policy?
David Carrington, director of the Baring Foundation, speaking at a South Bank University Seminar at Lazards in early 1994, made the point that funders look at reserve levels of those to whom they are making grants. He stressed that they should explain clearly the need for and uses of the reserves in the grant request by the trustees and expand on the policy at the grant application interview. He also suggested that trustees should explain in the annual report what the organisation's policy on reserves was and how it was reflected in the accounts. If reserve policy issues are thought through and declared, then a voluntary organisation can no longer be put on the

defensive by media attack on the level of its reserves. If they are not, then funders will wonder why the applicant needs to look for funds.

4. How does a voluntary organisation establish a reserves policy?
This will be a lengthy process. Projected income streams and how dependable they are will have to looked at. Risk factors that could affect legacies, fees, grants, sales must be assessed. Dividend yields and interest rates must also be taken into account. The voluntary organisation must also look at its forward expenditure for future uses – fixed versus variable revenue versus capital.

CASE STUDY ➤ RSPCA

The Royal Society for the Prevention of Cruelty to Animals recently faced criticism for allowing reserves of over £75 million to build up. Members of the charity's governing council accused headquarters staff of allowing the reserve to spiral out of control while volunteers struggled to raise money for animal welfare.

The financial services director, Mark Watts told Adrian Marks of The Sunday Times that the growth of reserves had been 'partly accidental' and caused largely by an increase in legacies. The reserves target had been £45 million, which would have allowed the RSPCA to maintain operations for 18 months, including the work of 300 inspectors, 48 animal homes, 32 clinics and 24 animal welfare centres. The charity has now drawn up plans to use the extra £30m to expand its network of animal homes over the next four years.

CASE STUDY ➤ Cancer Research Campaign

The Cancer Research Campaign (CRC) has recently revamped its reserves policy. Previously, CRC put aside money for what was loosely described as 'a rainy day'. As a grant making charity, CRC felt the need to refine this approach as it was essential that it provided cover for its future commitments both legal and moral. In 1990, following four years of rapid growth with income up 70 per cent over the period from £25.7 million to £43.6million, CRC carried out a review of its reserves policy. As previously the policy review took account of all risks then seen to be facing CRC, and undertook a full SWOT analysis (strengths, weaknesses, opportunities and threats) before arriving at the final revised policy.

After approval by the organisation's council, the policy was amended to one of 'maintaining free reserves in the range of six to nine months total forward expenditure where six months is the absolute minimum and nine months the desired level'. Free reserves were defined as total reserves net of tangible assets and are primarily invested in the stock market.

As the reserves were then above the range approved, the forward planning for 1991/92/93 was set to reduce the level of reserves by going in for planned deficit budgeting. The proposal was to increase research expenditure above voluntary income for a number of years but eventually to return to a neutral budget once reserves were down to within the approved level.

However, from 1991 to 1993 income increased less than it had in the previous four years. Indeed in 1991 there was a very small reduction but this position was reversed in 1992 when income returned to the 1990 level followed by a 10 per cent increase in 1993. CRC's research spending during the same period grew, as planned, at a much faster rate and by the end of 1993 was 26 per cent higher than it had been in 1990.

Increasingly the charity incurred deficits, which were effectively being funded from reserves to support its research commitments. Had the deficit not been planned within a defined reserves policy, then this situation would have given more cause for concern that it did.

Expenditure could not exceed income indefinitely even given a reserve policy. As the minimum level of reserves was approached, measures were taken, as part of the strategic planning process and the reserve policy to increase reserves to the top end of the desired range. Budgets for 1994/95/96 were set so as to reduce research spending below the level of income so that reserves were once more increased. Having a reserves policy enabled this organisation to take a gradual phased approach rather than dramatic steps. Without a reserve policy, CRC would not have been in a position to take the very hard decisions then facing it.

Opportunities for learning

Keith Manley, a visiting fellow in charity financial management at South Bank University spent almost 20 years in the voluntary sector. He says:

"For many years financial managers in charities tended to come from industry, but now they are moving the other way. For example, Andrew Hind is moving from Barnardos to head finance at the BBC World Service. Charities are also tending to recruit their financial managers increasingly from within the sector.

"Fundraisers have learnt a lot from the private sector. There is now an Institute of Fundraising Managers with a recognised qualification. The sector as a whole is becoming more professional and there are now career structures for financial managers in the larger charities."

Some voluntary organisations have followed the private sector by introducing computerised detailed monthly and weekly financial reports to minimise fraud and increase efficiency. However, there are still far too many whose financial reporting is too basic to allow critical and timely insights.

Voluntary organisations could also protect against fraud by running their own internal audits alongside the external one. Again it is mainly the small and medium sized voluntary organisations who have some catching up to do in this respect.

A great deal of exchange of best practice is taking place through secondments by accountancy companies to voluntary organisations. This mutually beneficial approach has led to significant improvements in some voluntary organisations.

Educating volunteers in financial management

Volunteers are the backbone of most charities, and the most important volunteers are the trustees who are liable for any losses unless the charity is incorporated as a company or a mutual and provident society. Under the 1913 Charities Act, the trustees have increased responsibilities for ensuring proper financial administration and there are criminal penalties for default. It is vital that volunteers responsible for or handling the finances have some training in financial management. The Downs Syndrome Association has tackled this by running workshops for branch and group treasurers. It is currently overhauling its constitution to reflect the recent changes in the Act.

Managing investment

It is quite difficult to gauge the size of the voluntary sector's long term investments simply because the sector is so diverse and many of its participants relatively small. The Henderson Top 1000 Charities indicates that the largest 1,000 charities control assets (including property and cash) of over £21 billion. This list excludes smaller charities as well as large charitable bodies such as the universities and the NHS charitable trusts. According to John Harrison, a director at Fleming Investment Management, in his book, 'Managing Charitable Investments' it seems likely that the sector has long term investments worth well over £20 billion. This is a tiny amount compared to the UK pension fund sector's £400 billion. But nevertheless, the charity sector is a significant part of the economy with an annual income of £17 billion, or 3 per cent of GDP. 'The fund management industry has moved quite rapidly to service an area of perceived growth, with many firms establishing specialist charity teams in recent years,' explains Harrison.

'The trend to professionalism seems set to continue with the resulting increase in a demand for more sophisticated investment techniques and products. Investment practitioners should recognise that charities will become increasingly demanding clients, with trustees who expect their investments to contribute fully to their other activities.'

The main decision-making body in a charity is the Board of Trustees. So the legal responsibility for any investment decision rests with them. The employees of a charity may have the same titles to those in the commercial world such as chief executive, financial director, but legally they cannot be trustees. The majority of larger charities give discretion to their appointed manager to make investment changes within broad parameters of policy. The charity retains control of policy and the power to appoint and fire the manager. The finance director will, however, have a major influence on the trustees' decisions. The trustees will often form a separate investment subcommittee comprising three or four trustees, with perhaps lay advisers included as well. 'The size of the charity is a key determinant of the formality of the organisational structure. In a sector where individual charities can grow very quickly, it is important that trustees recognise the need for internal structures to evolve. 'Many of the recent charity frauds have arisen because the internal framework for control was not suited to the current needs of the organisation,' warns Harrison.

The new rules and regulations on charities' fund management

The Charity sector had its hopes raised by provisions in the Charities Acts 1992 and 1993, which allowed for outdated legislation governing investment in charities to be reformed. In Spring 1994, the Charity Commission published in draft form its policy in respect of granting wider power schemes for the investment of charitable monies which gives charities the opportunity to widen their investment powers on an individual basis. The Government then amended slightly the Trustee Investments Act (TIA) which governs the investment powers of many charities.

The new powers enable charities of all sizes to invest direct in investments of member countries of the European Union, Austria, Finland, Sweden, Iceland and Norway. This is beneficial to large charities, but it may not be so desirable for the smaller ones who use pooled funds as the most appropriate method of diversification. This change also throws up a peculiar anomaly. It allows charities to invest direct in countries such as Greece and Portugal (which could still be termed emerging markets in some ways) whilst continuing to exclude direct investment in the US and Japan – the largest and two of the most mature markets in the world.

Another problem with the TIA has been the need to maintain such a high proportion in narrow range assets which cannot be invested in equities. At the end of January 1995 the Home Secretary announced planned changes of this proportion which should improve the situation. The Draft Changes (Investments Act 1961) Order 1995, which went before Parliament at the end of March 1995 proposed a change in the ratio of wider:narrower range investments from 50:50 to 25:75, allowing greater access to equities.

Sarah Hamilton, from Fleming Investment Management in the Investors Chronicle, writes:

"Although some progress has been made, the legal framework remains overly prescriptive and outdated. There is still much that should be done to modernise the TIA allowing charities greater scope to secure attractive investment returns."

Investment objectives

Harrison details four key parameters of policy which should be recognised in any statements of investment objectives:

♦ **Time horizon**.

♦ **Income needs**.

♦ **Legal powers**.

♦ **Non-financial criteria** (i.e. ethical returns).

Managing a charity investment fund constantly involves balancing income and growth. According to Harrison it is not uncommon for objectives to be phrased in terms of 'an income yield of 6 per cent per annum with growth at least in line with inflation. In practice this approach is woolly and potentially dangerous.'

The dangers of setting unrealistic objectives are two-fold. First, according to Harrison, an objective should be more than a broad statement of intent. It should be a working tool for judging success. If the objective is wrong then the trustees may come to the wrong conclusions.

But as Harrison points out, 'The second and more serious danger is that the wrong objective will produce the wrong investment policy.' This is particularly true if the income yield is set high either as a comfort factor for the trustees or as a means to 'keep managers on their toes'. Income returns can be judged straight away but growth (both of income and capital) takes longer.

By maintaining a high standard of prudence and diversifying voluntary organisations can avoid the risks that accompany investment. Although there have been some spectacular failures of the system (for example, the collapse of Barings), the private sector tends to limit exposure with clear guidelines on the extent to which individuals can take investment decisions on behalf of the company. Best practice in the voluntary sector is similar.

A key issue here is prudence. It is essential for charities to maintain a balanced portfolio which spreads investments to minimise risk. Many private sector companies actually lose very large sums of money through speculating on treasury bonds, for example, but despite pressures from the investment community this is not an allowable option for charities.

Ethical investment

Ethical investment has been an issue in the charity sector for many years. However ethical investment by trustee bodies tends to be frowned upon by the legal system. It views charity trustees as guardians of the assets on behalf of other people. It expects trustees to act in the best interests of the beneficiaries and is wary of areas which could be seen as personal prejudice. The Bishop of Oxford test case is the most relevant landmark test case to illustrate this point. The case came in 1991 after the Bishop of Oxford sought to change the Church Commissioners' investment policy. The bishop wanted to exclude companies involved in certain activities counter to Christian principles and more controversially, to invest in ethically desirable activities despite poor financial returns. Specific examples included low-cost housing projects which would further the work of the church, but which offered returns below commercial rates. The case was lost, but not before the courts set out a number of exceptions to the 'maximise financial returns' principle. In particular, the court recognised that investing in assets which directly conflicted with the charity's objectives in a way which was clear to all could be damaging to the charity's fundraising work. The cases cited were a cancer research charity investing in tobacco shares and a Quaker charity investing in arms companies.

The onerous duty placed on trustees, then, is to balance the narrowing of any investment criteria against its impact on investment performance, whilst at the same time taking into account any problems of attracting support that investing in certain categories of investment might cause.

There could be serious ethical problems, for example, for a Third World development charity with investments in arms manufacturers. It seems likely, however, that charities will have to wait for further test cases to clarify the position.

Harrison, a specialist charity fund manager, writes: 'The Church Commissioners case does allow ethical investment but does not give carte blanche. The tests it applies in terms of 'direct conflict with the charity's objectives' which should be 'clear to all' are tough. For example, it is by no means clear that a geriatric hospital could avoid tobacco companies whilst a cancer hospital certainly could.'

Summary

In general, voluntary organisations are far more conscious of the need to avoid wasting money than private sector organisations. Frugality is part of the operating philosophy.

The problems (and opportunities) lie in seeing the larger picture. Making best use of resources requires planning for the long term, developing systems to match planned activities with funds, and controls to ensure that funds are wisely invested and spent.

In general, the voluntary sector is rightly conservative in its management of funds. But there is plenty of room to develop more imaginative approaches that allow a more strategic, systematic use of resources.

Checklist

1. Who decides what **financial reserves** your organisation should keep?

2. Who in your organisation is responsible for **investment decisions**? Are they qualified for the role?

3. Are staff trained in **basic financial management** techniques? Do they need to be?

References

1. Keith Manley, *Financial Management for Charities and Voluntary Organisations*, ICSA Publishing, p.35

2. John Harrison, *Managing Charitable Investments*, ICSA Publishing, 1994.

3. Sarah Hamilton, *'Investment Powers a Time for Change'* Annual Charities Review, Investors Chronicle, 11 November 1994, p36

4. Adrian Randall, Neil Finlayson, *'Vital to have a policy on reserves'*, Annual Charities Review, Investors Chronicle, 11 November 1994, p38.

5. Steve Boggan, *'Charity ignored warnings about £7 million deal'*, The Independent, February 26 1993

6. Jimmy Burns, Andrew Jack and Roland Rudd, *'Charity guidelines breached'*, Financial Times, Weekend, 27 February 1993

Chapter 8

Is the voluntary sector prepared for radical change?

Key issues

♦ *Do voluntary organisations have the management skills to cope with change?*

♦ *How can they match private sector and public sector organisations in using their resources more efficiently?*

Change for today's organisations comes in several guises. One of the most important is societal change, the inevitable evolution (and sometimes revolution) of the society in which they operate. Societal change raises fundamental questions about the role of the organisation and the people in it.

Growth change occurs as a result of increases in size or as a process of maturing – or both together. Growth puts strains upon the fabric of the organisation, upon the ability of managers to control critical activities and upon the collaborative relationships that provide cohesion of purpose. Growth change frequently occurs at a time of crisis, rather than as a reaction to opportunity.

Operational change usually occurs as a result of either growth or a change in the organisation's environment – for example, a change in the pattern of giving, or new opportunities such as contracting out – although it can also result from the enthusiasm of a senior level champion to improve some aspects of the way the organisation works. The critical question in each case is: are you driving the changes or are they driving you?

Societal change

It is difficult to remember a time when the role of the voluntary sector was the centre of as much controversy as at present. When it was published in October 1993, for example, 'Voluntary Action' (1) – the report by the independent think-tank Centris – created an immediate furore.

Written by Barry Knight and two other former advisers to the Home Office's Voluntary Services Unit, the report claimed that charities are a medieval concept with no place in the modern world. According to Knight:

"The medieval classification of charities should be abolished. Tax breaks should be assigned to organisations based on their performance against agreed criteria."

More recently, comments made in a speech by the Duke of Edinburgh in June 1994 triggered a backlash among charitable organisations which disagreed with his suggestion that absolute poverty no longer exists in Britain and that many charities no longer deserve charitable status.

Viewed from a distance it is to be hoped that these public wrangles are simply the opening rounds of a more mature debate still to come. However, they also indicate that the voluntary sector – along with a great many other areas of British national life – is entering a period of re-evaluation and rapid change.

At a time of great social uncertainty it is not surprising that questions about the future role of the voluntary sector are surfacing. Indeed, such questions are to be welcomed as long as they represent the best interests of the people affected.

Moreover, most voluntary organisations would agree that they will have to confront a whole range of issues in the coming years. It is likely, however, that those voluntary organisations that plan for change and find ways to lead the debate will do more to serve their cause than those that simply bury their heads in the sand. The aim must be to ensure that what emerges from the current uncertainty is a stronger, more accountable and effective voluntary sector better able to cope with national and local social needs.

The starting point must be to improve and professionalise the way the voluntary sector is managed. In planning for the future it is vital to take account of trends – both national and international – affecting the environment in which voluntary organisations operate.

A recent report[2] published on behalf of the Association of Charitable Foundations (ACF), the Charities Aid Foundation (CAF) and the Corporate Responsibility Group (CRG), identified a number of trends affecting the management and funding of voluntary organisations. Five issues were highlighted which have particular bearing on future planning by voluntary organisations:

♦ The new **contractor/provider relationship**.

♦ A shift from core funding to **project funding**.

♦ The **shrinking state**.

♦ The **fragmentation of government**.

♦ **Localisation**.

The contractor/provider relationship

Statutory bodies are increasingly moving away from direct service provision to arrangements whereby they contract with private or voluntary sector organisations to provide a particular service or outcome. As Osbourne and Gaebler noted in their excellent book 'Reinventing Government'[3], this trend is evident in most developed countries. This new direction in service provision offers a number of opportunities for

Mega trends in society

Business in the Community's David Grayson identifies ten "megatrends", which are shaping corporate community involvement by companies and demand a corresponding response in the voluntary sector.

Trend	Business response	Voluntary sector response needed
1. Win-win-win	Companies insist on seeing business benefits from corporate community involvement (CCI)	Voluntary sector organisations (VSOs) must look for new ways to collaborate that take companies' aspirations into account.
2. People power	Companies are involving employees, encouraging them to volunteer for community projects, recognising that transferring skills and experience is one of the most valuable forms of CCI	VSOs need to identify the skills they most need, which could be transferred by corporate volunteers and plan campaigns to access this valuable resource
3. What, no education?	Education and training are priority issues for companies	VSOs must learn to include educational dimensions in projects, where this makes sense for both partners
4. From feel good to doing good	Results in terms of community benefit are becoming most important to companies	Broader-based partnerships with community agencies will become more common
5. Glocalisation	"CCI is becoming more international and more local".	UK-based VSOs will need to link with similar organisations overseas to access the corporate budgets of multinational companies; and develop close relationships with local branches
6. Drops in the ocean to changing the ocean	In the United States in particular, companies are increasingly willing "to translate their CCI experiences into public policy positions" – often at a high level of public influence	VSOs may be able to combine forces with the private sector in new and powerful ways
7. Mainstreaming CCI	"CCI is being integrated with other business functions" – marketing, human resources and public affairs	VSOs can use the change in role to get closer to the strategic heart of partner companies
8. Shared destinies	"Companies will move from one-off, in-out contributions towards more strategic relationships with partners"	VSOs must be ready to initiate and manage partnership relationships
9. Do and tell	Companies will be more active in publicising their CCI activities, especially to shareholders	VSOs can build on and profit from this publicity – and help to leverage the companies' efforts
10. In pursuit of excellence	CCI departments are becoming more professional	VSOs have to match their professionalism – but VSOs also have a lot to teach CCI departments

the voluntary sector. It also creates problems for voluntary organisations and their funders. In particular:

♦ The voluntary sector will increasingly be in **competition** with private sector (and other providers) when bidding for contracts.

♦ Contract funding is for the **direct provision of services** and is not intended to support the other functions of the voluntary sector such as advocacy, policy development, experiment, community development and advice.

♦ The contractor/provider relationship favours the **larger professionally organised voluntary organisations** at the expense of the smaller ones, which are in danger of being squeezed out.

♦ The demand for **measurable outputs and detailed costings** places increased demands on management to develop and monitor effective tools to evaluate performance. New levels of public accountability may also mean that in the long-run it becomes more difficult to persuade high-calibre individuals to take on the responsibilities of trustees and committee members.

♦ The definition of **required outcomes** calls for careful negotiation to ensure that what is measured is meaningful in terms of the services required and not simply what is easy to measure and easy to achieve. The danger otherwise is that the targets set fail to take account of more difficult clients such as people with special needs.

♦ Problems may occur with **double funding** or **unfair competition** if a voluntary organisation receives core funding from a public source, which is not included in some way in comparing its bid with those of other providers, particularly those from the private sector.

The switch from core funding to project funding

Core funding for many voluntary organisations was once seen as the Government's responsibility at local or national level. But government departments and local authorities are increasingly reluctant to act as core funders because it ties their hands in the future by committing them to increase funding year after year as more organisations join the core-funded ranks. In effect, core funding restricts the grant-making process eroding the discretionary component, which might otherwise be used to fund new ideas.

The shrinking state

In the UK as in all other OECD countries, the period since the early 1980s has seen a major reappraisal of the role of the state in the provision of direct services. In the UK, this has led to a questioning of the need for some services, while at the same time the government has sought to have more of its programmes delivered by private sector or voluntary sector organisations. For example, the creation of Training and Enterprise

Councils and the shift of fair rent housing provision to housing associations reflect this trend.

These developments have simultaneously increased the importance of the voluntary sector and made its funders more wary of becoming involved with government programmes. One cause for concern among commentators from all sectors is that future governments might assume that if they withdraw funding from a particular programme other funders would automatically step in to fill the gap. Neither the private sector nor the voluntary sector have the funds or the inclination to do this.

The 'Resourcing the Voluntary Sector' report found that where the reduction of state funding led to voluntary organisations being asked to fund the **provision** of what were previously statutory services, trusts and companies were particularly reluctant to become involved. This, the report said, was demonstrably happening in education and to a lesser extent in health services. In addition, it noted:

"Where bodies which were previously clearly in the statutory sector (e.g. providers of education, health and housing services) have been switched to the voluntary sector in whole or in part, a number of complex legal and accountability questions have arisen, with many of the new bodies being unsure of their powers, duties and responsibilities."

The fragmentation of government

Since the early 1980s, but particularly with the spread of Agencies and privatisation over the last five years, central government policies have been developed and delivered in a much more compartmentalised way than was previously the case. This has led to much more specific and clearly defined objectives for individual government units. Increasingly, these units are left to achieve their set objectives in their own way with less recourse to consult with other parts of government. Greater regionalisation has also occurred with the creation of government offices in the regions which are responsible for the delivery of local programmes such as the Single Regenerative Budget. This has been accompanied by a devolution of decision-making to the community level. For example, Care in the Community means that many decisions about buying services from outside are now made at the level of social workers, and in the area of health provision, by fund-holding GPs. While local authorities have retained more of their own identity than their central government counterparts, they too are subject to the same pressures to delegate and decentralise. From the perspective of the voluntary sector these developments mean:

♦ Even within government departments it is difficult to secure much in the way of a consistent or co-ordinated approach to voluntary bodies.

♦ The role of the Home Office Voluntary Service Unit in attempting to secure such an approach across departments is made very much more difficult, especially so as a result of the low political clout of the Unit.

♦ Programmes and projects which, when viewed from a wider perspective such as that of the Exchequer or Government as a whole, would make good financial and policy sense tend to fail to find funding as they have to be justified in terms of the narrower objectives of one of the fragmented parts of government.

There is a compelling argument for government to take a more coherent view. As the report notes, however, even if it were possible to establish (or return to) a more coherent government approach this would have important drawbacks for the voluntary sector. If all departments were required to follow the same procedures and priorities and to consult with each other before taking decisions about whether to support or use the voluntary sector, the government would almost certainly develop a much more monolithic approach. Decisions would take much longer and innovative proposals would be likely to fall foul of centrally imposed rules.

While it is frustrating that government finds it difficult to develop a more coherent approach to social policy issues – for example there appear to be conflicting policy streams on homelessness – there are nevertheless some advantages for voluntary organisations in the present diversity of approaches between departments.

Localisation

The trend towards pushing decision-making out from the centre to a local level is well established now both in government and in the private sector. In the context of government this often involves working directly with local communities by missing out local authorities. Among companies there is a move away from allocating funds for voluntary organisations (once the prerogative of the chairman's office) at the centre, towards letting local branches allocate funds in their own communities. In the private sector, this shift reflects the move among UK businesses to flatter management structures.

The new emphasis on making decisions at a local level has important implications for voluntary organisations. In particular it means there is less scope for cross-subsidy from wealthy to poorer areas. There is a very real danger that neglected areas requiring high levels of voluntary activity will be unable to attract funds. New approaches are required to overcome this difficulty. In the crime prevention area, for example, liaison groups have been established at Borough level in London involving the police, local authorities, other statutory services and voluntary organisations to try to improve and co-ordinate efforts to reduce crime. Such approaches place a premium on partnership relationships across sectors.

Centris Report

Finally, it is important to consider the more radical proposals for the voluntary sector that have been made in recent months. Foremost among these are the recommendations contained in the Centris Report.

The report recommended that voluntary organisations should have their charitable status withdrawn and that the voluntary sector should be split into two separate categories: those that provide services and those that campaign, with no overlap between the two groups as is currently permitted.

In the first category, the report said, should be voluntary service providers, mainly the large organisations already bidding for government contracts in the new purchaser-provider markets emerging in health, education and social services. But those organisations in the second category should return to the traditional role of voluntary bodies; that of challenging the existing social order and concentrating on campaigning for change.

The report drew widespread criticism from the voluntary sector, not just because it advocated withdrawing tax concessions from charities and abolishing the Charity Commission, but because it also accused many of the larger voluntary organisations of losing their vibrancy and strength as a result of becoming more dependent on government funds. Some senior staff, the report, claimed, were more interested in pay, status and company cars than in the clients their organisations were set up to serve. Some charities, it said, had highly hierarchical management structures, with up to 14 different levels of management. The report claimed:

"Some organisations are so cumbersome, moribund, outdated and riddled with error that nothing could touch them. The real problem is how to close them down, yet no one seems to have devised a method of removing voluntary organisations that have outlived their useful life."

Strong criticism indeed. But some commentators saw more sinister forces at work. 'The Independent' in its Leader column on 13 October 1993 warned:

"A revolutionary movement has been launched to destabilise Britain's charities. Its chief theoreticians, from a little-known think-tank, want their status abolished." The newspaper went on to observe: "The charitable sector should not be complacent. This document bears the fingerprints of government. Though produced by the Centre for Research and Innovation in Social Policy and Practice, it was paid for by three government departments and its authors are former Home Office advisers... it may not be long before ministers echo the revolutionary message."

The Centris report also drew sharp criticism from the voluntary sector itself. Director of the NSPCC Christopher Brown, for example, dismissed it as 'maverick'.

Talking to 'PR Week', he said of the recommendations to split the voluntary sector into service providers and campaigners:

"Society and the clients with whom voluntary agents work would be the poorer for this split. It is vital that service provision should inform advocacy work: severing the link could weaken the democratic process and the representation of vulnerable groups."

Save the Children director general Nicholas Hinton and press officer Don Redding said:

"Do as [Barry] Knight proposes, and you will render charities 'difficult to sustain on either track and deprive the UK of what is internationally recognised as one of its greatest strengths."

Charities which currently combine both functions were quick to point out, too, that the sorts of changes proposed would affect not only the basis on which they campaigned, but their relationships with business supporters.

Katrina Dunbar, head of the press office at Shelter, said that for a charity like her own it would be like cutting a tree off from its roots.

"In terms of Shelter's campaigning work, although we are non-party political, the work we do is clearly attacking government policy, yet a lot of companies are willing to be linked with us because of our direct services work – it gives us credibility and the knowledge with which to campaign."

Many from the voluntary sector saw the report – which claimed to be the most comprehensive review of voluntary organisations since Beveridge's special report on the sector in 1948 – as a wasted opportunity. But in one area, at least, it was an unqualified success; it provoked debate. Head of campaigns at SCOPE Brian Lamb told 'PR Week':

"It's right to identify the concern in a lot of voluntary organisations that by contracting out they will become simply service providers. But it's a mistake to think that contracting out means there will be a fundamental change in the voluntary sector. The Government wants the voluntary sector to play an increasingly large role, not just in service provision but to represent clients' needs."

In a letter to the 'Financial Times' published on 16 October 1993, Judy Weleminsky, former director of the National Council for Voluntary Organisations wrote:

"Our sector is very aware of the high standards demanded by our unique position as recipients of gifts from individuals and funding from statutory funders. It would be naive to believe everything in the charitable world is rosy, but this [the Centris] report exaggerates the problems and fuels unnecessary fears."

Fred Heddell, chief executive of Mencap, the leading charitable provider of residential services for the mentally handicapped added that the size and £60 million turnover of his organisation brought "power and political influence" which were vital in campaigning on behalf of disabled people.

"At a time when statutory services are failing to meet so many of the needs of people with a disability," he told the 'Financial Times', *"it is irresponsible to make proposals which, if implemented, would throw the organisations that provide so much of the limited care available into structural turmoil."*

Defending the report in a letter to 'The Independent' published on the 26 October 1993, its principal author Barry Knight wrote:

"My report is designed to improve the access of groups based on social solidarity – gender, ethnicity, disability, sexuality, or other binding characteristics – to resources they deserve so that they can change the basis of society in favour of social justice and equal opportunity.

"Any report that has a critical analysis will, of necessity, challenge the status quo. It is therefore natural for the large charities to defend their position. Our report, however, does not attack them, but sets out a positive vision to achieve the aims identified."

In a letter to 'Third Sector' magazine, Knight also observed:

"Tucked away among the tables [in the report] is one neglected finding: the bigger the income the smaller the membership or, to put this another way, the bigger they [charities] become the less democratic and accountable they are."

While it is unlikely that the Centris recommendations will be implemented by the government in the foreseeable future, the voluntary sector would be unwise to dismiss its findings altogether.

Managing societal change

Like private sector organisations, the voluntary sector can cope with societal change by strengthening its competence in strategic planning. In particular, it needs to:

♦ Assign clear executive responsibilities and resources to **monitoring its environment**.

♦ Become part of **a wider range of networks** that provide insights to thinking not just in the voluntary sector, but in government, business, social organisations and elsewhere.

♦ Ensure that **threats and opportunities** are included as standard items for discussion at Management Committee or Trustee meetings.

♦ Adopt **flexible forms of strategy setting**, such as scenario planning, which allow the organisation to develop alternative futures to meet environmental uncertainties.

Mike Hudson, a consultant at the Compass Partnership who has advised some 45 voluntary sector organisations on strategic planning, told 'Third Sector' magazine, December 1994, that the principle is now well established in the sector with many charities having completed two if not three planning cycles.

VSO's strategic plan for the 1990s, 'Investing in People' was approved in April 1992 and is widely regarded as a model for the voluntary sector. There was opposition at the outset, but director David Green was determined to push through the planning process. He believed that VSO wasn't clear where it was going and he had been concerned to find the equivalent of several different mission statements being produced around the organisation.

After a year-long consultation process with stakeholders, including funders, serving and returned volunteers, staff and local groups, a five-year plan emerged, consisting of a statement of purpose and values and detailed financial, fundraising and service delivery targets.

The benefits of the plan, which was widely publicised, were immediate, according to Green. Being able to present such a strategy document to politicians and corporate donors helped improve VSOs credibility. Management decision making was also simplified; in the past, for example, long debates were held as to which countries VSO should operate in. Now decisions as to whether to withdraw or enter a country can be referred to a clearly defined plan.

Green stresses to 'Third Sector' magazine that the plan should only be seen as a management tool. He also plays down the risk that failure to meet widely publicised targets could later rebound on the organisation

There are other potential dangers in the move towards strategic planning, however. Many companies in the private sector are reducing their planning horizons. Recognising that rapid societal change can make detailed plans obsolete overnight, they are opting instead for very broad long-term plans and very detailed six-monthly plans. This is perhaps an area, from which the private sector might usefully learn from the voluntary sector.

Another danger is that charities adopt inappropriate models of strategic planning. Says Shirley Otto:

"There's a great danger with voluntary organisations trying to become too much like businesses. Take strategic planning, for example. In companies it is very much command driven. Where voluntary organisations have tried it they often produce a document which then isn't actually referred to. We've been teaching people to plan for years – I suppose it's giving it kudos to call it strategic planning – but the process often assumes that the world in which organisations operate is somehow manageable. In reality, of course, planning isn't something you do on a one-off basis, it's a way of life.

"A key question is how you can use command structure models based on the private sector in organisations where people are driven by their own values. In most voluntary organisations people feel themselves to be pretty equal and are less likely to accept hierarchical power. But many voluntary organisations are going over to hierarchies via the adoption of strategic planning. We're seeing a swing back in the direction of the traditional power model of white male leaders which can wreck the values-driven element."

Blundering into formulaic approaches to strategic planning without recognising the unique values and purposes of the voluntary sector can be equally deleterious. Says Otto:

"From a process angle, there is a way of thinking about a changing world. The ability to build those mechanisms into an organisation's processes is a strength. The whole idea of the learning organisation – which is a fashionable concept now in the private sector – is very voluntary sector. What they have to realise, however, is that change is something that has a negative side for some people. It wrecks careers. Change causes a lot of pain along the way.

"Another thing to realise is that the niche a voluntary organisation needs to be in may not match where the funding is available from. You can't simply move in the direction indicated by funding because it may not be where the beneficiary needs it to be. If you start dabbling with the intrinsic purpose of a values-driven organisation it can cause a lot of problems and frustration."

A more informed exchange of experience between private and voluntary sectors is called for by Tom Jennings. He explains:

"I do think the voluntary sector could learn from business in the area of strategic planning. But from my contact with the voluntary sector I've often thought that there is great scope for learning in both directions. A lot of companies, for example, have made the mistake of thinking they can introduce empowerment from the top down – but to work it has to be introduced from the bottom up. If a leader from a voluntary sector organisation has a clear vision, he is much less likely to try to use the power from his position to force it on the organisation. He may have a hard time bringing people along with him, we often hear that cited as a difficulty, but change is likely to come from persuasion. Private sector managers are more likely to try to use their hierarchical power."

Managing growth

All the textbooks on organisational collapse refer to the problems that arise from rapid growth. It is very easy for an organisation to allow itself to grow more quickly, in terms of meeting demand, than its resources of finance, technical and management competence and delivery capability can cope with. The result, very often, is implosion. Even those organisations that have coped with rapid expansion, sometimes of 100%, 200% or more annually can become victims of their own success, if the growth suddenly stops. The organisation may simply have too much momentum – resources tied up in production or delivery systems planned on continuing growth – to switch suddenly to lean and mean operation. For a voluntary organisation, a slowdown in funding can have an equally dramatic effect, leading equally quickly to insolvency.

Managing rapid growth demands a ruthless focus by the top team on the things that really matter in fulfilling the organisation's purpose. It requires very effective information systems, to ensure that cash flow retains a positive balance. And it requires an extra level of attention to the attraction and selection of staff.

Feed the Children

FTC's chief executive, David Grubb, believes that rapid growth was achieved without major mishap by a combination of the following:

1. Early appointments, with the exception of one person with field experience, were all people who had no experience of other aid agencies. We wanted proactive self-starters, who could be creative in their approach.

2. We also hired people who were extremely aware that there was no-one else to blame or lean on if it didn't work.

3. We took a very proactive attitude towards the media. I went on TV even before we went out to Romania. We put an ex-editor of the local paper on the staff, who emphasised that if it was a good story, we should go tell it. Everyone was ready to stand in front of a customer.

4. Total realism that as a start-up company, our financial management and awareness had to be of a very high order. We focused on the commercial realism by continuously asking: "why will people continue to give to you?"

Managing operational change

Operational change can affect any aspect of the organisation and its activities. The private sector is constantly organising and reorganising in efforts to achieve greater productivity and efficiency, or better to meet customer needs, or both together. So much so that employees often complain of initiative fatigue – the exhaustion of commitment and enthusiasm that occurs when changes come one after the other interminably. Initiative fatigue can be permanently crippling, if it is not well-managed.

An important lesson the private sector (or some of it) has learned is that a lot of small, apparently unconnected changes are often more difficult to cope with than a major change, which acts as an umbrella for multiple smaller initiatives. This is particularly true when the changes involve a transformation of culture.

The umbrella concept can be almost anything that inspires and challenges yet is widely accepted as desirable. The most common concept co-opted in this way is Total Quality Management.

TQM and the philosophy of continuous improvement

Total Quality Management (TQM) – a management approach that advocates incremental change through continuous improvement – has much to recommend it at a time when the environment in which many voluntary organisations operate is itself changing very rapidly. But TQM is no quick fix. It requires a fundamental shift in thinking at all levels in the organisation and a culture change that can involve many years of work. For those organisations prepared to stay the distance, however, the potential benefits are considerable.

In the past ten years TQM has become a by-word for efficiency and success throughout the business world. But its origins can be traced to manufacturing companies in Japan in the period after the Second World War. What these Japanese companies did was to analyse and document what was required of each worker to ensure a high quality product. In this way they built consistency into their operating procedures so that every car or television set that rolled off the assembly line was of the same standard regardless of which workers were on that shift or other variable factors. In this way and in sharp contrast with other industrial nations they were able to build-in quality. (Some people may remember British Leyland in the 1970s, for example, when the term a 'Friday car' was used to describe a substandard vehicle that had apparently been built shoddily because workers were in a hurry to start their weekend.) In addition, because the procedures in Japanese companies were documented it was possible to continually make small improvements which enhanced the quality and productivity of work throughout the company.

It was largely due to the application of TQM among a highly disciplined workforce that Japanese companies were able to out-perform their rivals in America and Europe during the 1970s to become the economic force they are today. It is ironic, too, that two American management thinkers, Dr W. Edwards Deming and Dr Joseph Juran, were instrumental in developing the approach that came to be known as TQM and which enabled these Japanese companies not only to catch up with but in many cases to overtake leading US companies in the short space of 25 years.

For a while in the late-1970s and early 1980s the Americans put the Japanese success story down to the availability of cheap labour. But when the Japanese car manufacturer Honda opened a plant in Marysville, Ohio, which used US workers paid at market rates and which outstripped the US car giants in Detroit, the penny finally dropped. American companies realised that the Japanese were doing something fundamentally different in their factories. The mid-1980s were characterised by a scramble among Western companies to understand how the Japanese companies were managed and to implement their own TQM initiatives. Indeed, such was the impact of TQM during this period that by the end of the 1980s it seemed possible almost to divide the world's top companies into two categories: those that had introduced TQM; and those that were just about to.

As with all good ideas, however, there was no clear consensus on the best way to apply TQM, and a great many variations on the TQM theme emerged as different companies applied its basic tenets to their own circumstances. Also, because it was applied first to heavy manufacturing processes many of the TQM techniques that were developed at that time involved complex statistical analysis of variables such as temperature and material tolerances which are less easily applied to processes involving human interaction. In reality, however, the success of TQM was in many respects less to do with the minutia of these techniques and much more to do with the new patterns of thinking that it inspired.

Moreover, in recent years the Total Quality approach has also been applied successfully to service industries and within the public sector. There are indications, too, that it is now beginning to spread to the voluntary sector.

The underlying philosophy of TQM has much to offer voluntary organisations. The basic principles of TQM are:

♦ A fundamental change of emphasis from quality control (checking that work already carried out meets the necessary standards) to **quality assurance** (whereby quality is built into the process so that only work of an acceptable standard is carried out).

♦ An adoption of the philosophy of **continuous improvement.** Everyone within the organisation (not just managers) is responsible for trying to improve the way that work is done. Improvements can include ways to reduce costs, shorten the time a task takes, avoid wastage, make life easier for suppliers or customers or any other sort of desirable change in the way work is carried out. The point is that everyone in the organisation is continually on the look-out for such improvements. In this way, adjustments to processes and procedures are carried out on an on-going basis rather than once and for all every few years when the old way of doing it has become hopelessly out of step with the competition.

♦ A change to a **customer-oriented approach**. Under TQM every decision starts with what the customer wants or needs and works back to the action the organisation should take. The notion of customer-orientation also extends to internal customers. Every department (and every team within a department) has a set of customers to whom its work is directed. So, for example, the marketing department is expected to meet the needs of its internal customers in other departments.

♦ A commitment to **getting everything 'right first time'**. The procedures followed by everyone within the organisation are developed to ensure that everything that is done is of an acceptable standard. This eliminates the wasted effort required to put right substandard work and removes the need for a quality control department checking work.

♦ The **participation of everyone** in the organisation in achieving its objectives. In a TQM culture, the old view of managers overseeing the work of others is replaced by the idea that everyone is responsible for the quality and improvement of their own work; the role of managers is to support them in their efforts.

♦ A commitment to TQM at the **very highest level** of the organisation. Only if top management invests the time and resources that are required – including attending training themselves – will TQM deliver real benefits.

♦ The acceptance that it is only by finding appropriate ways to **measure performance** that it can be evaluated and improved over time.

♦ A recognition that **prevention of errors** is more effective than curing them.

♦ A switch from the traditional adversarial management style to **Quality Management Systems** which encapsulate the underlying principles of TQM.

What makes the TQM approach attractive to many organisations is that by applying to an external accrediting agency – such as the British Standards Authority in the UK – organisations can achieve Quality assurance accreditation.

Some voluntary organisations are already in the process of applying for BS 5750 and its derivatives – the British equivalent of the International Quality standard IS 9000. The theory is that those which are successful will in effect become members of the world-wide TQM club.

Most organisations require the assistance of consultants to help them introduce TQM. There are a number of specialist consultants in the UK experienced in advising British voluntary organisations in this area. For example, Charities Evaluation Services (CES) – itself a registered charity – runs one-day seminars on the basics of Quality Assurance and provides advice on this and a wide range of other ways to evaluate performance.

However, the tide now appears to have turned against BS 5750. Many companies have found BS 5750 to be a source of bureaucracy, hindering change, and both the standard and the awarding bodies have themselves come under increasing criticism.

But, accreditation aside, where it truly takes root TQM can be a powerful engine to create competitive advantage. Any organisation that is capable of changing to new circumstances by continuously improving everything it does has an important advantage over those that simply react to a crisis when the current of change becomes irresistible. This will be particularly critical in the coming years when the current of change in the voluntary sector is likely to become a torrent.

CASE STUDY ➤ The Leonard Cheshire Foundation

In November 1993, the Leonard Cheshire Foundation, Britain's biggest provider of care for people with disabilities, completed the first stage of introducing the Quality Assurance standard BS 5750.

The Foundation, which was formed in 1948 by the late Group Captain Leonard Cheshire, VC, and provides care to more than 45,000 people through its 85 UK homes and 38 care at home services, completed a pilot scheme at three homes in Surrey and Hertfordshire, and a domiciliary care at home service in East Dorset.

All four – The Grange at Poole; Bell's Piece at Farnham in Surrey; the Hertfordshire Home in Hitchin; and East Dorset Care at Home service – received BS 5750 accreditation in little over a year. In doing so, the three homes in Surrey and Hertfordshire became the first voluntary sector residential homes in Britain to achieve BS 5750.

According to the Foundation's quality assurance officer Richard Whitmore, staff, residents and volunteers were all involved in the accreditation procedure.

"In seeking BS 5750 accreditation we have demonstrated our commitment to the pursuit of excellence in delivering the highest possible standards of care to our residents", he says. "Through clearly defined written procedures drawn up by our staff these standards are now visible to all. The procedures guarantee consistency and continuity and provide a valuable training tool for new staff.

"The system also ensures continuous critical review of our procedures. Areas of concern are quickly identified and appropriate corrective action not only taken – but seen to be taken", he adds.

Spurred on by the success of the pilot project, the Foundation is now pushing ahead to get a further 20 homes and services in the UK accredited.

James Stanford, the director general of the Leonard Cheshire Foundation, says: "Quality assurance is about the assurance of standards. It means that we are meeting our own standards, those of our purchasers, and those of our clients. We are the first major voluntary agency of our kind to receive BS 5750 and we hope that many more of our homes and services will follow suit.".

Homes and services involved in the second phase of the programme include those in Liverpool, Hull, Colchester, Surrey and Devon.

Making change happen

Apart from TQM, the principal tool voluntary organisations have to help them manage change is business or strategic planning. Two other tools are also becoming increasingly important, however – best practice benchmarking and client research.

The business plan

A business plan, as its name suggests, is a plan for how an organisation will put its aims into action in the coming months or years. In other words, how the organisation will go about its business. Such planning is as relevant to voluntary businesses as it is to private sector businesses. Without clear objectives and careful planning voluntary organisations are more likely to fail their donors and beneficiaries. A business plan has two primary functions:

+ **Internal planning** – it enables an organisation to take an overview of its activities and to ensure that its resources match its needs over a given period.

+ **External review** – it enables the organisation to demonstrate the feasibility of projects and services to vital audiences especially funders and business partners.

Both of these functions are becoming increasingly important to voluntary organisations for a number of reasons. For example:

+ Recent legislation, such as the NHS and Community Care Act 1990, is leading to **more formal relationships** between statutory funders and voluntary organisations in the new contracting culture, and increasingly requires voluntary organisations to submit detailed tenders to obtain funding for services.

+ Increasing competition among voluntary organisations for all forms of funding is placing greater pressure on them to demonstrate **efficiency**.

♦ Business partners and donors are requiring ever higher levels of **professionalism** from the voluntary organisations they support.

♦ The squeeze on statutory funding since the late 1980s makes it vital for voluntary organisations to identify future shortfalls and develop **strategies to top up funds** from other sources using marketing and fundraising campaigns.

♦ The government's 'Efficiency Scrutiny of Government Funding of the Voluntary Sector' published in 1990 increased the pressure on voluntary organisations to be both **accountable and efficient** in their operations.

According to Nicholas Martin and Caroline Smith in their book 'Planning for the Future' there are six key steps involved in creating an effective voluntary business plan. These are:

♦ **Setting objectives**.

♦ An **environmental analysis**.

♦ Developing a **marketing strategy**.

♦ An analysis of **operational requirements**.

♦ Preparation and presentation of **the finished document**.

♦ **Implementation** of the plan.

Setting objectives

According to Martin and Smith there are many areas for which objectives must be set. Among them:

♦ **Service range** – the types of services or activities the organisation will provide.

♦ **Target users** – the groups and numbers of people the organisation plans to provide assistance to, such as people with learning difficulties, for example; and the organisations it will do so through, social service departments, for instance.

♦ **Intended benefits** – the benefits that users will receive from the organisation's activities, e.g. development of skills, improved quality of life etc.

♦ **Service outcomes** – the results of providing a service.

♦ **Other features** – including internal objectives such as developing distinctive skills among staff through training; and the enhancement of the image and reputation of the organisation.

The organisation should also be clear about the objective of the business plan itself i.e. whether its main function is to meet the criteria of external audiences such as funders, or to provide a tool to enable the organisation to reinvent itself internally by altering the attitudes of employees and volunteers.

Leading-edge private sector companies now publish their business plan (expurgated only of genuine commercial secrets) to all employees. To do so they have to overcome a mass of cultural barriers and fears amongst executives and line managers. For voluntary organisations, which tend – at least in theory – to have more open cultures, there seems to be no practical barrier to such formal disclosure other than lack of precedent.

An environmental analysis

Any business plan must be set in context. Analysis of that context begins with gathering relevant information about the environment – internal and external – in which the organisation operates. The key at this stage is to ensure that the plan is based on real data and not simply on the perceptions of a few people at the top.

According to Martin and Smith there are five main types of information required for an effective environmental analysis. These are:

♦ Information on the **needs and opinions of current and potential users** of the organisation's services. (The views of past users may also be useful for assessing strengths and weaknesses.)

♦ Information on **important trends and influences** on the organisation's environment.

♦ The **criteria used by grant makers** and other funders in deciding whether to support funding applications.

♦ **Existing patterns of service** in areas of activity with which the organisation wishes to become involved.

♦ The **activities of organisations** with similar services.

These five types of information can be assembled from three main sources.

♦ **Internal sources of information** – through discussions with staff, particularly frontline staff and volunteers who collect an enormous amount of valuable information as they go about their jobs.

♦ **'Secondary' sources or desk research** – using published materials from magazines and journals, libraries and additional sources such as materials published by other voluntary organisations.

♦ **'Primary' sources or field research** – by surveying beneficiaries and funders; setting up discussion or focus groups; visiting other organisations; and attending exhibitions and conferences.

SWOT analysis

Once information has been gathered from these three sources it should be possible to do a SWOT analysis: a review of the **Strengths**, **Weaknesses**, **Opportunities** and **Threats** that face the organisation. In the main, strengths and weaknesses will pertain to the organisation directly, whereas threats and opportunities are more likely to arise from features of the external environment in which it operates.

♦ **Strengths**: what the organisation is good at, particularly areas in which it has an advantage over other similar organisations. For example, a high public profile, or high levels of user satisfaction for services.

◆ **Weaknesses**: areas where the organisation is at a disadvantage or is outperformed by other similar organisations. For example, low levels of specialist training in key areas, or poor geographical coverage in certain areas.

◆ **Opportunities**: trends or circumstances that favour the organisation or provide an opening which it can fill. For example, contacts that present opportunities to form strategic partnerships with companies or other voluntary organisations, or a government-led public awareness campaigns.

◆ **Threats**: developments that are potentially dangerous for the organisation. For example, a decline in statutory sources of funding, or new legislation placing added responsibilities on the organisation.

From the SWOT analysis – a report in its own right – the organisation should be able to summarise the management actions required to maximise opportunities and minimise threats. For example, if a source of funding seems likely to end then the organisation should review new opportunities and have an alternative fundraising strategy in place.

Developing a marketing strategy

As indicated in Chapter 5, marketing is essential to any organisation and involves matching services and other activities to the needs of key audiences. In the context of the voluntary organisation's business plan, the marketing strategy explains how the organisation intends to reach the people on whom it depends for success. It will typically include:

◆ **Marketing objectives** i.e. what the marketing strategy intends to accomplish. These may be financial objectives – for example, raising £X thousands from corporate donors and £Y thousands from members of the public; organisational objectives – enhancing the reputation of the organisation among the users and funders; or strategic – launching a new service or campaign by attracting national media coverage.

◆ The **target market segments**. For example, if research shows that there are 10,000 potential beneficiaries in the area not currently using the service, this might be an important market segment. Similarly, if the organisation requires additional people to meet its objectives it might target potential volunteers, or approach a large company in the area to take advantage of an employee volunteering scheme

◆ A breakdown of the **marketing tools** and the 'mix' of those tools it will use to reach the identified market segments. For example, the use of radio advertising to reach potential service users confined to their homes; or displaying posters asking for volunteers at community centres and in company canteens. The business plan itself is one of the marketing tools the organisation can utilise to market itself to funders.

Operational requirements

This is an analysis of the resources required to carry out the plan against what is available. For example, it will involve a review of equipment, staffing levels and management capability, as well as the preparation of detailed financial projections. One important component of this is to identify skills gaps that the organisation needs to fill through training.

The preparation of financial projections can be divided into two parts. It begins with an analysis of 'inputs' such as:

♦ **Income** – from grants, contracts, membership fees, donations, legacies etc.

♦ **Costs** – expenditure on salaries, rent, telephone, heating and lighting, insurance, postage and stationery, equipment, maintenance, training, travel etc.

♦ **Service take-up** – the numbers of service users or customers (including estimated increases or decreases in the take-up of services).

Detailed figures are required for each of these headings, together with assumptions made in preparing them such as that the level of membership will rise by 10 per cent over the next three years, or that salaries will rise by 5 per cent in the coming year.

The 'outputs' of the organisation's financial projections will be budgets that enable it to allocate the required level of resources where needed whilst providing an effective financial controls on spending. Typically budgets will be prepared for:

♦ **Income and expenditure** – this provides an estimate of whether the organisation will have a surplus or deficit of funds.

♦ **Cash flow** – this should identify potentially 'cash dry' periods and allow the organisation to make provision for these in its planning. For example, it should include the dates when grants will be received and times of the year when large expenditures occur such as quarterly utility bills etc.

In addition to financial projections a business plan should also indicate the financial controls the organisation has in place. In particular, it is essential to have a clear system of financial reporting which enables the organisation to monitor its finances. Financial reporting allows the organisation to compare income and expenditure projections against actual income and expenditure and make any necessary adjustments as it goes along.

This should enable it to avoid a crisis at the end of the period if the income and expenditure streams do not balance. Effective financial reporting also allows the organisation to check the financial assumptions it made to see how well they hold up and to anticipate future problems resulting from invalid assumptions.

Grouping activities into clearly defined 'cost centres' is one way to simplify financial reporting. Each cost centre – for example, training, publications, advice – reports to the management committee which monitors financial performance against the allocated budgets. The creation of cost centres also enables the management committee to see which areas of the organisation's activities perform well and which require changes or should be dropped altogether.

A key component of effective financial reporting is to identify the variance between projected costs and income from budget. This should also include the levers for remedial action such as who should address the problems and when.

Preparation and presentation

Organising material to produce a finished document which best serves its intended purpose is an essential part of creating an effective business plan. Much of the work at this stage is concerned with boiling down the large quantity of information that has been gathered into a workable first draft. It may also involve identifying and resolving inconsistencies in the different sections of the business plan. For example, objectives which cannot be met from existing resources must either be dropped from the plan or the shortfalls addressed by explaining how additional funds will be raised in the marketing strategy.

At first draft stage the contents of the business plan should be reviewed to ensure:

♦ it meets the need for which it was intended – i.e. it fits with the criteria of funders or clearly sets out the required change in strategic direction

♦ There are no serious gaps in it that require additional work or research to fill.

♦ The assumptions made in different sections of the plan are consistent with one another.

♦ It is a convincing and professional document.

♦ It is a document that enjoys the support and respect of the management committee and other key audiences such as senior staff and clients.

Implementation

The existence of a business plan is no guarantee of success unless the necessary steps are taken to turn it into action. It will have little impact unless responsibility for tasks is assigned to the appropriate people. A process of cascading the requirements of the plan must also be embarked upon so that people know what is expected of them in the plan and have any additional information they require to fulfil their role.

What period should a business plan cover?

The period covered by the business plan varies from organisation to organisation and will also depend on external factors such as how rapidly the environment in which the organisation operates is changing. Most plans cover a period between one and three years. Trying to plan any further ahead is unlikely to be helpful as the circumstances and assumptions on which it is based will almost certainly be overtaken by events.

Martin and Smith recommend a two-year rolling business plan as a sensible compromise for voluntary organisations. This, they say, should be reviewed at the end of its first year and a revised plan introduced at that time for the next two years. We would advocate a three-year rolling plan.

What gets measured gets done

There is a saying in business that what gets measured gets done. Behind it is the acceptance that managers are often too busy fighting fires to implement changes they know are required to improve the efficiency and performance of the organisation over the long-run. Whether TQM is the adopted approach or not – and there are plenty of people who would say that the claims made on its behalf have not materialised in many of the organisations that have introduced it – the fact remains that an organisation can only make real improvements if it knows how it is doing. That means measuring performance.

In its insistence on evaluating performance by measurement which is then used to focus on the key issues, the business world has much to teach the voluntary sector. There are two techniques in particular that do not require the full adoption of TQM, but which could be used by voluntary organisations to good effect. These are:

♦ Best practice benchmarking.

♦ Customer and employee satisfaction surveys.

Best practice benchmarking

The principle behind best practice benchmarking is very simple: if you want to improve a particular aspect of your organisation or the service it provides, you find another organisation that is extremely good at the aspect you want to improve and you use that organisation as a benchmark for your own performance. Benchmarking involves:

♦ Establishing what would make the difference in the eyes of service users between an ordinary supplier and an excellent one.

♦ Setting new standards in the key areas according to the best practice the organisation can find among other organisations that lead in these areas.

♦ Finding out how the best organisations achieve their superior performance.

♦ Applying both the lessons from the other organisation and new ideas to meet the new standards – and if possible to extend them.

Benchmarking is *not* about aiming to clone the success of other organisations, or indulging in industrial espionage. Nor is it measurement for measurement's sake. The goal is to build on the success of others to improve future performance. Very simply, why waste time and effort trying to reinvent the wheel, when you can be refining its applications and adapting them to your own particular needs?

So, for example, if a voluntary organisation felt that its fundraising campaigns were ineffective it might want to benchmark itself against another voluntary that was particularly successful in this area. The first measurement would be the ratio of revenue generated by a campaign to the cost of running it. By comparing the performance of the two organisations on this measure it should be clear how much better one does than the other. So, for example, perhaps the poor performing organisation achieves a ratio of £3 raised for every £1 spent, whereas the organisation it benchmarks against regularly raises £10 for every £1 spent. The next step is to look at why this is so.

It could be, of course, that the only distinguishable difference between the two organisations is that the high performer has a 'sexier' cause. However, even if that is so a number of questions follow from this finding such as: what does it do to make its mission more appealing to the public and corporate donors? How does it communicate with them? How does it organise its collection channels?

In most cases, an analysis of what the high performer does will reveal other differences such as the marketing mix it uses. With research it should be possible to identify the areas where the high performer is stronger than your organisation. Clearly, some judgement is required here and perhaps some trial and error to determine which strengths are actually making a significant contribution to performance.

Other voluntary organisations might want to benchmark in areas such as the logistics of providing a rural home care service. They might want to compare say the transport per capita costs of providing the service to each customer against that of an organisation that performs a similar service well.

Many of the companies which use best practice benchmarking have actually found it much more useful to benchmark themselves against organisations in very different lines of business. For example, a manufacturing company might benchmark the performance of its delivery fleet against that of a specialist freight carrier. In this way it can learn from an organisation which excels in the activity it is looking to improve. Also, because the organisations are not in direct competition, it is often easier to obtain information about how the benchmarked company manages its operation, to ask for advice or to study the operation at close quarters.

There is no reason why voluntary organisations, too, should not form best practice benchmarking partnerships with companies or other voluntary organisations. It's an 'I'll show you mine if you show me yours' arrangement from which both partners can benefit greatly. After all, what better way to form a working relationship with a company than to ask for non-financial help of this kind? Ultimately, of course, it may also lead to other sorts of partnerships that are mutually beneficial.

For example, areas of performance voluntary organisations could benchmark might include:

♦ Transport and logistics.

♦ Cost of administering payroll.

♦ Cleaning and maintenance of sites.

♦ Recruitment procedures.

♦ Database management.

♦ Career development programmes.

♦ Direct marketing campaigns.

♦ Internal communications strategies.

As with all management tools, of course, it is one thing to understand the theory of benchmarking and quite another to obtain the benefits claimed on its behalf. Consensus – not least on what the organisation hopes to achieve by benchmarking – is vital to its successful implementation. Properly used, benchmarking focuses on 6 important questions:

1. **What shall we benchmark**?

2. How do our **internal processes** work at present?

3. What **measurements** shall we apply?

4. **Who shall we benchmark against**, and how?

5. What is the scope and nature of the **performance gap** identified?

6. How can we translate the data we have gathered into **real improvements**?

Each of these in turn breaks down into a number of subsidiary questions. Question 1 prompts the question 'In which areas will improvements add the most value to the organisation as a whole?'. Question 2 leads on to What, if anything, do we measure at present, and why?' And so on.

Customer surveys

Customer surveys are now such a standard activity in the private sector that customers are complaining they are inundated with requests for comments on the service and products they receive.

The reason companies expend so much effort in gathering this kind of date are numerous. Getting "close to the customer" pays off in more rapid response to customer needs, early warning of failures in service or product provision, and greater customer loyalty.

The most common methods private sector companies use are telephone and postal surveys. However, there are problems with these methods – not least that you only get answers to the questions you ask, and these may not be the most important issues to the customer. Best practice companies supplement surveys with methods of gathering qualitative data. Among these:

♦ **Customer panels.**

♦ **Complaints analysis.**

♦ **Critical incident reporting** (getting front line staff to interview customers who appear pleased or displeased).

♦ **Hot line,** usually toll-free.

Voluntary sector organisations can use all of these approaches and some are beginning to do so.

Summary

Change can be very difficult in the voluntary sector, because voluntary organisations do not have the command and control structures that enable private and public sector organisations to direct change. Rather, they have to achieve change largely through consensus and influence. On the other hand, once consensus is achieved, change is often easier to implement, because the level of genuine commitment is so high.

Comprehensive application of strategic planning, Total Quality Management, benchmarking and customer research will enable voluntary sector organisations to become even more effective at managing change.

There is no reason, if they do, why voluntary organisations should not in due course provide the best practice model for other sectors to follow.

Checklist

1. What **changes** does your organisation face in the next five years? Does it have a long-term plan?

2. How will its **sources of funding** alter in the next few years?

3. Does the organisation have the **skills** to prepare detailed costings for contract bids?

4. Is it investing in **training** to acquire the skills it will need? Is It investing in information technology and research and development to add value in the future?

5. How does it **evaluate its performance**? Which activities get measured?

6. Does the organisation **benchmark itself** against other organisations? What could it do better?

References

1. 'Voluntary Action', Centris, 1993.

2. 'Resourcing the Voluntary Sector: The Funders' Perspective', edited by Robert Hazell and Ted Whybrew, published by the Association of Charitable Foundations (ACF) on behalf of the Charities Aid Foundation (CAF) and the Corporate Responsibility Group (CRG), 1993.

3. Osbourne and Gaebler, 'Reinventing Government'.

4. 'Uncharitable proposals from the state', The Independent, 13 October 1993.

5. Steve Bevan, 'Charities defend their position', PR Week, 21 October 1993.

6. Judy Weleminsky, *'Proposal to split charities' role destructive'*, Financial Times, 16 October 1993.

7. Barry Knight, *'Charity begins with a positive vision'*, The Independent, 26 October 1993.

8. Barry Knight, *'Large charities cannot cope with change'*, Third Sector magazine, 18 November 1993.

9. Nicholas Martin and Caroline Smith, *'Planning for the Future: An introduction to business planning for Voluntary Organisations'*, NCVO, 1993.

10. Clutterbuck, Clark and Armistead, *'Inspired Customer Service: Strategies for Service Quality'*, Kogan Page, 1993.

11. Andrew Cornwell, *'Forward Thinking'*, Third Sector magazine, December 1994, p13.

Chapter 9

How far will the voluntary sector have to change?

Key issues

♦ *Should the voluntary sector adopt more private sector organisational structures?*

♦ *How can it take better advantage of the IT revolution?*

Organisations in the private sector tend to reappraise their structures frequently. In part, this is because new leaders bring in new people and adapt structures to the key people at the top. In part, it is also a direct result of the dictum *structure follows strategy* – as new strategies emerge, the organisation has to change around them. It is not surprising, therefore, that US companies, which operate on relatively short planning horizons, tend to restructure more frequently than Japanese companies, whose strategies remain relatively stable.

In general, such restructuring has remained true to the basic hierarchical model, which has its origins in military command and control systems. In recent years, however, a number of factors have combined to make companies undertake more fundamental reviews of how they can make their structures best fit the business objectives. Among those factors are:

A redefinition of the boundaries of the organisation

Even the largest organisations now recognise that they are but part of a chain, in which value is added at every link. A gut reaction in decades past was vertical integration – buying up your suppliers and your customers to manage as much of the change as possible. The superficial attractions of this approach hid massive inefficiencies (even though the rationale for vertical integration was efficiency) and meant that the companies involved were too broad to focus on doing a few things well. Today's private sector organisations are learning that it is better to invest resources, research and intellect into strengthening their position in the chain and into *influencing* their customers and suppliers. Supplier management programmes often involve extensive exchanges of personnel between the organisation and its suppliers; customer retention programmes seek to involve customers and make them feel part of the company. One US company even invites customers to audit its systems each year!

The mass market-testing of the British public sector is another manifestation of this new perspective on organisational boundaries. The critical question: "what is the proper focus of this organisation's activities?" leads inevitably to a discussion of whether non-core activities should be contracted out. The trend towards subcontracting in the private sector began with peripheral activities such as cleaning, security or running the staff restaurant, then extended into expensive and high-aggravation tasks such as payroll management. More recently, many companies have contracted out their entire IT functions and, in a few cases, most or all of their Human Resources function.

In some cases, these expulsions from the corporate centre have been motivated primarily by monetary savings (which do not necessarily emerge). Where the decision is genuinely strategic, however, it comes from an assessment of how the company can best free up management attention to focus on the things that will genuinely deliver its objectives.

One way of looking at outsourcing is according to its strategic importance to the organisation. In other words, how important is it for us to maintain control over this aspect? how critical to our customers is it?

Activities can then be seen as:

♦ **Peripheral** — every organisation has to have this activity but it adds little or nothing to its reason for being or its ability to fulfil client's needs. In most cases, there will be numerous suppliers available of suitable quality.

♦ **Support** — an important activity, where a major failure would have an impact on the organisation's ability to function and/or on its reputation; but one which is not critical to the business purpose. For example, engineering maintenance in a factory. The more management time and expertise it takes to keep up to date, the greater the case for subcontracting these activities to specialists.

♦ **Strategic** — not a core activity, but nonetheless one that has a significant impact on the organisation's ability to gain or maintain competitive advantage. For example, the Quality management function.

♦ **Core** — those activities, which are the organisation's reason for being.

Voluntary sector organisations have been relatively slow in following this trend. Nonetheless, legitimate questions for trustees and other stakeholders to ask are: "What are our core and strategic activities? Are we giving these sufficient attention and resources? Could we focus more clearly on them if we subcontracted peripheral and support activities to external organisations, either in the private sector or perhaps to other, more specialised charities?"

It is difficult to make valid predictions without examples to draw upon. However, it seems clear that, if voluntary organisations do follow this route, they will increasingly find themselves in new alliances. The goal and challenge will be to ensure that the *clarity of purpose* of the organisation is sustained and reinforced, while other people take on activities that have traditionally been "in-house".

Business process re-engineering (BPR)

Once a business has established its place in the activity chain of its markets, it is but a small step to examine the intricacies of the logistics chain in its own operations. This inevitably leads to structures based on processes rather than functions; to integrating activities according to their ultimate impact on the customer, rather than on keeping similar activities together.

As described in The Business Magazine, BPR "involves fundamentally rethinking and redesigning the processes, which we often take for granted, in order to achieve dramatic improvements in business performance". It requires managers to map and analyse core business processes in detail, from beginning (for example R&D) to end (e.g. checking customer satisfaction after delivery). Departmental barriers are ignored in this exercise – it is the *process* that counts. The result is often a much simpler process, with fewer layers of managers and radically different organisation structures.

At Sun Life, for example, BPR resulted in a change from an organisation based on functional specialists to one based on multi-skilled employees. Seven levels of hierarchy were reduced to three – customer service, managers, team leaders and teams. The results, says 'Management Today', include "40-90% improvements in process turnaround times; 10% reduction in the unit costs of some processes; and 50-80% quality improvements (work performed right first time). Sun Life confidently predicts a significant increase in job satisfaction among employees and greater customer satisfaction leading to increased business".

Again, the voluntary sector has been relatively slow in following this trend. Indeed, our study found none that had implemented a BPR programme. This is, we believe, partially because the voluntary sector always takes time to come to terms with new management jargon. Equally, however, the voluntary sector has greater difficulty in applying concepts such as BPR, which demand a rigorous, centrally-inspired review of all activities. In a consensual organisation, it takes time to achieve the buy-in to carry out such a review.

Nonetheless, the need to evaluate and improve business processes at the organisation level (rather than just at the activity level) will become increasingly urgent. As more private sector companies have experience to share, trustees will ask penetrating questions about business processes in charities.

Closeness to the customer

The increasing emphasis upon customer responsiveness has forced companies to re-examine how best to meet the conflicting demands for flexibility and personalised service on the one hand and consistency and reliability on the other. A variety of solutions has emerged, but common themes are:

♦ Decentralisation wherever possible, to place decision-making authority on customer issues with local units and people on the spot.

♦ Keeping operating units small (some companies deliberately spawn new small companies rather than growing existing companies beyond the point where they know and value individual customers).

The customer in a charitable context is first and foremost the group of people that the organisation was formed to help. At one time, charities that worked with the disabled would have had few disabled people in the organisation. Now charities are making a concerted effort, where possible, to involve their beneficiaries, whether it be on the board of trustees, as employees or through consultation with members. The Royal National Institute for the Deaf (RNID) now has a profoundly deaf person as its chief executive. The Royal National Institute for the Blind (RNIB) has taken steps to involve the visually handicapped at every level of its organisation and has a blind chairperson.

Other constituencies that can be thought of as 'customers' include volunteers, donors and purchasers of contracted services.

Beyond these, there are other 'potential customers' that voluntary organisations should consider. These include people who don't currently use their services but who should be catered for in future if it is to fulfil its stated purpose. In other words, a voluntary organisation should not define customers narrowly as the people whose needs it serves when there are other equally legitimate customers whose needs it does not. In fact, the range of customer constituencies voluntary organisations have to manage is actually much wider than those that private sector companies address. As a result, companies can often view customer segments as distinct markets whereas voluntary organisations face a much more difficult task in juggling customer constituencies.

Each requires a different approach, taking into account their expectations as well as their perceptions of the organisation and their relationship to it. Establishing these expectations and perceptions allows them to be managed. Private and public sector companies gain deep insights into their customers by using a variety of media, from extensive and detailed surveys (e.g. London Underground, British Gas) to videoing customers unpacking computers and attempting to interpret the manual (ICL).

The voluntary sector typically uses a much narrower range of methods to understand its customer segments. However, it is now increasingly common for them to carry out regular donor surveys. So, for example, NCH: Action for Children annually commissions independent market researchers to survey companies' attitudes to charitable giving. Volunteers from a much smaller charity, Christian Mission Aid (CMA) visit local churches to canvas the congregation for details on which charities they prefer to give to and why. Larry Davidson of CMA explains, "This way we can perhaps tailor the way we market ourselves to fit in with what people believe they want from a charity."

Impact of information technology

Faster, more comprehensive information technology helps decentralisation by making it possible to coordinate activities without the need for intervening layers of management. Complex networks of organisations function simply because everyone shares information about customers, order progress and so on. The IT revolution has already brought many benefits, but according to Jim Cannon, a management consultant specialising in the interface of IT and the organisation, these are just the tip of the iceberg. He explains:

"Every technological revolution has its periods of consolidation followed by a time of fast growth. We are on the brink of another technological leap forward as people become aware of the benefits of the latest developments. E-mail suddenly has over a million new subscribers a month. As more and more key organisations have e-mail, it then becomes the best way of communicating. There had been a vast takeoff on the Internet with over 32 million subscribers worldwide."

All this has a powerful effect on the way businesses are run. For example, British Airways has reservations offices around the world. When you phone for a ticket you do not know if you are speaking to Dallas, Bombay or London. Companies are increasingly making use of cheap skilled IT labour in the Far East. With modern telecommunications, the operators or programmers could be in the next office.

As a brief overview, the principal benefits tend to be in the following areas:

♦ **Customer service**. Insurers such as Direct Line have brought major cost benefits to their customers by eliminating middle men and by using the computer to provide faster, more personalised service with a minimum of hassle to the customer.

♦ **Administrative efficiency**. (This doesn't always work to the benefit of the customer – witness the withdrawal of personal contact by banks, who have closed small branches to concentrate backroom activities in regional centres.)

♦ **Marketing**. By gathering more data about customers and using it to time contact renewals, companies have increased sales and customer loyalty.

♦ **Measuring processes**. Systems to monitor activities real time put more power in the hands of customer-facing employees and sometimes in the hands of customers themselves. For example, leading consumer goods importing and manufacturing companies can tell their customers exactly where their orders are in the production system or on the high seas. In some cases, customers can simply dial into the company's computer to find out for themselves.

Many voluntary organisations make excellent and intelligent use of IT. Among examples of imaginative use of computer power are:

◆ Victim Support Schemes have made very constructive use of IT to measure how effective their services are. These schemes help victims of crimes by offering emotional and practical back up. So, for example, if an old person has been mugged, they can be so shocked that they refuse to go out. A volunteer from the scheme will then make sure that he or she is available to go shopping with the victim. Some inner city estates, for example, the Stonebridge Estate in Brent, are so dangerous that volunteers and police go in pairs to visit victims. To check that they were sending people into the more difficult areas, the scheme built a database and compiled statistics on how clients were dealt with. It recorded whether the person was visited once or twice, whether somebody from the scheme went along to the court appearance and if they were referred from the police station or the estates. With this information to hand they could then measure the frequency the more deprived areas were visited and ensure they were adequately supporting the people who needed it most.

◆ Age Concern in Doncaster has a sitting scheme for which it charges £2 an hour. The sitter receives £1.50 of this and the charity takes a 50p cut. It also has a similar scheme which offers cut-price cleaning to the elderly. This is administered by computer so the organisation can monitor the services and instantly see, for example, who is cancelling regularly. Steps can then be taken to find out why.

Margot Lunnon of the Community Computing Network cites the example of the Childrens' Society, which with 100 sites and 1,500 employees, is one of the bigger charities. Its former Computer Development Manager, Ian Pritchard, was intent on making maximum use of IT with the resources available. He promised every office a computer as long as they sent members of staff to be trained on the computers and the software packages. He also overhauled databases and fundraising software.

Not every voluntary organisation is so professional about IT says Lunnon:

"Many charities are willing to invest in the equipment and then fail to train their staff how to use them. This is a terrible waste of resources. I know of one charity where the local offices were begging for computer training, but HQ refused to allow any money to be allocated to it.' Others such as The British Trust for Conservation Volunteers leaves the outlying offices to acquire and train themselves on their own computers. One organisation in North Humberside had raised £2,500 for computer equipment. It then looked into training. Unable to afford the £2,000 quoted, the organisation is now muddling along. Some members of staff produce a document on the machine and then type in the page numbers afterwards because they don't know how to operate the programme.

"Many organisations are using volunteers who know about IT, but this has its own problems. Volunteers aren't always available when you need them. To set up a database, it is necessary to follow a project over a long period. For whatever reason, volunteers often have to break off midway through. In addition, volunteers aren't always in a good position to gain the co-operation of members of staff.

"Volunteers and employees who don't know about IT can make a lethal combination. Some years ago two elderly lady volunteers were given the job of keying in a large survey at one charity. Neither they, nor the employee supervising them, realised that if the hard disc filled up they were liable to lose everything they had typed in. Unfortunately this is exactly what happened."

To many private sector organisations, widespread competence in the use of IT has been a fundamental building block in their restructuring. It is unusual, if not impossible, to use IT strategically without a fairly high level of IT literacy throughout the organisation – not least because the involvement of users and operational managers is critical in understanding where and how real benefits can be obtained.

The voluntary sector in general runs a real risk of missing out on many of the benefits of the next stage of the IT revolution, because it has insufficiently absorbed the possibilities of the current technologies. This is one area where partnership with the private sector could have very great advantages for charities. Instead of waiting for hand-me-downs of obsolete equipment (which can be more expensive to operate than the new generations) voluntary organisations should seek to acquire volunteers from companies, with a view to keeping abreast of the current technology. We recommend that larger charities should have an IT director, responsible for ensuring that the organisation maximises the benefits of computer technology for its operations; and that any charity with a marketing advisory panel should also have an IT advisory panel, to guide its strategic use of technology and to provide expert advice.

The extent to which all this will affect the structure of voluntary organisations is debatable. Better information and control of processes will allow highly centralised voluntary organisations safely to devolve responsibilities to the field. But for federalised organisations the main impact may be to reinforce the structures they have, while allowing them to gain the benefits of greater coordinations; or it may allow the centre finally to exert more control over critical activities to ensure consistent standards. Either way, this is a transition that should be managed. Given that voluntary organisations are not in the IT business, it behoves them to partner either with organisations that are, or with private sector organisations, which have already made similar transitions and which are willing to share their experiences.

While it is clear that this is a difficult area for many voluntary organisations – not least because creating an IT infrastructure can involve a substantial investment – there are nevertheless very serious issues involved. For one thing, IT offers enormous scope for voluntary organisations to become more efficient and at the same time reduce their running costs – something that they have a duty to their donors and beneficiaries to achieve.

In the past few years, many private sector organisations have invested heavily in new technology to reduce their wage costs. Many have been criticised, too, for making employees redundant as a consequence.

However, the fact is that wages make up a very large proportion of service provision in the voluntary sector. As the economy picks up this means that services may be squeezed by increases in earnings which are not matched by increased income and are not directly linked to general price rises. Investing in information technology is one solution.

At the same time, there is a great deal of evidence to indicate that in the past many companies invested millions of pounds in technology which did not deliver the savings or performance improvements that were promised. There are valuable lessons that voluntary organisations can learn from their experience. These include the following dos and don'ts:

Do not:

♦ Invest in **immature technology** (i.e. technology that is still in its development phase).

♦ Allow IT people to **fall in love** with the technology.

♦ Spend so much of the budget on **hardware and software** that you cannot afford to train your people in how to use it.

♦ Go **'Live' with critical services** on a new IT system overnight (as the example of the London Ambulance Service demonstrates it is vital to have a back-up until the reliability of the system can be guaranteed).

♦ **Make employees redundant** who have a deep understanding of how the organisation works and could be re-trained to use the new technology.

♦ Base purchasing decisions on cost criteria alone – reliability and upgradeability are often more important.

Do:

♦ Consider IT as **part of the organisation's strategic plan.**

♦ Verify that the IT supplier can **deliver what is required** (through consultation with other organisations that have used it).

♦ Remember that **industrial tourism** (visiting companies and other organisations) is an extremely cost effective way to carry out IT research.

♦ **Include service contracts** in budgeting for IT.

♦ Make the most of **IT expertise** from the private and public sectors through secondments and donated consultancy.

♦ Ensure that **technology is used appropriately** – i.e. to enhance and support human interaction with beneficiaries, not instead of it.

How to develop structures

A key objective for increasing numbers of private sector companies is to establish structures that are customer-focused, efficient, responsive and capable of continuous evolution. Best practice varies with the nature of the industry and the operating culture – there is no "right" way of structuring a company. However, the broad consensus favours the approach, typified by Sweden's ABB, which has split itself into multiple small units, operating with a high degree of autonomy within a broad framework of strategy and investment controls.

ABB's structure would not be suitable for all companies (it would be difficult to make work in, say, a car factory, although a great deal of devolution of authority can still be made to shop floor teams). It allows a variety of structures – suited to local needs – to operate in the same greater organisation. There may be, for example: a research and development joint venture, several varieties of wholly owned trading companies, a separate subsidiary to manage properties (particularly common among retailers and multinational companies), a captive insurance subsidiary, an IT function outsourced to a facilities management partner, and so on.

Voluntary sector organisations exhibit a wide variety of structures, too, but they are noticeably less responsive to change. As organisational purpose evolves, as social priorities and competitive positions change it will become increasingly important for strategic reviews to lead automatically to reviews of structures.

The evolution of voluntary sector structures

Some voluntary sector organisations already have structures similar to those private sectors aspire to. For example, the British Red Cross was until recently made up of independent groups of the same name, each registered as a separate charity.

Such structures are not without their problems. The local groups of supporters tend to be more conservative about the activities of the organisation. Headquarters often has a great deal of difficulty controlling the branches. One large charity with a network of shops decided some years ago to install electronic tills. This brought outcry from the volunteers who ran the shops. The volunteers, often elderly ladies, insisted they did not need such technology. The organisation in question had to come to a compromise, but not before it had made clear to its helpers who paid the lease on the shops and footed the bill for any maintenance and repairs.

Other voluntary organisations have the opposite problem. Says a consultant for CAF Consultants, the management consultancy for charities, 'Organisations set up with boards of trustees rarely have a flat management structure. The trustees take on the bulk of responsibility for running the organisation because of the controls imposed by legal requirements. This leads to a hierarchical management structure.'

What sort of structures are available to voluntary sector organisations?

The new structures emerging in the private sector are many and varied, but tend to fall into one or other of the following categories:

♦ **The star**

Star organisations are built around a small number of large customers. Everything they do mirrors a customer need. They may typically operate from the customer's premises and may even have absorbed some of the customer's former staff. The majority of people in the organisation are concerned with delivery and they are supported by a relatively small core of experts and administrative staff. The pace of organisational change is partially or wholly dictated by that of the customer organisation, although part of the customer expectation may be that the star organisation stimulates the cultural and technical innovation its own people cannot. Typical star organisations would be IT contractors such as Perot Systems or FI Group.

♦ **The boundaryless organisation**

Boundaryless organisations have abandoned the attempt to maintain the distinction between their operations and those of their suppliers and customers. They operate through networks of expert sub-contractors, mostly smaller businesses than themselves or self-employed freelancers. They enter into joint ventures with customers and freely second their own staff into customers' organisations. They retain their identity by remaining within a clearly defined market niche and venturing outside that niche only in partnership with other, similar organisations. Typical boundaryless organisations are specialist management consultancies. Their culture is pragmatic, strongly individualistic and heavily reliant on relationships.

♦ **The amoeba organisation**

Amoebas grow fast and split instinctively when they feel they are beginning to lose touch with their customers. They also have strong instincts of customer-orientation and innovation. People in these organisations are motivated by the chance to run their own show – empowerment is built into the structures and systems. Amoebas may also be characterised by disorganised systems, especially around the "soft" issues of management – they rarely stand still long enough to put these in order. Typical amoeba organisations might be young, entrepreneurial high technology companies.

♦ **The chemical soup organisation**

The chemical soup organisation differs from the boundaryless organisations in that while the latter has a clear framework of fixed structures, in which people find their own freedom to operate, the former often appears to have no fixed structures at all. The main driving force, outside the top management vision is a motley collection of ever changing project teams. No job or task is permanent; changing circumstances arising from customer need, market opportunity or some internal drive for efficiency dictate that teams and their members come and go constantly and often at short notice. Working in a chemical soup organisation is unsettling, challenging, sometimes frustrating (people often feel that nothing ever gets finished) but the outputs are frequently rapid growth and high returns for both the companies and the people who work in them. Chemical soup companies are often relatively large organisations, going through rapid growth or cultural transformation.

For the voluntary sector organisation, some of these structures may seem completely off the wall. (They are to many private sector organisations, too!) For the moment, most voluntary organisations undergoing restructuring are adopting more conventional approaches. Like companies, they aim to become flatter, more empowering and more focused on fundamental tasks.

CASE STUDY ➤ NSPCC

Back in 1989 the NSPCC realised that it had become inward looking and was not concentrating on its prime purpose -to prevent cruelty to children. With the help of management consultants, the Coverdale Organisation, the NSPCC undertook a major restructuring and a fundamental review of strategy.

Before doing so it consulted every one of its 1300 staff and shaped a way forward with a series of nine regional conferences to discuss key issues.

The outcome of the nationwide consultation was the document 'NSPCC Strategy for the 90s which came before the annual council meeting in 1991 and gained unanimous approval. This document paved the way for a reform of the organisation's management structure.

Explains director Chris Brown, 'Our strategy provided a vital sense of direction and has been absorbed deep into the heart of the NSPCC, governing, guiding, and channelling every thought and action towards preventing cruelty to children. It has prompted a revolution.'

In the restructuring that followed, eight new regional directors were appointed and responsibility for budget and projects in their area was devolved from head office. An internal inspection unit was established to check on standards throughout the organisation. And, as more responsibility was devolved, Brown was released from a stifling bureaucracy to fulfil his role as spokesman nationwide, travelling widely meeting and encouraging staff.

Since the upheaval, the NSPCC has gained an increasingly high profile and funds have swelled – £41 million was raised in 1993, a 33 per cent increase on the previous year. The 64 teams working with abused children have now been expanded to 88 through cost effective partnerships with other agencies.

CASE STUDY ➤ Childrens Society

The Childrens Society campaigns for vulnerable youngsters as well as providing support for the most disadvantaged and their families. In the late 1980s the society had become a disparate organisation scattered throughout England and Wales made up of isolated teams of five or six people. Managers came from different backgrounds -social work or fundraising – and had problems communicating and working together; this resulted in a lack of cohesive management which was proving demotivating and inefficient.

The society set out to bridge a gap between the director and the workforce, foster a common approach and language and create a cohesive management. It brought in management consultants who provided training for directors and senior management together through a series of five day courses. This was followed up with participants back at work.

After the society had developed a common purpose, it embarked on a major restructuring. The six regional offices were replaced with twelve in which social work and fundraising managers worked side by side.

The director, Ian Sparks was also encouraged to change his management style. Senior staff filled in an appraisal questionnaire and Sparks met regularly with a consultant to discuss his management style. He now tries to give people the space to think and contribute.

Summary

There is no doubt in our minds that voluntary sector organisations need to look more imaginatively at structures. Among questions that need to be asked are the following: What structure would best meet clients' needs? How flexible does it need to be at the client interface? In the backroom operations? Could we make better use of ad hoc and permanent teams?

In doing so, however, it is important that voluntary organisations do not simply adopt practice from other sectors without criticising it deeply. For example, says Tom Jennings, formerly of IBM:

"It concerns me that parts of the voluntary sector are trying to become too businesslike, when business is moving in the opposite direction. Take the example of management tiers. Some voluntary organisations are putting in additional layers of management on the advice of government agencies, which say they need them to be more accountable. Yet people inside the organisation don't see any reason to do so and we all know that business is trying to strip management layers out."

The main problem we foresee, however, is convincing stakeholders of the need to change structures. After all, most voluntary organisations have much the same structures now as when they were founded – why change what has worked so well so far? In some cases, the existing structure may well still be the most relevant and effective. However, every organisation, whatever sector it is in, should ask itself regularly – at least once every two or three years – *does our structure truly enable us to maximise the way we use our resources?*

Checklist

1. If you were starting from scratch, what **structure** would best fit the needs of your organisation? What changes would enable the current structure to more closely resemble the ideal?

2. How can the organisation **alter its focus** to get closer to customers/ end-users? For example, should customers be involved in designing new services and fundraising campaigns?

3. Are there **opportunities to use IT** to link up with other voluntary organisations to add value? Do employees and volunteers have their own PCs which could be networked?

4. Could **partnerships with IT providers** enable the organisation to work more effectively?

References

1. James Richardson, *'A third lane on the infobahn?'*, NCVO News, December 1994/ January 1995 p.14.

2. Ranu, Nicole, *'Rebuilding from Scratch'*, The Business Magazine, January 1994.

3. Oliver, Judith, *'Sun Life's New Policy'*, Management Today, August 1993.

Chapter 10

Can the voluntary sector exist alone?

One of the most significant trends in the voluntary sector over the last few years has been the growth of partnership relationships between voluntary organisations, business and government. These relationships – known in the United States as public purpose partnerships – involve a much greater degree of involvement by the company partner than simply writing a cheque. Typically the company is prepared to invest considerable time and effort into developing a relationship that best meets the requirements of all parties.

The growing popularity of these sorts of relationships reflects a move away from companies simply throwing money at the voluntary sector in an unfocused way, towards a more strategic view of community investment. In the partnership model companies see their support for voluntary organisations not in terms of old-fashioned philanthropy, but as enlightened self-interest. In the best partnerships the business partner recognises that it has a vested interest in supporting the communities in which it operates and that strategic alliances with carefully chosen voluntary partners can bring real benefits to the business. As such, companies in these sorts of relationships require a more professional relationship with voluntary organisations. For voluntary organisations which can meet these needs, the emergence of the partnership model opens the door to a much more integrated approach to addressing social issues.

Public purpose partnerships

In the UK, public purpose partnerships already cover a wide range of activities such as:

♦ Supporting **education**.

♦ Fostering **urban regeneration**.

♦ Tackling **crime**.

♦ Supporting the **arts**.

♦ Cleaning up the **environment**.

♦ Reducing **illiteracy** among adults.

♦ Tackling **homelessness**.

♦ Assisting **young offenders** to find jobs.

These partnerships take many forms, including:

♦ Companies focusing their community investment activities on **a single voluntary partner** or group of partners for a given time period. For example, the Argyll Group, which owns the Safeways chain of supermarkets, gives its entire charitable budget to the St John Ambulance.

♦ Companies **supporting community projects** developed in conjunction with voluntary partners. For example, Community Links in East London is supported by a number of local companies.

♦ **Cause Related Marketing**, whereby products or services are promoted to consumers on the understanding that companies will donate part of the revenue from sales to the named voluntary partner. For example, Kleenex owned by Kimberley Clarke recently promoted its paper products through a campaign with the RNLI (Royal National Lifeboat Institution). Coupons on promotional products allowed customers to send £5 to the company to receive a model of a lifeboat. The company donated £1 to RNLI for every model bought.

♦ **Local partnership alliances**, where a group of companies co-ordinate their community investment efforts to support local voluntary projects. For example, the Hull Compact aims to foster and develop education business activities.

♦ **Employee volunteering schemes**, where companies encourage employees to support specific voluntary activities through voluntary work. For example, Eurocamp has a special relationship with Feed the Children, Superdrug has a partnership with NCH: Action for Children and Kingfisher has one with Crime Concern.

The difference between sponsorship and partnership

Sponsorship is usually a relatively passive relationship. At its best it becomes a partnership as both parties work closely together in planning and in ensuring mutual benefit.

In general sponsorship tends to be relatively short-term, tied to a specific project or contract. The relationship is not expected to evolve beyond the contractual. Partnership is for the longer term and carries an expectation of increasing understanding, cooperation and effectiveness of working together.

Companies considering sponsorship tend to ask a number of basic questions in considering voluntary organisations to collaborate with. Among them:

♦ Is there a **clear project** to support?

♦ Is the project **realistic** and properly budgeted?

♦ **What will it do** for our business?

♦ What **reputation** does the voluntary organisation have? Will it enhance, compliment or reduce our own?

♦ To what extent can we **link** this initiative with others in our portfolio?

♦ What is the **best way** we can become involved (money? project support? goods in kind?)

A high degree of demonstrated competence in managing sponsored projects can lead rapidly to more substantial, long-term partnerships, as some of the cases in this chapter testify.

Building effective partnerships

Between companies in the private sector, there is a lot more talk about building partnerships between customers and suppliers than genuine experience. Suppliers, having apparently more to gain from the relationship, are the main seekers of such partnerships; but the partnerships that do take place tend to be ones initiated by customers, who are concerned to maintain the quality and reliability of supply and who perceive the economic benefits of a few long-term, stable relationships, as opposed to a lot of unstable ones.

Many of the arrangements referred to as partnership sourcing bear about the same relationship to the real thing as a holiday fling does to an enduring marriage. A genuine partnership is an intimate relationship of sharing over the long term. It involves a great deal of self-knowledge and a willingness to really get to know the other party. Genuine partnerships are characterised by the way in which the parties share:

♦ **Information**, including their medium- to long-term plans.

♦ **Learning** (especially from mistakes).

♦ **Accountability**.

♦ **Rewards**.

♦ **Resources** (including people and skills).

♦ **Goals**.

The same basic principles apply to relationships between the private sector and voluntary organisations. A relationship can be:

♦ **Transactional**
Commitment is limited to the project or contract in hand
benefits may be unequal
duration may be quite short
there is little or no requirement of cultural affinity

♦ **Alliance**
commitment extends beyond contractual to the spirit of the agreement
benefits tend to be mutual but different
duration is medium- to long-term
some cultural affinity required

♦ **Partnership**
commitment extends to integration of objectives

benefits are shared; each side is concerned that the other received the benefits expected

duration tends to the long-term

strong cultural affinity is important

Amanda Jordan of National Westminster Bank community investment department points out that "most voluntary sector organisations are still suspicious of businesses as partners". However, our survey reveals that voluntary organisations tend to have a much more positive view about the potential for forming partnerships with private sector organisations. In some ways, this is not surprising, for the balance of power in these relationships still tends to rest with the private sector company, as the source of funding. Companies may well be coloured in their perceptions by their experience of customer – supplier relationships, seeing the voluntary organisation more in the guise of supplier than potential partner.

Creating genuine partnerships between voluntary organisations and public sector organisations may be even more difficult. The nature of government contracting arrangements, with mandatory tendering and a heavy reliance on contractual agreements, mitigate against long-term relationships. Yet such relationships do exist and flourish. In every partnership between voluntary organisations and public sector agencies, which we are aware of, there have been:

♦ A **strong match** between the goals of the agency and those of the voluntary organisation (indeed, in most cases, the task has been fundamental to the purpose of the voluntary organisation).

♦ A willingness on both sides to **address problems** and inefficiencies in operations in an open and constructive manner.

♦ A recognition that **both parties must gain** substantial benefits from the arrangement.

♦ A willingness to **extend the relationship**, with increasing interchange of expertise and personnel.

The following cases illustrate how some voluntary organisations have used the spectrum of transaction, alliance and partnership to further their goals.

CASE STUDY ▶ Feed the Children

Feed the Children has developed a series of close partnerships with private sector companies as a strategic response to its operational needs. From FTC's inception in 1990, it aimed to acquire and distribute goods rather than funds and it has been consistently delivered to children in the world's trouble spots £2 of aid for every £1 of cash donation. At a transactional level, it recently received 30,000 obsolete corporate blouses from Nationwide Building Society. Other organisations donate seconds and surplus cereals, medical equipment – almost anything that might be of use to children who have nothing.

Transactional relationships frequently (and quickly) evolve into alliances. For example, Oxford University Press started by giving product and soon began to provide expertise in warehousing. International transporters TNT approached FTC with a large volume of food parcels it had collected from its depots around the UK, for distribution in the former Yugoslavia. FTC, at that time still learning how to deliver goods, suggested that TNT take the food to Split itself. TNT has since donated a second-hand truck and trailer. In both cases, the increasing involvement by the company has been good for employee morale and motivation.

Among alliances that have evolved into partnerships is FTC's relationship with Eurocamp. Until approached by FTC, Eurocamp replaced and destroyed all its equipment after two seasons. The initial transaction was to agree to give FTC all its old tents, cooking gear and so on. But both Eurocamp and FTC benefited by highlighting the relationship in the company's brochures. As the two organisations grew closer, Eurocamp employees have become more and more involved in promoting and fundraising for FTC. Children's paintings, produced in camp competitions, now hang in hospitals in Bosnia. The two organisations now review regularly how they can deepen their collaboration.

Jon Scourse, Corporate Liaison Manager of FTC used to be marketing director of shoe retailers Millwards. "It always used to niggle me that old shoes were thrown away. So we hatched a scheme with FTC, where, every time a child buys a new, larger pair of shoes, we ask the mother if we can keep the shoes the child has grown out of. We started in 1991 and have just passed the 500,000 pair mark in 1994. After food and medicine, access to shoes is the most important thing for these desperately poor children. The staff at Millwards have been very motivated, designing and running a whole series of events to fundraise for FTC."

One of the earliest partnerships for FTC was with transporters Christian Salvesen. "This was always going to be a time-limited relationship," says FTC's chief executive David Grubb, "but that didn't stop it being very much a partnership. Christian Salvesen was interested in the marketing value of being seen to be in Bosnia; we desperately needed help in transporting goods to where they were needed.

"I wrote to 13 trucking companies in the UK to say we would be going into Eastern Europe and would they help. There was a big recession in the industry at that time and Christian Salvesen were the only ones at that point to say yes. They gave us a transportation capability freely when we had nothing. They were very surprised by the response from the workforce. Drivers were queuing up to donate their holidays.

"Christian Salvesen's main interests for sponsorship lie with schools, road safety and trucking safety. We learned from them how to operate our own fleet of trucks. We didn't become a burden; we learned the logistics skills quickly that they were willing to teach us. We no longer have a partnership, but we can still go back to them at any time for advice on trucks, driver training, maintenance and so on."

CASE STUDY ▶ National Westminster Bank

Nat West has moved in recent years to develop a number of strategic partnerships with voluntary organisations, among them one with Citizens Advice Bureaux. Explains Amanda Jordan of the Bank's community investment department: "It was a good strategic use of our money to help people get their finances back in order. We have gone from giving conscience money to more of a partnership.

"In addition to financial support, we have given advice to CAB about designing premises and CAB has helped our internal working party on advances policy. It gives us anecdotal information about Natwest. We take that information seriously and use it to change the way we deal with customers.

"We have no interest in undermining their independence. We have a clear policy of offering information and advice to customers, but at a certain point it's appropriate they should have an independent source of information.

"It took time to build confidence in each other. Some people in the Bank showed hostility and suspicion, seeing CAB as a bunch of amateurs and radicals, who would cause us problems. Some people in CAB saw us as a conservative influence interested only in money. It's still not a trouble-free process. We've made a lot of progress at national level, but we still have a long way to go locally.

We have taken someone from our branch network to manage the relationship. This is very useful in letting CAB know what help and advice we can give them."

Another strong two-way relationship is with SCIP, the schools curriculum developers. Explains Jordan: "We had a long-term relationship with SCIP, but it never amounted to much more than giving money. Then Carol Kay, the new chief executive got involved in helping us develop a programme to promote financial literacy in schools and joined our steering committee. SCIP wrote the materials and are now getting involved in training our staff, who will deliver the programme in schools."

It wasn't all smooth sailing, both parties admit. "One of the issues we had to resolve," says Kay, "was whether the intellectual property belonged to SCIP or Natwest." There was also the question of whether SCIP would survive. "They had faith that I would pull it off," recalls Kay, "and that helped our confidence. We see the relationship as a partnership because the benefits on both sides are quantifiable and there is a genuine exchange of expertise."

Case Study ➤ Threshers and Radio Lollipop

Threshers partnership with Radio Lollipop, which provides a radio service to children's hospitals, was initiated by the charity in 1979, when it was near to shutting down for lack of funds. So the story goes, one of the radio station's staff was buying drinks at Threshers for a last broadcast party, when he had the inspired idea. If the charity paid for all the off-license's plastic carrier bags and put its own logo on them, would the company sell them on the charity's behalf, rather than give them away, as was the practice then? Explains Jayne Bridges, Threshers marketing director:

"One of our directors had a child in hospital who had listened to Radio Lollipop. He realised that, for some children – for example, those needing bone marrow transplants, who have to stay in hospital for a long time – the radio station was their only lifeline. Play therapy is integral to a child's development, so Lollipop was important in preventing their education regressing.

"It has now become an integral part of our business to focus customers' minds on raising large sums of money for this charity, to the extent that we raised over £1 million over five years. Most has come from customers, although when customers make big purchases, we may give them the bags and pay for them ourselves.

"The arrangement appealed to us because we were having difficulty identifying a national charity we could get close to. Being in drinks and cigarette retail we have to be careful to choose the right partner. We already had a lot of fundraising at branch level, for local causes such as hospices, but even £1000 is a drop in the bucket to a national charity. The association with Radio Lollipop has given us a focus for local staff events, too, especially in areas where there is a children's hospital."

Case Study ➤ Kingfisher Group and Crime Concern

Tim Clement-Jones, until recently Kingfisher's company secretary, explains the reasons behind the formation of what has become a very close partnership – so close, in fact that he has become chairman of Crime Concern.

Crime prevention is one of Kingfisher's four corporate social responsibility priorities. Its relationship with Crime Concern dates from the charity's earliest days. Kingfisher worked with Crime Concern to identify a project which, says Clement-Jones "had all the right elements which back up the image of our retail brand with their target audiences – essentially consumers – and which had the right appeal to our corporate target audience of local and national opinion-formers and Group employees.

"The project we chose was called the Greenwich Junior Citizens Award Scheme. This was founded by Sergeant Joe Lynch, the local Crime Prevention officer and the Greenwich Crime Prevention Panel and essentially was a scheme in which children between the ages of 10 and 11 came for half a day to a selected site to take part in simulated scenarios in which they can learn key crime prevention and safety messages.

"With Crime Concern we developed a number of pilot projects, first changing the name to 'Crucial Crew' – after an opinion poll of primary school pupils showed this to be the overwhelming favourite – and over a period of two years sponsored a number of pilots in England and Scotland and Wales.

"It proved to be overwhelmingly popular. Almost all the schemes which we initially funded have continued to thrive with local sponsorship.

"An important part of the scheme is the participation and sponsorship of local emergency services and utilities. After two years of pilot schemes, we produced a pack designed to show local authorities, schools, police etc, how to set up and run a successful Crucial Crew scheme. A copy of the manual was distributed to every local authority and Police Force in the Country.

"After the production of the manual in 1992 our next step was to help Crime Concern with the resource required to roll out Crucial Crews across the Country. It was clear in many cases that the manual was not enough by itself to ensure the rapid growth of Crucial Crew schemes. We decided to do this by sponsoring a member of staff at Crime Concern whose role it is to advise local organisations on Crucial Crew in addition to the guidance that they receive in the manual and in particular to advise on how to attract local sponsorship. There are now at least some 40 Crucial Crews across the country.

Our connection with the scheme is well known. Certainly when it comes to looking at the evidence of market research and our own research amongst opinion formers and amongst other major FTSE 100 companies, the connection between Kingfisher and crime prevention generally and Crucial Crew in particular is much more clearly the case than with any other of the causes that we support."

To understand how and why these sorts of partnerships have developed it is necessary to consider the context in which companies and voluntary organisations now operate. A number of factors underpin the move away from the old notion of philanthropy towards partnerships.

Companies face growing expectations from employees and other stakeholders, including shareholders and the public, to act in a socially responsible manner. Some of these expectations are enshrined in law, such as the duty of care regulations under the 1990 Environmental Protection Act, which makes firms responsible for the safe disposal of their waste even if they are paying someone else to do it. Others, such as companies' involvement with local community projects to help the disadvantaged and links with schools represent a combination of enlightened self-interest and altruism.

There is also greater awareness among the business community in general of the benefits of strategic partnerships. This is indicated by an increase in joint venture activity between companies across a range of industrial sectors. For example, joint ventures in the car and information technology sectors are increasingly common, not just across companies but across national borders.

Voluntary organisations, too, have had to adjust to greater competition for funding and in many cases reductions in government funding, making them more aware of alternative forms of support. At the same time, the vacuum created by the State's withdrawal from community service provision is increasingly being filled by the private and voluntary sectors. Where there is scope for collaboration it is logical that the two sectors should combine forces.

In other cases, local government has played an active role in fostering partnerships between the private and voluntary sectors. For example, a number of Training and Enterprise Councils (TECs) and local authorities have formed strategic partnerships with their business communities aimed at forging a common vision and strategy for the economic development of their localities. Initiatives from central government such as the invitation for local areas to create partnerships to bid for a 'Business Link' (one-stop shop for business support) franchise have also encouraged the move towards partnerships.

The convergence of all these factors means that the once clear-cut boundaries separating the public, private and voluntary sectors are becoming blurred. As we approach the next century it is inevitable that a debate – only in its infancy at present – will gather momentum over the sort of society we should become. At the heart of that debate will be the role and the responsibilities of the three sectors and the extent to which partnerships between them can support social needs and aspirations.

What all this means for voluntary organisations is that in the second half of the 1990s the soil is particularly fertile for the growth of strategic partnerships across sectors. Voluntary organisations that are able to create meaningful relationships with business partners stand to reap enormous benefits, not least in terms of continuity of funding. For example, it would be much easier for them to be able to plan projects three or five years in advance with a committed partner rather than having to raise funds on an annual basis.

To realise the potential that these sorts of partnership offer, however, there are a number of important issues for voluntary organisations to address. In particular they must find ways to get closer to potential partners in order to better understand:

♦ **Why companies support the voluntary sector**.

♦ **How the two sectors see each other** – particularly in terms of each other's strengths and weaknesses.

♦ **What companies initially look for** in voluntary partners and vice versa.

♦ **The potential for new kinds of strategic partnerships** in the future.

♦ **How to target** potential partners.

♦ **How to make the initial approach**.

♦ **What companies expect** from a successful partnership and how to avoid exploitation.

♦ **What sorts of support** both partners should expect from the relationship.

♦ **How to manage** these sorts of relationships.

Challenges for partnerships

In a thought-provoking paper in 1994, BITC's David Grayson painted a picture of private sector companies and public sector agencies facing radical upheaval in their operating environments. He points in particular to seven factors – constant change, new focus on the competitive advantage of regions, education and training being seen increasingly as a tool of economic development, "glocalisation", clustering of growth businesses, a drive to "upscale" local development programmes, and targeting society's excluded. Each poses different and severe challenges for community partnerships.

Much of Grayson's analysis is applicable to partnerships between either private or public sector organisations and the voluntary sector. For example:

♦ **Permanent change**:

Are the managers of voluntary organisations scanning their environment frequently and widely? Who takes responsibility for this role vis-a-vis the partnership, as opposed to the individual partners?

♦ **Competitive advantage**:

Have we pulled together the right mix of partners? Would we achieve more by bringing in erstwhile competitors?

♦ **Glocalisation**:

Can we increase local impact by linking up with similar organisations in other regions or countries?

♦ **Small business clusters**:

Can voluntary organisations link up not just with big companies, but with networks of smaller businesses?

♦ **Upscaling**:

Do we have strategies for, as Grayson expresses it "leveraging additional responses"? Most charities are set up to ameliorate a social problem. It takes a leap of vision and far greater resources to eliminate a problem. Whose interests could be mobilised to make this a possibility or even a likelihood? And can we as an organisation cope with the trauma of making itself obsolete?

♦ **Including the excluded**:

How can we help beneficiaries become more involved in managing/ influencing organisations operating on their behalf? Can we tap the vast and increasing reservoir of people who have little or no stake in modern society, with a view to their helping both others and themselves.

A recent example of what can be achieved is the BEAT programme, run by Birmingham's Probation Service to help young offenders find jobs and keep out of trouble. The young people are paired with mentors, ordinary people from the local community, who offer their friendship, guidance and advice. The majority of mentors in the pilot scheme were themselves unemployed, some for long periods, and a proportion had themselves been young offenders some years before. Not only did none of the young people in the scheme re-offend, but the mentors gained so much self-confidence helping someone else that many of the long-term unemployed also found jobs during the period of the scheme.

A broad extrapolation from Grayson's summary of social change might be that whole new areas of social need will open up in the coming decades, along with new opportunities for fruitful partnerships between sectors and between the voluntary sector and groups within the community. These do, indeed, pose challenges.

Why do companies support voluntary organisations?

The starting point for voluntary organisations wishing to develop effective strategic partnerships with companies is a greater understanding of what potential partners from the private sector are looking for. If they are to build mutually beneficial relationships, voluntary organisations must recognise that the key to such partnerships lies in the convergence of objectives. The aims of both parties must be a sufficiently good fit to enable them to work towards common goals. The effect, otherwise – to add another analogy – can be likened to two men rowing the same boat in different directions. At best the boat will move in the intended direction of the stronger rower; what is more likely, however, is that a great deal of energy will be expended in going round and round in circles. Worse still the boat may capsize.

An obvious, but fundamental, issue is that of motivation. It is essential that voluntary organisations have a realistic understanding of what motivates companies to become involved with the voluntary sector. Clearly it would be naive to assume that all companies support voluntary projects out of the kindness of their hearts alone. A cynical and in most cases equally misguided view would be that companies have a secret agenda that involves using the voluntary partner as a cover for unscrupulous ends. (In the very small number of cases where this happens the voluntary partner is nearly always equally culpable itself for ignoring the danger signals and entering into the relationship in the first place.)

Nor is it sufficient to assume that a company is motivated simply by some sort of nebulous notion of the public relations value of involvement with a voluntary organisation. The best run companies no longer operate their community involvement activities on such vague lines.

If, as is quite likely, a company believes that some of the positive image of the voluntary organisation will rub off on it in the public's mind, and if the voluntary partner is aware and happy for the association to work in that way, then it is sensible on all sides to recognise that that is the motivation. In this case one of the explicit objectives of the partnership should be to publicise its achievements to key audiences.

Indeed, often one of the strongest benefits a voluntary organisation brings to the partnership is a high public profile and a reputation as a worthy cause. For that reason alone, voluntary organisations should be extremely careful that they understand the motivations of private sector partners to ensure that their image does not become tarnished by the wrong sorts of bedfellows.

It would be wrong, too, to assume that improving image through association always works in one direction. Many companies enjoy a very high professional standing among the public. A company such as IBM, for example, has much to offer a voluntary partner in terms of enhancing the voluntary's professional image.

As an integral part of the research for this book, we conducted our own survey among business leaders and voluntary organisations to find out more about how these partnerships work. In particular, we hoped to identify areas of the relationships which could be improved.

Between November 1993 and January 1994, the views of 600 chief executives and chairmen and 200 voluntary organisations were sought on a variety of issues contained in two separate questionnaires. In particular, we were keen to understand more about the way the two sectors see each other both in terms of perceived strengths and weaknesses; and the factors that affect decisions on both sides to form strategic partnerships. The results were revealing.

Our findings confirm that community involvement by most companies is in fact prompted by of a mixture of altruistic and business motives. This perception was echoed by the voluntary organisations in our survey when they were asked how the business case was best made.

However, a sizeable minority of companies said that their motives were wholly altruistic (23 per cent) while only one voluntary organisation felt best results would come from appealing to altruistic motives. Interesting as this finding is – it suggests perhaps that voluntary organisations believe companies are more hard-nosed than they actually are – motives will vary from company to company and project to project.

In another survey conducted at the end of 1993, Andrew Wilson at the Ashridge Management Research Group (part of Ashridge Management College) looked at how and why companies give to voluntary organisations. His findings were based on a postal survey of 2,000 companies located in the UK, including the 1,000 largest businesses, plus a sample of 1,000 small and medium-sized firms.

The Ashridge survey revealed that overall the level of company support for the voluntary sector held up well during the recession, with the larger companies continuing to dominate the scene. It also showed that by no means all large companies adopt a professional approach to community investment.

Only 44 per cent of the large companies which responded to the Ashridge survey said they had a formal policy on charitable support. Slightly more than half had a specific budget set aside for the purpose. (Our own survey indicated a much higher percentage of companies had some kind of policy on the type of voluntary organisation they prefer to support and the sorts of relationship they try to develop. The large difference between the findings of the two surveys reflects perhaps that our sample was a smaller number of very large companies. If so, then this would suggest that formal policies are more common in the very largest organisations.)

However, when we asked voluntary organisations whether they had a formal policy on the relationships they seek with companies, only 57 per cent gave a positive answer. As a basic starting point, creating a policy would seem an essential step in developing relationships that deliver results. But our findings suggest that in this critical area voluntary organisations actually lag behind companies and still have some way to go to establish a coherent approach to partnership. More promising was the response of several voluntary organisations and companies which indicated that they are in the process of developing policies across a broad range of external issues.

Based on the Ashridge findings, Wilson draws the very reasonable conclusion that rather than thinking of the world of corporate support as being divided into small and large players, a more accurate picture is one of companies that can be categorised as adopting either a hands-off approach, or alternatively a partnership approach to their involvement with voluntary organisations.

The former, he says, is characterised by companies that, whilst wanting to give something back to society by helping a charitable organisation, seek to delegate this function as far as possible by making the voluntary organisation responsible for decisions on how the money can best be spent. Within such companies the process of corporate giving is externalised and management decisions are passed over to the voluntary organisations themselves. Typically, the company is seeking a minimal level of involvement and accepts that it will receive largely external benefits (for example, improved corporate image). In effect, the company requires voluntary suitors to function much like any other supplier by offering the best deal available and a quick, efficient and effective service. This approach was summed up in a comment from one respondent to the survey:

> "We're in business to make money, not run charities", he said. "When we choose to donate, it's your job to do something with it."

In contrast, Wilson says, companies which have adopted a partnership approach look to internalise the management of their corporate giving as much as possible. Typically, these companies are prepared to invest resources in investigating the potential benefits of different types of charitable support. They contribute management time in building links with voluntary organisations and in return expect to gain internal benefits such as staff development opportunities and improved staff morale. In this case, the company seeks to work closely with voluntary organisations, jointly managing the programme of corporate support within the context of a partnership. Again the approach was epitomised by a comment from a respondent who said:

> "We need them [voluntary organisations] to act as an agency or consultancy. That way we can work with them to put into action properly structured events."

It is with the latter of these types of company that we are mainly concerned in this chapter. Both the Ashridge survey and our own suggest that companies which take the partnership approach are more likely to have a formal policy. Where a formal policy exists a much clearer view of an individual company's motivation can be gained.

Our research indicates that many of the more enlightened companies now have such policies and are happy to discuss the way they manage their community investment programmes publicly. For example, in a recent article in the 'Financial Times', the chairman of Kingfisher Plc Sir Geoffrey Mulcahy outlined his company's four principles of community involvement:

> *"Underpinning our policy is the belief that a healthy business needs a healthy community. Policy is directed by a social responsibility committee, which includes our corporate affairs and human resources directors, as well as one of our non-executive directors, Lady Howe. The committee meets quarterly and each of our businesses reports to it twice a year."*

He went on to outline four guiding principles for Kingfisher and its operating companies – which include household names in UK retailing such as Woolworths, Superdrug, B&Q and Comet, as well as Darty on the European mainland.

> *"The first and firmest is that any issue we support must be relevant to our mainstream commercial objectives. It may be by addressing social problems which ultimately affect our profitability, for example, by improving our corporate reputation. We support crime prevention because this ties in with the high street environment. The safer people feel, the more likely they are to come out and shop.*

> *"The second principle is that we are very clear about the target audiences we are trying to reach. While our businesses will focus cause-related marketing on their customers, our audiences at the centre include opinion formers, shareholders, employees and national and local government. We support women's issues because two-thirds of our employees are women.*

"Principle number three is to limit ourselves to a manageable number of issues instead of trying to cover the field.

"Finally we try to build up a leadership position, to give us a competitive edge with particular target audiences. This may be by anticipating issues which will become important, or by not shrinking from those that may prove controversial. We are helping, for example, to fund a Stonewall study on attitudes of and towards gay men and lesbians in the workplace."

The point here is that for those who make the effort to find out, the motivation of Kingfisher and its operating companies is clearly set out. The four principles provide would-be voluntary partners with clear guidelines to ascertain their fit with the organisation's aims.

In the same article Mulcahy outlined the way these guiding principles are used to make decisions on voluntary partners.

"It is important to recognise that the objectives of a voluntary organisation are different to those of a commercial one", he notes. "The essence of successful projects is to identify the mutual benefit for each of those involved and then for them to work in partnership. Once we have identified a particular cause – such as homelessness or equal opportunities – choice of project becomes the next step. This is as important as the choice of charity which must be well-run and have an acceptable brand.

"We will ask ourselves how material the project is to our business objectives. How innovative is it? What value can we add? How much support do they want, relative to what we can afford? We will look at the quality of the organisation's management and operating plan and at how they will evaluate progress and report back. We may also seek the views of the relevant government department."

This then is the approach of one major community investment player from the business world. Not all companies have such well organised or articulated policies, of course, but many are moving in this direction. To engage in a profitable dialogue with them voluntary organisations need to follow developments closely and to ensure they are in step with the aims of a target company. To do so, they require antennae in the business community and in particular contacts on the corporate social responsibility conference circuit.

What do companies look for in voluntary partners?

It is clear from the Kingfisher example above that the motivation and objectives of companies are likely to vary depending on the nature of their business. So, for example, the projects that a retailing organisation such as Kingfisher supports – in areas such as crime reduction and women's issues – may be very different to those favoured by a chemicals and pharmaceutical company such as ICI, which might want to position itself as a champion of environmental issues. This means that voluntary organisations, which in the past may have taken little interest in the differences between companies, must become more familiar with the business world if they are to anticipate the changing priorities of companies and instigate new types of partnerships which meet those needs.

It is also apparent that different business sectors are moving at different speeds. For example, the growth of environmental pressure groups in the 1980s undoubtedly influenced the pace with which companies in industries such as the oil and chemicals sectors developed corporate social responsibility policies. The strength of public feeling meant that these companies would almost certainly have developed policies even if new legislation to prevent pollution had not been introduced.

What is perhaps surprising about the last few years is that moves towards greater social responsibility in other industries has continued despite recessionary pressures in the UK economy. As the economy comes out of recession the number of companies looking to form strategic partnerships with voluntary organisations is likely to increase.

The Ashridge survey also found that certain causes were more likely to attract the support of companies than others. In particular, the findings indicated that:

◆ **Local charities** were the most popular cause among the companies that responded.

◆ Other types of charitable organisations in the top five were those that help **children and youth**; people with disabilities; medicine and health; and national charities.

◆ By far the **least popular** type of charities with companies was religious causes.

◆ Other charities in the bottom five of most popular causes were those that support animal welfare; housing; the arts; and international charities.

However, as interesting as these findings are in broad terms, they simply confirm that some voluntary organisations are 'sexier' to companies than others. Based on these findings, for example, it would appear that a local charity involved in researching medical cures for children with disabilities will find it much easier to find corporate support; while an international charity providing housing for gifted animal artists may find it considerably harder. In the future, we believe that the key to forming strategic partnerships will lie increasingly in finding companies with which voluntary organisations have a good fit. By targeting the right companies this means that even the less popular causes should be able to attract support. Other general points that emerged from the Ashridge research were:

◆ **Small businesses** are almost twice as likely to support local charities rather than national charities.

◆ The most popular form of charitable support is a straightforward **cash donation**. The second most popular form is sponsorship.

♦ The data also underlined the **wide variety of activity** that takes place under the broad term of 'corporate giving' – more than half the companies were involved in three or more different types of activity.

♦ The least popular method of corporate giving is through a **company trust fund**. This lends weight to the widely held perception that most corporate charitable support is not handled in a tax efficient manner.

♦ **Secondment and staff volunteering** occurred in just over 30 per cent of the companies that responded.

♦ **Decisions about charitable giving** are spread amongst a wide variety of people. Most frequently, it is the chief executive who decides, although the chairman, board of directors and a range of other people also have an important influence over the decision-making process.

♦ 24 per cent of firms responding to the survey said there were **no benefits to the company** from supporting charities, even though between them these companies gave almost £600,000 to charities in 1992 in one form or another.

♦ The three most **common benefits** of corporate giving perceived by companies were an improved company image; being seen as part of the local community; and improved staff relations and morale.

However, Andrew Wilson also notes that many respondents put forward several reasons why there companies were involved with charities. Some of these were altruistic, while others were self-interested. He observes:

"This underlines the point that the motivations for corporate giving, and the benefits that are derived from it, are not one-dimensional. Rather, an individual firm's propensity to offer support is likely to be affected by a complex web of drives and incentives."

Wilson's point is well made. In order to build the sort of relationship which will form the basis of an effective partnership, it is necessary to delve deeper. Only by attempting to understand each other's motivations and expectations in a given set of circumstances can effective relationships be forged. That said, in any partnership both parties should be clear on two basic questions:

♦ **What they want** out of the partnership
♦ **How they will judge** its success.

Business and voluntary perceptions

In a great many cases partnerships between voluntary organisations and companies work extremely well. However, to gain an insight into how these relationships might be improved we asked both sides how they perceived their partners.

Companies in our survey showed both a high level of agreement and disagreement over the strengths and weaknesses of the voluntary organisations they dealt with.

There was general agreement about the strengths and weaknesses of voluntary organisations.

Strengths:

♦ Having a **sense of purpose** (92 per cent of responding companies agreed).

♦ **Capacity to innovate** and accept new ideas (77 per cent of companies agreed).

♦ **Ability to communicate** (62 per cent of companies agreed).

Weaknesses:

♦ Knowledge of and interest in **the company's objectives** (89 per cent).

♦ **Organisational structures** (76 per cent).

♦ Ability to **relate on equal terms** with private sector partners (75 per cent).

♦ **Quality of management** (63 per cent).

Experience on 'ability to deliver what they promise' was clearly mixed, as 50 per cent of company respondents said this was a strength and 50 per cent a weakness!

However, the list of perceived weaknesses suggests that the reason companies do not look for 'ability to understand our needs' and 'high quality management' may be that the track record of the voluntary organisations they have dealt with in the past have been poor in these areas.

Voluntary organisations were equally forthright about the strengths and weaknesses of the community investment departments of companies they deal with There was general agreement that these departments are strong in:

♦ **Marketing expertise** (73 per cent of voluntary organisations agreed).

♦ Knowledge of and interest in **the company's objectives** (70 per cent).

♦ **Quality of management** (68 per cent).

♦ **Ability to communicate** (65 per cent).

♦ **Sense of clear purpose** (59 per cent).

And weak in:

♦ **Capacity to innovate** and accept new ideas (71 per cent).

♦ Ability to relate to (voluntary organisations) on **equal terms** (63 per cent).

Slightly more than half of voluntary organisations also criticised community investment departments on their ability to deliver what they promise.

In many respects, our survey confirms the received wisdom about the way the voluntary and private sectors relate to each other. However, it was interesting to note that elsewhere in the survey when we asked what companies look for in a voluntary partner (and what voluntary organisations think they look for) the findings indicated that companies are less demanding than voluntary organisations expect in a number of key areas. In particular, companies had lower expectations of their voluntary counterparts in terms of: high quality management; demonstrably efficient use of resources; the ability to understand the company's needs; and the ability to work as a team with company managers.

The overview, then appears at first sight to be a healthy situation, with the general perception of voluntary organisations about what their performance should be exceeding what companies actually expect. However, we were not able to test whether companies' low expectations in these areas were an accurate picture of the importance they attach to them or were the result of experience of poor performance by voluntary organisations they have dealt with in the past. In other words, we cannot be sure whether companies genuinely require a lower level of performance than voluntary organisations think; or whether they expect less only because they have a generally lower opinion of voluntary organisations compared to their own standards. Clearly, if the latter is the case voluntary organisations have some work to do in convincing private sector partners that they can be regarded as their equals.

Partnerships of the future

One point that is clear from our research is that it is no longer enough for voluntary organisations to take a scattergun approach to selecting corporate partners. While it is true that in a few cases historical links or personal contacts will be enough to bind a voluntary organisation to a corporate partner, in the future there will be an increasing onus on voluntary organisations to develop relationships with companies with which they share real mutual interests. Voluntary organisations which take a lead role in developing the case for such relationships stand to gain greatly.

We believe that in the new environment of the late 1990s partnerships between business and the voluntary sector could look very different. But a step change in thinking is required if voluntary organisations are to realise the potential that exists. There are already some early indications of a revolution taking place in the way business and the voluntary sector interacts.

For example, at first sight there may appear to be little synergy between a campaigning environmental organisation such as Friends of the Earth and an industrial polluter. Yet, while it is true that FoE is unlikely to benefit in the long-run from a close association with an unrepentant polluter, developing a partnership with a company which currently has a poor environmental record but which has a strategic goal of improving its environmental performance could be extremely beneficial for both, provided that the voluntary organisation manages the relationship on a tight rein.

For example, what began as an adversarial relationship between Friends of the Earth and the chemicals company Fisons has since developed into a constructive dialogue. Where once FoE pilloried Fisons for the negative impact its operations had on the environment, it now advises and monitors the company's moves to become more environmentally responsible. The partnership has a good fit with FoE's mission to clean up British industry, and makes a very good flagship for a model it is anxious to persuade other companies to adopt. At the same time FoE knows that if the company should backslide it can embarrass it publicly all the more effectively for reneging on its commitments.

For its part, Fisons knows its environmental image will enjoy a much more rapid rehabilitation with the public as a result of its constructive relationship with FoE. It also benefits from the environmental expertise that FoE has developed from its work in this area. What binds the two partners together in this case is that they both have a strategic reason for working towards improving the environmental performance of the company.

As companies become more aware of the interests of their stakeholders – customers, employees, shareholders and suppliers – there are increasing opportunities for strategic partnerships with voluntary organisations which enhance the brand image of the company. We have already discussed the growing trend towards cause-related marketing in Chapter 5, but there are clear benefits for companies and voluntary organisations in partnerships where the association is not used so explicitly as a marketing or fundraising tool.

So, for example, there is a natural fit between companies such as Mothercare and voluntary organisations such as the NSPCC and Save the Children which champion children's welfare issues. Here the rationale of the partnership flows from the concern of the company's customers – predominantly parents – with the protection of children everywhere.

Similarly, it is not difficult to see why a pet food manufacturer might support the RSPCA, since the company would be well aware that its customers take an interest in the prevention of cruelty to animals.

Other companies are linked to voluntary activities by less direct but equally logical concerns. As a large employer of graduates, for example, Shell UK has a vested interest in the UK educational system and plays an active part in supporting educational projects including its sponsored Science and Technology Education Project (STEP) award scheme, whereby students in their final year of study are matched with companies to work on specified projects. In the future, a typical basis for a strategic partnership might be where:

♦ **Both organisations have a direct interest in an outcome** (e.g. Fisons and FoE).

♦ The mission of the voluntary organisation is **directly relevant to the company** (e.g. Crime Concern and Kingfisher).

♦ The voluntary organisation has a **high profile among the company's stakeholders** (e.g. Mothercare and Save the Children pet food manufacturer and RSPCA, The Body Shop and conservation projects to preserve endangered species).

♦ There is **clear synergy** between the two partners (e.g. Shell UK and schools projects).

♦ The company has **an established reputation in a particular area of voluntary activity** (e.g. Barclays Bank or Digital and the Arts).

♦ A business leader takes a **personal interest** (e.g. Waterstone's the Bookseller has a close relationship with Shelter partly because of the personal concern of its chief executive Tim Waterstone in the plight of the homeless).

Targeting potential partners

In order to create the sorts of strategic partnerships that will provide real benefits in the future, voluntary organisations will have to become more adept both at understanding the needs of business and at interpreting and managing their own needs.

To do so they will have to do their homework. A number of basic areas should be covered before an approach is made. These include:

♦ An assessment of the **voluntary organisation's fit** with the company's objectives for community involvement.

♦ A thorough **understanding of what the company does** including its market positioning, key products and services and the positioning of any brands. This analysis should include an understanding of the company's main competitors and also take account of recent developments.

♦ A clear idea of whether the proposed partnership should be based on **developing a specific project** tailored to the goals of the target company, or whether an application for **core funding or support** is more appropriate.

♦ The **scale of involvement** sought – this will be determined in part by how wide a portfolio of voluntary partners the company favours. Clearly, if the company prefers to commit itself to a single voluntary partnership for a given period then the scale of support proposed would be greater than if it allocates its favours more widely.

Where a target company has a formal policy statement for its community investment objectives this should be the starting point for research. These can usually be obtained direct from the appropriate department (usually community investment or corporate affairs), or may be gleaned from their annual reports (available on request from the company and kept at Companies House) and from Press coverage.

In fact, a great deal of general background on a company can be extracted from its annual report, including the names and special interests of non-executive directors who can sometimes be used to add leverage to a proposal. Other sources of information include: the trade press for the industry in which the company operates; internal magazines and newsletters (often available in the reception area), business sections of national newspapers; talking to people who know the company and stockbrokers reports.

Before approaching a target company, voluntary organisations also need to find out whether the company prefers to support individual projects or to provide core-funding to voluntary organisations.

Some 25 per cent of companies in our survey said that they preferred to support individual projects rather than voluntary organisations and vice versa some 23 per cent preferred to support organisations rather than projects. A similar picture emerges from the voluntary organisations, with 34 per cent preferring to develop specific initiatives or projects, then seek business support and 20 per cent preferring to establish relationships first then seek suitable joint ventures. Just over half the voluntary organisations, however, preferred to choose between these approaches according to circumstances. Clearly this last approach provides the greatest flexibility in tailoring partnership proposals to companies.

Our survey also indicates there is a divergence of opinion among companies over whether to spread commitments and resources thinly over numerous voluntary organisations and initiatives or to focus on a few carefully chosen initiatives. Nearly 40 per cent of companies preferred the latter, but slightly more opted for a balance between the two – leaving 20 per cent who preferred to distribute their largesse far and wide. To some extent this will reflect the structure and culture of the company. A heavily decentralised, multi-site organisation will often tend towards local autonomy in allocating giving, while a more centralised company will often find it more convenient to focus on a few selected voluntary organisations. But the survey results also reflect the state of maturity of companies' giving behaviour – the leading edge companies tend to mix some local autonomy with a highly focused approach at the centre.

Voluntary organisations were also divided over the issue of focus, with 11 per cent scattering their net, 26 per cent preferring to build close relationships with a small number of companies, and the rest preferring a mixture of both approaches.

Most companies still think of relationships with voluntary organisations as charitable support despite the language of partnership.

To some extent this is because the private sector remains blinkered in its view of the opportunities available. However, many companies (and voluntary organisations) also seem unclear about the difference between sponsorship and partnership. We define the two terms as follows:

Sponsorship is where a voluntary organisation provides certain services for a payment or gift. For example, a company might sponsor an event – say at Lords cricket ground – whereby the voluntary organisation provides hospitality for corporate clients or managers.

Partnership is where both organisations share an interest in an issue and work together to try to do something about it. For example, as a high street retailer Kingfisher Plc has a vested interest in tackling street crime and has therefore formed a partnership relationship with Crime Concern whereby the two organisations operate joint programmes.

Making the initial approach

Our research indicates that despite the business logic of partnership relationships with voluntary organisations, there is still a long way to go before the business community at large becomes attuned to the potential benefits they offer. Certainly our survey suggests that businesses are generally less concerned about building effective partnerships. Even where they use the language of partnership, the practicalities of relationship management suggest that they are often thinking more of traditional charitable support. Only four companies in our survey said this was their main approach, while 46 per cent relied upon voluntary organisations to approach them. Others used a mixture of both and one company employed an outside agency to help make the choices. The survey also indicated that only 21 per cent of companies keep a database of potential voluntary partners.

This suggests that voluntary organisations have an important role to play in educating companies. Unfortunately, people in the voluntary sector often don't see the opportunities for working with business in other ways because they focus their attention on the short-term aim of obtaining money. In the next few years, however, they will have to make the initial approach and do most of the running to get public purpose partnerships off the ground.

At present, matchmaking by voluntary organisations appears to be equally variable. Some 13 per cent of voluntary organisations in our survey chose targets by size and known policy of giving; 29 per cent by relevance of their activities to the companies' business objectives; others used a mixture of both. Use of sponsorship agencies was remarkably low in our sample, with only two voluntary organisations saying they employ an outside agency to make approaches.

Where voluntary organisations take the initiative they generally make approaches through a mixture of personal contact and letter. Only 11 per cent said that approaches generally come to them from companies. 56 per cent maintain a database of potential business partners as part of their marketing management.

Part of the problem for voluntary organisations is knowing **who** to contact. Asked who makes the decision in their organisation, the companies gave varying replies:

- Community affairs manager/ director   19%
- The corporate affairs manager/ director   14%
- Another director   5%
- The board   10%
- A management steering committee   29%
- An employee steering committee   14%

Other responses to the question included:

- A grants committee for small grants
- Board subcommittee
- Independent trustees
- Senior managers
- Charitable trust
- Charities subcommittee (centrally) and locally by the operating businesses
- Local business chief executives
- Staff vote
- Group trade marketing manager
- Group charities committee

A handful of companies surveyed (7) generally delegate decisions to the local operating units. The rest of our sample were roughly equally split between taking decisions at head office or sharing the responsibility between head office and the field.

To make the initial approach effective, voluntary organisations should ideally identify:

- **Who decides** what gets put in front of the decision making committee.
- **Other influencers** such as non-executive directors with a particular interest in community investment or social issues who might be used to add leverage to a proposal.
- The **timing** of budget allocation or community investment programme decisions.
- **Mutual contacts** who could make an introduction.

In addition, some companies provide guidelines for what a proposal should include. For example, the community affairs department at Allied Dunbar reports that it has on occasion returned proposals that were in an inappropriate format to a voluntary organisation with recommendations for changes to the application. But not all companies are as conscientious and failure to follow guidelines may result in the application and the research behind it being wasted.

As far as possible voluntary organisations should always put the case for the partnership in a business-like way – this is slightly different to presenting the business case, which may or may not be the best approach depending on the policy of the company concerned and the strength of the case itself. There is no point, for instance, in putting forward a proposal with a hard business rationale if it does not stand up to hard business criteria such as quantifying the effect on the bottom-line. However, where there is a good fit with the company's business this should be emphasised and facts and figures used to substantiate it wherever possible.

In the future, as companies become more aware of the effect community investment programmes can have on staff morale, we would expect to see decision-making on which voluntary organisations to support increasingly devolved to employees. For example, Virgin Atlantic already tries to involve employees at all levels in its charity giving policy. For over five years, the company has operated its 'change for good' policy whereby the loose change of passengers is collected at the end of the flight for a charity chosen on rotation every six months by Virgin's Healthcare Foundation and cabin crews. Since 1988 this one programme alone has raised over £5 million for UK-based charitable causes.

As employees become more influential in the decision-making process there will be greater scope for voluntary organisations to market themselves and their projects to these audiences. With the company's permission the voluntary might promote itself via presentations and the distribution of information within the company. Voluntary organisations that find ways to work closely with the company's management to maximise employee involvement will enhance their appeal.

What do companies look for in a voluntary partner?

Beyond the initial approach it is clear that voluntary organisations which conduct the dialogue with a target company in a professional manner will stand a better chance of developing a true partnership relationship.

In another part of our survey we sought to compare what businesses look for in the voluntary organisations they support and the voluntary organisations' perceptions of what companies were looking for.

The picture that emerges from the results is one of relatively strong agreement on almost all counts, although the companies seem to be generally less demanding than voluntary organisations expect.

Overall, this would seem to bode well for the future of partnership relationships. However, again we were not able to test whether companies' low expectations of teamwork come from experience of failure in the past, from poor penetration of the concept of partnership throughout British firms generally, or from a perception that the best way to manage the relationship is to let the voluntary organisations get on with what they do best and not interfere.

	Companies %	Voluntary organisations %
Relevance to the company's priority areas of community interest	100	96
High quality management	44	53
Demonstrably efficient use of resources	61	80
Ability to present well-thought through and argued plans	63	70
Ability to understand the company's needs	39	63
Ability to work as a team with you and your colleagues	42	51
Willingness to incorporate an agreed process of evaluation of results and a project review	42	40

What should partners expect from each other?

An integral part of developing a partnership relationship with a company is clarity about the sorts of support the voluntary organisation is seeking. A growing number of voluntary organisations now recognise the benefits of a more sophisticated approach than simply asking for money. The status of 'partner' within the relationship can also be greatly enhanced by having a clear idea of what the voluntary organisation will provide in return for company support. Voluntary organisations should also consider what they require from companies in terms of the commitment of senior managers. Where partnerships prosper it is usually because they enjoy the enthusiastic support and commitment of the company from the board of directors down. Many companies encourage voluntary partners to make presentation to the board. Again, these should be handled with the utmost professionalism.

A recent study by Michael Fogarty and Robin Legard entitled 'More than Money' and published by the Joseph Rowntree Foundation, (March 1993), examines the well-respected Community Investment Programme run by IBM in the UK. Fogarty and Legard conclude that, whilst cash is always welcome, voluntary organisations can gain far more than straight gifts of money from companies. Significantly, too, they find that the transfer of skills from private firms to voluntary organisations emerges as the greatest source of 'added value' from a relationship with IBM.

At the same time, Fogarty and Legard observe that some voluntary organisations are able to offer a service to their corporate partners, ensuring that the notion of a two-way relationship is explicit in the partnership. For example, the Terrence Higgins Trust not only benefits from support from IBM but also contributes by advising the company on issues of HIV and Aids in the workplace and by backing an IBM-led initiative to raise awareness of these issues among other companies.

In another case, a two-way partnership grew out of the existing relationship between the company and Haven Products which provides employment for people with disabilities and is based near IBM's factory in Greenock. The relationship has led to Haven – which started out as a workshop offering undemanding charitable jobs – becoming a supplier of quality commercial components to IBM and other companies.

Fogarty and Legard's wider analysis of the IBM community investment programme suggests lessons for both the voluntary and private sectors.

Lessons for voluntary organisations can be summarised as:

♦ **Preparing for partnership**: the most effective relationships between companies and voluntary sector organisations are founded on mutual advantage. (The organisations supported by IBM expected to give as well as to get, as did the company).

♦ **A clear and confident approach**: voluntary sector organisations should not be afraid to take the initiative and show the company what a two-way relationship could achieve. A clear divide emerged during the study between the tentative and unimaginative approach of voluntary organisations which did not know what to expect from a company like IBM and the more confident and targeted approach of those who were more familiar with the company. Voluntary organisations need to have a clearer view of their own potential and the ways in which company support might add to it.

♦ **More than money**: 'in kind' contributions can be more valuable than cash. Money is only worth as much as the services or equipment it can buy. Often, therefore, it will be more profitable to ask for personal input, equipment, or facilities from a company, and to 'cut out the middle stage of money' as one voluntary project organiser put it. Voluntary organisations also need to achieve an efficient and businesslike operation; companies can help them make better use of information technology, for example, and management skills for making sound strategic and financial planning decisions.

♦ **The people resource**: the transfer of skills from the private sector to voluntary organisations emerged from the study as the greatest perceived source of 'added value' from a relationship with IBM. Voluntary organisations welcomed the company's policy of encouraging volunteering among present employees and those who have recently retired. In general, IBM staff were valued not only for their own services but for providing access to the company's other resources and for opening doors elsewhere in the private sector. Organisations which seek the involvement of company managers may hope to receive help in improving their strategic planning, setting targets and monitoring progress. The involvement of individual members of staff from IBM proved a stepping stone to increasing help from the company. In only one case did local volunteers become frustrated by the extent to which IBM employees were dominating their activities. Training courses in Creative Management Skills offered by IBM were also highly rated.

Lessons for companies can be summarised as:

♦ **Replication**: firms are individual, with their own markets, their own communities and their own special interests. Clearly, it is not possible to duplicate another company's community investment programme, but many of the principles underlying IBM's approach are relevant to other companies.

♦ **Basic principles**: a considered and businesslike approach to community investment based on mutual advantage is a style that any company can adopt. IBM's achievement is founded on a strong commitment from its board and chief executive. Any company should be capable of creating a climate of collaboration with voluntary organisations by making the personal service and skills of its staff available and taking steps to encourage volunteering. A main ingredient in the success of IBM's model for community investment is the company's holistic approach: not just reacting to specific requests for support, but sitting down with the voluntary organisation to take an overview of its needs. Any firm could do the same either through its own staff or by enlisting the help of intermediaries such as community trusts or Councils of Voluntary Service.

♦ **Scale of support**: the scale of some IBM contributions is such that only a large company or a consortium of companies can provide it. But even small and medium-sized companies can encourage employee volunteering by offering time off and company approval and can contribute the advice of non-executive directors, experienced managers or specialists. While smaller firms probably cannot afford a substantial community relations department, they can seek help with publicity and promotion through intermediaries such as community trusts.

♦ **Timing**: a business that decides to have a coherent community investment programme and to transmit it throughout the company can put the necessary processes in place in a relatively short space of time. IBM's community investment programme, for example, has only taken on its present shape since the late 1980s.

Fogarty and Legard draw three conclusions from their study:

1. The type of partnership between a company and voluntary organisations as illustrated with IBM, and based on mutual advantage, have proved valuable both to the company and in empowering voluntary organisations.

2. Although the IBM model has distinctive features, it is not too exceptional to be replicable in other companies by drawing on IBM's experience for lessons that can be adapted to the particular circumstances of the company.

3. The promotion of partnerships between voluntary organisations and private business depends on both sides showing initiative. Voluntary organisations need to be aware from the start of their own potential and the range of company support that could be made available.

Managing the relationship

Over and above the issues already discussed there are a number of key issues involved in managing partnerships between voluntary organisations and companies. These include:

♦ Clear definition and agreement of objectives on both sides.

♦ A genuinely high level of mutual trust.

♦ Flexibility.

♦ Effective planning to achieve both sides' objectives.

♦ Good communications.

♦ Sharing of problems at an early stage.

The importance the two sides attached to these issues in our survey are indicated in the following table:

What they considered to be the most important aspects of partnerships

	Companies %	Charities %
Clear definition and agreement of objectives on both sides	92	90
A genuinely high level of mutual trust	63	75
Flexibility	35	51
Effective planning to achieve both sides' objectives	56	71
Good communications	75	75
Sharing of problems at an early stage	42	54

Companies also suggested other aspects of the relationships, including:

♦ Good **evaluation and feedback** on a regular basis.

♦ **Commitment by the board**.

♦ Ability to **deal with 'real' issues** – not problems on the surface.

♦ Ability to help **motivate staff**.

♦ **Businesslike approach** on both sides.

♦ Good financial and resources **planning**.

♦ Clear lines of **accountability and responsibility**.

♦ **Review** milestones and approved points set and met.

- Clear identification of **deliverables**.
- **Risk analysis**.
- **Time planning**.

Setting clear and achievable objectives is a critical issue yet it was given a relatively low emphasis placed by both sides on evaluation and project review gives cause for concern. Until companies ask for measurement, they are unlikely to change the practices of voluntary partners.

However, it is notoriously difficult to set measurable targets for people-related projects.

Relevant "hard" measurements might include:

- Number of **people reached** by an initiative.
- Number of **recruits** to the charity/new customers to the charity.
- Volume of **press coverage** for the initiative for the company/for the charity.
- Degree to which sponsored event is **self-supporting**.

Soft measurements might include:

- Changes in public perception about the cause.
- Changes in public perception of the company.
- Clients' perceptions about the service quality.

What can go wrong with partnerships

As with all relationships some friction and problems are to be expected. In general, where these occur they should be dealt with before they threaten the long-term objectives of the partnership. Most can be resolved if they are handled appropriately at an early enough stage. However, our survey revealed some generic problems on both sides which we have chosen to list to help those involved in partnership relationships understand the issues that can niggle their colleagues from the other side of the fence. Many of these we suspect are based on stereotyped perceptions which will become less of a problem over time, but at present they are real enough to those who experience them.

The most commonly cited problems with partnership relationships
As seen by companies:

- Failure to appreciate each other's different objectives.
- Poor communications.
- Failure to meet and agree timetables.
- Independence – charities don't always give reference to the company.
- Lack of professionalism.
- Over estimation of management timetable devoted to the charity.
- Lack of focus – too many projects running at one time.

- Need for a clear and succinct brief – to reduce management time/ 'obvious' issues not dealt with.
- Recognition of the need to be accountable.
- Marketing abilities.
- Financial management and resources/ budgetary control – going back and asking for more.
- Lack of understanding of financial pressures with a plc.
- Failure to appreciate a need for 'quid pro quo' relationship.
- Lack of understanding of each other's aims/ motivation.
- Under-estimation of each other's skills and resources.
- High staff turnover in voluntary organisations.
- Over-ambitious objectives.
- Different pace of activity.
- Attitude of private sector managers to voluntary sector.
- Saw voluntary organisations as off-putting – over-inflated, smug idea of their own importance – especially the arts.
- Tend to employ Sloanes – puts people off.
- Mistrust on both sides.
- Cost under-estimates.
- Unrealistic mutual expectations or mismatch of expectations.
- Low level of business acumen.
- Lack of flexibility.
- Inadequate administration capability.
- Reluctance to accept evaluation.
- Ignorance of commercial pressures, objectives.
- Failure to recognise need for commercial return.
- Different management styles.

And by voluntary organisations:

- Lack of communication.
- Lack of clearly defined objectives.
- Lack of voluntary sector management – usually try to apply business rules to the charity.
- Unrealistic targets set for ventures (time and financial).
- Company expecting and the charity offering more than can be provided (promising too much – both sides can be guilty).
- Lack of appreciation by the company of the cost of developing proposals and implementing them.
- Long lead time re company budgeting.
- Inability to appreciate each other's needs and motivation.
- Partners want innovative projects and not to reinvest in proven success formulae.
- Change of goal posts mid project.
- Voluntary expected to do a lot for a little money.
- Lack of communication between marketing and community department.
- Patronising acceptance rather than realistic commercial respect for skills in the voluntary sector.
- Assumption that any money is better than none.
- Corporate Community Investment departments are peripheral not mainstream.
- Poor understanding of voluntary sector.

- Generally it is not so much sectors but the individuals representing the private sector partner. It is often to do with relationships, trust, communications, as well as strategic management objectives.
- Lack of understanding of the environment that the voluntary sector operates re. professional advice, photocopying, people resources and decision making
- Inability of private sector to develop 'strategy' in the partnership if not similar to own mission statement.
- Lack of long-term commitment.
- Concealing their motives – honesty pays.
- Asking companies to donate without a clear case being presented.
- Decision making processes of charities.
- Frequent change of personnel in companies leading to lack of continuity of partnership.
- Charities' inability to sell themselves strongly enough.
- Identifying any advantages for the sponsorship company.
- Lack of imagination from company.

A mismatch of expectations?

Perhaps one reason why problems occur is because companies and voluntary organisations have different expectations over the nature of partnership relationships. Our survey found that more than three out of five companies expected partnerships to last just for the duration of the project, compared with just over a third of voluntary organisations. Nearly half of the voluntary organisations expected partnerships to become long-term, multi-project arrangements, compared with only one fifth of companies.

Voluntary organisations are also more optimistic about the growth of partnerships with business. While 55 per cent of companies expected to increase the role of partnerships with the voluntary sector, 94 per cent of voluntary organisations expected to increase their partnership activity over the next two years.

To recap, there are a number of clear steps for voluntary organisations seeking to establish effective partnerships with companies. These can be summarised as:

- **Doing the homework** – identifying and targeting companies which would make good partners.
- **Making the initial approach** – opening a dialogue and presenting the business case for a strategic partnership.
- **Setting targets** – agreeing clear, measurable targets that are relevant to all parties and which can deliver real benefits.
- **Managing the relationship** – ensuring good channels of communication and accountability to facilitate the achievement of objectives and make the partnership work.
- **Renewing partnerships** – building on past successes to ensure that partnerships are truly long-term and have a strategic focus.

Each of these steps requires careful management planning according to the particular circumstances of the organisations involved.

If partnerships do continue to grow rapidly – which we believe they will – there may be greater opportunities to share best practice between the business and voluntary sectors. However, there is a major discrepancy between the voluntary organisations and the businesses about the potential for transfer of management expertise and ideas from the voluntary sector. While 80 per cent of charities believe there are 'lessons the private sector can learn from the way voluntary organisations are managed', only 34 per cent of companies agree!

In the future, voluntary organisations that find ways to convince companies that there is real scope for learning in both directions will do themselves, the voluntary sector and British business a great service. One of the most useful techniques is for voluntary managers to put themselves in the shoes of business managers to make their point.

By analysing the voluntary operation in terms that a business manager understands the facts often speak for themselves. So, for example, rather than talk with missionary zeal about what the organisation is trying to achieve, a voluntary sector manager might explain that he or she is responsible for providing X number of services to Y number of customers with a staff of Z people scattered in different locations around the region. For good measure they could then throw in the size of the budget. Alternatively, faced by a private sector manager who says he is responsible for a budget of £1 million the case might be made another way by the voluntary manager pointing out that that is almost a third of his or her own. As CAF's David Wickert explains:

"I regularly meet directors of companies who say I probably won't understand the sorts of sums of money they deal with. Then they tell me they have to manage an annual throughput of £15 million. I usually nod my head and agree but what they don't realise is that that represents about a month for us."

Better yet, at present there are a number of very topical issues in the private sector where voluntary managers have directly relevant experience. If voluntary managers can win the trust of business managers so that they confide their concerns about for example devolving responsibility to work teams, then the voluntary manager can say 'yes it is difficult, but this is how we do it'. In this way, voluntary managers can begin to win the respect they deserve from their private sector colleagues. In doing so they will greatly enhance the potential for relationships between the two sectors which are partnerships in the true sense of the word.

CASE STUDY ▶ The South Bank Homelessness Project and IBM

The London Enterprise Agency' Guaranteed Accommodation, Training and Employment (GATE) project originated in the concern of IBM staff based at London's South Bank about the nearby 'Cardboard City' where homeless people sleep rough. It was seen as both a human problem – especially for young people and a public nuisance. It was a particular nuisance to IBM, whose visitors arriving by rail or tube would be confronted with this environment before they reached the haven of IBM's high tech offices.

When appeals to the voluntary sector, the government and the police produced no action, the view grew among staff that the company should take the lead in establishing a demonstration project. What emerged was an imaginative scheme where young people could be offered immediate accommodation and training. This was done under strict conditions but with the guarantee of a job at the end with British Rail, a major local employer. As a final step, a major housing project was to be made available, offering young people a permanent home. The scheme has been so successful, not least from the point of view of British Rail, who have been delighted with the quality of young people recruited.

The impetus came from IBM, as one of the 21 members of the London Enterprise Agency (LENTA) and gained the support of Citibank and Shell, neighbours of IBM on the South Bank. The LENTA members agreed to provide £2,000 each to pay for a project manager. LENTA also commissioned research which produced the outlines of a scheme. A board was set up with IBM's location manager in the chair. His initial contribution involving 'a day a month or more', was identified as:

♦ Presenting to the board the initial proposal.
♦ Leading the brainstorming process by which the project was clarified and support secured from a range of employers.
♦ Setting clear objectives, including mission statements, targets and timetables.
♦ Arranging and leading a launch at IBM South Bank, financed by the company and taking an active part in the TV and other publicity which followed.

The need for a broader understanding on all sides of what the sectors have to offer was underlined by David Grayson of Business in the Community, writing in The Ashridge Journal:

"There are skills and ideas in government, business and the third sector which can be transferred. Though the borders between the three are increasingly blurred, in the UK at least, there is little in the way of common language or debate. Without such discussion, two polarized scenarios for the future emerge.

"In the first, the gap between the have and have nots increases inexorably so that an exclusive society emerges. There is resistance to tax transfers to the poorer sectors of society. As a result, the poor urban underclass feel no obligation to abide by the rules of civil society.

"In the second, a skills revolution takes place. Resources are found to help with industrial and community restructuring. Citizens realise they have reciprocal responsibilities to government and are increasingly able to learn and achieve skills to the best of their individual levels."

Summary

In researching this book we have been struck again and again by the enormous potential for a two-way exchange in ideas between the voluntary and private sectors. Much of what we've highlighted has been in the area of voluntary organisations learning from business. Yet, the alternative trade is probably of equal value.

So what are the skills that can be transferred from the voluntary sector to the private sector and vice versa? Many of them have already been referred to in passing. They include:

♦ **Visionary leadership**. The voluntary sector has demonstrated great success in motivating the commitment of people through influence, vision communication, and challenge. The private sector has greater experience and success in creating management structures that ensure control over complex processes. Both have lessons to teach in the development of effective first line supervision.

♦ **Empowerment**. Because it relies on volunteers at all levels, the voluntary sector has had to empower. The way, in which the private sector is now learning to support empowerment with information, training and infrastructural changes, will increasingly be a source of transferable know-how.

♦ **Employment policy**: The voluntary sector tends to be more radical in the areas of equal opportunities and job flexibility; the private sector has led the way in opening job opportunities for the older employee. Says NCVO's Tim Dartington: "Our sector has gone for younger people, partly because we can afford them."

♦ **Lean, flexible organisations**. Voluntary organisations tend naturally to have small hierarchies and minimal overheads, because they try to minimise the proportion of funds spent on overheads.

♦ **Particular expertise** in dealing with social problems such as consumer debt (of interest to banks and building societies) personal health matters (of interest to insurance and health companies) innovative housing solutions (of interest to developers and financiers) crime (of interest to retailers) and so on...

References

1. Sir Geoffrey Mulcahy, *'The four principles of corporate giving'*, The Financial Times, 25 October 1993.

2. Andrew Wilson, *'Corporate Giving: 'It's your job to do something with it'*, Action Research, Ashridge Management Research Group.

3. *'Partnerships between the private and non-profit sectors'*, Clutterbuck Associates, January 1994.

4. Michael Fogarty and Robin Legard, *'More than Money'*, Joseph Rowntree Foundation, March 1993.

THE SURVEY
Partnership between the non-profit sector and business

Report of a survey carried out for Kingfisher Plc by Clutterbuck Associates between November 1993 and January 1994.

BACKGROUND

The survey is an integral part of a research project sponsored by Kingfisher Plc as part of a series of investigations of best practice in corporate social responsibility.

Phase I of this research looked at best practice in community involvement, responsible employment and other key social responsibility areas such as the environment, from the point of view of business. It resulted in the book *Working with the Community,* published by Weidenfield in 1990.

Phase II examined best practice in management of social responsibility issues by business. This, too, resulted in a book, *Actions Speak Louder*, published by Kogan Page in 1992.

Phase III is a broad look at best practice in management of non-profit organisations, and, in particular, how they can form effective partnerships with business and other sources of funding. It is widely assumed that businesses choose their non-profit partners on the perception of the professionality with which those organisations carry out their activities. This survey aimed to test that assumption and to examine how closely aligned business and the non-profit community are in their perceptions and expectations of each other.

The survey is also timed to coincide with the recent increasing demands placed upon charities by the Charities Act 1993 in terms of financial probity and effective management.

The questionnaire was mailed to 200 charities and 580 chief executives/ chairmen of companies. Many of the companies are members of Business In The Community. We received replies within the deadline from 70 charities and 57 companies – sufficient for a valid sample of both audiences.

The business respondents represented a wide spectrum of industry sectors and tended towards the larger company. The responding charities ranges from the larger national caring institutions to hospital trusts and included a small number of quasi-governmental agencies.

The Questions

Responses may add up to more than 100 per cent in some cases, where more than one answer is applicable.

Policies on partnership

We asked companies whether they had a clear policy to define the kind of relationships they seek with non-profit organisations and vice versa for charities. Some 79 per cent of companies said they did, compared with only 57 per cent of charities.

As a basic starting point, creating a policy would seem an essential step in developing relationships that deliver results, so many of the charities, in particular, have a long way to go before they can establish a coherent approach to partnership. However, several charities and companies indicated that they are in the process of developing policies across a broad range of external issues.

Business motives for community investment

We asked companies why they became involved with the community. A majority said that it was for a mixture of altruistic and business motives and this perception was echoed by the charities when they were asked how the business case was best made. However, a sizeable minority of companies said that their motives were altruistic (23 per cent) while only one charity felt best results would come from appealing to altruistic motives.

Supporting projects v. organisations

A similar minority of companies said that they preferred to support organisations rather than projects (25 per cent) and vice versa (23 per cent). A similar picture emerges from the charities, with 34 per cent preferring to develop specific initiatives or projects, then seek business support and 20 per cent preferring to establish relationships first then seek suitable joint ventures. Just over half the charities, however, preferred to choose between these approaches according to circumstances.

Breadth of focus or commitment

There was also divergence of opinion among companies over whether to spread commitments and resources thinly over numerous charities and initiatives or to focus on a few carefully chosen initiatives. Nearly 40 per cent of companies preferred the latter, but slightly more opted for a balance between the two – leaving 20 per cent who preferred to distribute their largesse far and wide.

Charities also disagreed over the issue of focus, with 11 per cent scattering their net, 26 per cent preferring to build close relationships with a small number of companies, and the rest preferring a mixture of both approaches.

Finding partners

Received wisdom says that companies are becoming more proactive about seeking non-profit partners. Only four companies said this was their main approach, while 46 per cent relied upon charities to approach them. Others used a mixture of both and one company employed an outside agency to help make the choices. Only 21 per cent of companies keep a database of potential non-profit partners.

Matchmaking by the charities was equally variable. Some 13 per cent chose targets by size and known policy of giving; 29 per cent by relevance of their activities to the companies' business objectives; others used a mixture of both. Use of sponsorship agencies was remarkably low in our sample, with only two charities saying they employ an outside agency to make approaches.

Charities generally make approaches through a mixture of personal contact and letter. Only 11 per cent say that approaches generally come to them from companies. 56 per cent maintain a database of potential business partners as part of their marketing management.

Who are the company decision-makers?

Part of the problem for the charities is knowing *who* to contact. Asked who makes the decision in their organisation, the companies replied:

- Community affairs manager/ director   19%
- The corporate affairs manager/ director   14%
- Another director   5%
- The board   10%
- A management steering committee   29%
- An employee steering committee   14%

Other responses to the question included:

- A grants committee for small grants.
- Board subcommittee.
- Independent trustees.
- Senior managers.
- Charitable trust.
- Charities subcommittee (centrally) and locally by the operating businesses.
- Local business chief executives.
- Staff vote.
- Group trade marketing manager.
- Group charities committee.

A handful of companies surveyed (7) generally delegate decisions to the local operating units. The rest of our sample were roughly equally split between taking decisions at head office or sharing the responsibility between head office and the field.

What do businesses and the non-profit sector look for in a partner?
We next sought to compare what businesses look for in the non-profit organisations they support; and the charities' perceptions of what business was looking for.

	Companies %	Charities %
Relevance to the company's priority areas of community interest	100	96
High quality management	44	53
Demonstrably efficient use of resources	61	80
Ability to present well-thought through and argued plans	63	70
Ability to understand the company's needs	39	63
Ability to work as a team with you and your colleagues	42	51
Willingness to incorporate an agreed process of evaluation of results and a project review	42	40

The picture that emerges from the results is one of relatively strong agreement on almost all counts, although the companies seem to be generally less demanding than the charities expect. We were not able to test whether companies' low expectations of teamwork come from experience of failure in the past, from poor penetration of the concept of partnership throughout British firms generally, or from a perception that the best way to manage the relationship is to let the charities get on with what they do best and not interfere. However, we can reasonably conclude that businesses are generally less concerned about building effective partnerships.

The low emphasis placed by both sides on evaluation and project review gives cause for concern. Until companies ask for measurement, they are unlikely to change the practices of non-profit partners.

What do charities and businesses think about each other as organisations?
Companies showed both a high level of agreement and disagreement over the strengths and weaknesses of the non-profit organisations they dealt with.

There was general agreement that charities are strong in:

♦ Having a sense of purpose (92 per cent).

♦ Capacity to innovate/ accept new ideas (77 per cent).

♦ Ability to communicate (62 per cent).

And weak in:

♦ Knowledge of and interest in your company's objectives (89 per cent).

♦ Organisational structures (76 per cent).

♦ Ability to relate on equal terms with private sector partners (75 per cent).

♦ Quality of management (63 per cent).

Experience on 'ability to deliver what they promise' was clearly mixed, as 50 per cent said this was a strength and 50 per cent a weakness!

The list of perceived weaknesses would suggest that the reason companies do not look for 'ability to understand our needs' and 'high quality management' may be poor past experience in these areas.

Charities were equally forthright about the strengths and weaknesses of community investment departments.

There was general agreement that these company departments are strong in:

♦ Marketing expertise (73 per cent).

♦ Knowledge of/ interest in the company's objectives (70 per cent).

♦ Quality of management (68 per cent).

♦ Ability to communicate (65 per cent).

♦ Sense of clear purpose (59 per cent).

And weak in:

♦ Capacity to innovate/ accept new ideas (71 per cent).

♦ Ability to relate to (charities) on equal terms (63 per cent).

Slightly more than half of charities also criticised community investment departments on their ability to deliver what they promise.

In which areas do charities train their staff?

The perception by companies that charities often have 'poor quality of management' and 'are unable to relate on equal terms with private sector partners' may be due for change. Charities are investing widely in training – an important signal of the trend to become more business-like. When asked what areas they trained staff in the responses were:

♦ Communications/ public relations   79%

♦ Project management   41%

♦ Financial management   50%

♦ Fundraising	63%
♦ Information technology	71%
♦ Marketing	49%

Other areas specified were: TQM, time management, teamwork, systematic approach to general management skills, service delivery, research, business management, law/contracts, counselling, relationships – external and internal, running corporate and community events.

What they considered to be the most important aspects of partnerships

	Companies %	Charities %
Clear definition and agreement of objectives on both sides	92	90
A genuinely high level of mutual trust	63	75
Flexibility	35	51
Effective planning to achieve both sides' objectives	56	71
Good communications	75	75
Sharing of problems at an early stage	42	54

Companies also suggested other important aspects of the relationships.

♦ Good evaluation/ feedback on a regular basis
♦ Commitment by the board
♦ Ability to deal with 'real' issues – not problems on the surface
♦ Ability to help motivate staff
♦ Businesslike approach on both sides
♦ Good financial/ resources plan
♦ Clear lines of accountability/ responsibility
♦ Review milestones/ approved points set and met
♦ Clear identification of deliverables
♦ Risk analysis
♦ Time planning

A mismatch of expectations?

Perhaps one reason why problems occur is because companies and charities have different expectations over the nature of partnership relationships. Our survey found that more than three out of five companies expected partnerships to last just for the duration of the project, compared with just over a third of charities. Nearly half of charities expected partnerships to become long-term, multi-project arrangements, compared with only one fifth of companies.

Charities are also more optimistic about the growth of partnerships with business. While 55 per cent of companies expected to increase the role of partnerships with the non-profit sector, 94 per cent of charities expected to increase their partnership activity over the next two years.

If partnerships do continue to grow rapidly, there may be greater opportunities to share best practice between the business and non-profit sectors. However, there is a major discrepancy between the charities and the businesses about the potential for transfer of management expertise and ideas from the non-profit sector. While 80 per cent of charities believe there are 'lessons the private sector can learn from the way non-profit organisations are managed', only 34 per cent of companies agree!

Differences between management in voluntary sector and private sector organisations

Companies produce goods and services which they market to customers. So do voluntary organisations. Companies, of course, try to sell the goods and services they create for a profit. Voluntary organisations, with the exception of those that generate income for their other activities by trading, do not. Yet in many ways that is where the differences between the two sectors ends.

In order to function, voluntary organisations rely on the support of volunteers and benefactors who may be private citizens, companies or government. At the same time, they provide services and other benefits – often to a different group of individuals who are their customers or members. Much has been made of this separation between funders and customers by commentators. Among the three sectors of the economy, it is argued, the voluntary sector alone has two such distinct markets. In reality, of course, both the private and public sectors also have to cope with more than one audience. Consumer goods manufacturers have to balance the interests of retailers and consumers; the justice system has to accommodate the legitimate demands of the accused, victims and witnesses – let alone other stakeholders such as the police and the lawyers.

Some parallels can be drawn between the members of a charity and the individual shareholders of a quoted company. Both can usually only have a voice collectively, although in the case of the company one shareholder can more easily gain control. There is a difference, however, in that charity members are encouraged to become involved in the activities of the organisation, whereas shareholders are generally discouraged from doing so.

The significance of all this is simply to underline once again that the perceived differences between the private and voluntary sectors are not as clear cut as first appears.

In her publication 'Managing Across Sectors', Diana Leat provides a useful summary of the supposed differences between voluntary and private sector organisations and compares them with the reality.

Our own analysis borrows from her findings to highlight six key areas of perceived difference:

1. **Not for profit**: voluntary organisations are not run for profit, whereas businesses aim to maximise profit.

   Reality: 'Profit', as Leat notes, is an unclear concept. Some voluntary organisations generate surpluses which in a business context might be called profits. Moreover, companies take a much wider view about the allocation of resources than the simple notion of maximising profit suggests. Indeed it is debatable whether pure profit maximisation is the primary goal of businesses. Investment in product research and development, training and staff benefits, for example, often take priority over short-term profit maximisation in order to safeguard the long term success of the business and its future profitability.

2. **No bottom line**: voluntary organisations have no bottom-line by which performance can be judged, whereas businesses use the bottom line as the basis for evaluating their performance.
   Reality: To say there is no bottom line for voluntary organisations is misleading. The question of whether any organisation is solvent – i.e. has an income that is greater or equal to its expenditure – in effect is its bottom line. Furthermore, both sectors face problems assessing the contribution of departments such as personnel and information technology which do not produce tangible results.

3. **Non-competitive**: voluntary organisations do not operate in a competitive environment, but competition is inherent in business.
   Reality: perfect competition rarely exists in either sector, but resources such as funding and staff are limited so there is always competition. Moves towards a contract culture between voluntary organisations and local government agencies also mean that competition between voluntary organisations -and private sector firms – is intensifying.

4. **No direct link between funder and customer**: voluntary organisations receive funding from a separate source to customers, whereas businesses generate a revenue stream from customers.
   Reality: the notion of 'the customer' can be misleading. Many companies sell their products and services to customers who are not the direct consumers. Companies also rely on the capital of shareholders who are often distinct from their customers. In some voluntary organisations, too, the funder and the customer are one and the same.

5. **Unpaid, part-time board**: voluntary organisations are governed by a board of unpaid governors or trustees, whereas companies are run by paid managers and paid board members.
   Reality: the role of trustees is very similar to that of the non-executive directors on company boards who represent shareholders' interests. In both sectors managers are largely full-time, paid employees and have considerable control over the supply of information that board decisions are based on.

6. **Voluntary sector ethos**: voluntary organisations are more participative and egalitarian in the way they are managed than businesses which tend to be run on hierarchical and undemocratic lines.
   Reality: organisations in both sectors are required by law to implement basic equal opportunities provisions. Beyond those requirements,

however, a wider commitment to equality and participation is not characteristic of all voluntary organisations. Many companies also now recognise that greater participation and equality among employees is essential to achieve quality, innovation and success. Such principles are enshrined in many of the modern management texts based on Japanese practices.

Trustees' liabilities

The NCVO and Charity Commission working party on trustees summarised the potential liability of trustees as follows:

"Once an individual accepts the office of trustee, he or she becomes jointly liable for the administration of the charity. A trustee cannot escape responsibility either by remaining inactive, leaving the other trustees to make decisions, or by delegating the administration to other individuals or committees (unless expressly authorised to do so under the governing instrument [constitution] of the charity). A trustee, for example, will not escape a liability for financial shortcomings on the grounds that the finances of the charity were a matter delegated to the treasurer or finance committee of which the trustee in question was not a member.

"The personal liability of trustees does not prevent their employing staff or agents to implement their decisions. They have a statutory power to do so. They will not be personally liable for the wrongful acts of employees or agents provided they exercise proper care in making the appointment and in supervising the appointee.

"Similarly, trustees may delegate their decision-making powers to sub-committees (whether consisting of trustees or non-trustees) provided this is expressly permitted by the governing instrument of the charity. Statutory powers of delegation are severely restricted and there is no implied power of delegation. Where trustees have power to delegate, they will not be liable for the faults of those to whom they have delegated discretionary powers provided they monitor the sub-committee in question. Otherwise they may be liable for losses suffered by the charity as a result of their lack of care and diligence."

Within the broad bounds of their legal responsibilities, trustees need to be aware of the different types of liability they are exposed to. These are:

♦ Liability for breach of trust
♦ Liability to third parties in contract and tort
♦ Liability under the Insolvency Act 1986
♦ Vicarious liability.

A fuller explanation of each of these is given in the Charity Commission leaflet CC3, but they may be summarised as follows:

Liability for breach of trust: all charity trustees may be personally liable if they fail in their duty of care – i.e. to act as reasonable and prudent businessmen and women – and the charity suffers financial loss as a result. For example, authorising speculative investments resulting in a loss for the charity, without taking appropriate professional advice. Liability for breach of trust can also arise if they do not have proper regard for the purposes of the charity or overstep their powers. For example, engaging in unpermitted political activities.

Liability to third parties in contract and tort: contractual liability arises where a charity enters into a contract, for example to supply a service. Liability for tort is liability for actions such as trespass, nuisance or breach of statutory duty. Where a charity is incorporated, the charity itself is deemed to enter into a contract and would therefore be sued as an entity, protecting trustees from personal liability. However, if the contract constituted a breach of trust they could still be liable.

Liability under the Insolvency Act 1986: directors of a charitable company (who are in effect trustees) can be personally liable to repay sums to an insolvent company where they have been guilty of wrongful trading. In other words, they are personally liable for allowing the company to continue trading when they knew or should have known that liquid assets could not cover liabilities.

Vicarious liability: charity trustees remain liable where an employee fails to carry out his or her duties.

Care and diligence: in carrying out their responsibilities, trustees are expected to act with the same diligence and care as men and women 'of ordinary prudence and vigilance would in managing their own affairs'. As indicated earlier, this has been interpreted to mean that they should act as ordinary prudent men and women of business.

To execute this duty of care and diligence, trustees must take appropriate action, for example, to satisfy themselves about the probity and of staff and the accuracy of financial records. Remember, too, that the absence of bad faith or dishonesty, does not protect a trustee from liability for losses suffered by the charity resulting from failure to take action. What constitutes 'reasonable action' in this context is judged against the facts that the trustee did or should have known.

The fact that duty of care and diligence translates into the actions of a prudent business man or woman implies that trustees have a working knowledge of financial and legal matters. In practice, this need not be a detailed understanding of the issues but at the very least an awareness of when it is advisable to seek professional advice. To have taken and acted upon professional advice will not necessarily provide a cast iron defence against claims that they have failed in their duties, but does at least demonstrate that trustees have acted with due care and diligence.

Index

ALSO AVAILABLE FROM DSC BOOKS

THE COMPLETE GUIDE TO BUSINESS AND STRATEGIC PLANNING
For Voluntary Organisations
Business plans and strategic planning, increasingly demanded by
funders, can also help your organisation achieve its aims. This
practical guide, supported by NatWest, will help you draw up
realistic plans and implement them effectively. Don't forget that
major lottery applications now have to be supported by a business
plan! *"Crammed with templates to organise your thinking and planning
...a winner!"* (BAFM Newsletter)

MANAGING QUALITY OF SERVICE
Measuring Performance for Voluntary Organisations
This new and fully revised edition addresses the ways in which
voluntary sector funding contracts now emphasise measurement
and accountability, and sheds new light on the potentially fraught
process of quality assurance. It shows how intelligent monitoring
systems and processes can be beneficial, can enable an organisation
to gain a sense of achievement, can increase internal knowledge of
which services and activities deliver sustainable and valued results,
and can create a feeling of purpose and progress within the
organisation.

THE GOVERNANCE AND MANAGEMENT OF CHARITIES
Published by Voluntary Sector Press
The definitive guide to maximising the effectiveness of your charity.
Derived from his unique experience at the heart of the charity sector,
Andrew Hind's authoritative model of charity governance and
management will transform the way you shape your charity's future.
Filled with case studies, specimen strategic and financial plans, job
descriptions for trustees and senior managers, and valuable
benchmarking data. *"Breathtaking in its scope, but very practical too -
people in charities of all sizes will find it immensely useful."* (Professor Ian
Bruce, Director General, RNIB)

For full details of these and around 90 other guides and handbooks
for voluntary organisations, contact us for a free booklist.

Directory of Social Change (Publications)
24 Stephenson Way
London
NW1 2DP
Telephone: 0171 209 5151, fax: 0171 209 5049